# Middle Eastern Subcultures

# Middle Eastern Subcultures

A Regional Approach

William E. Hazen
Mohammed Mughisudden
The American Institutes
for Research

Contributors
George N. Atiyeh
Abdul A. Said
Alan R. Taylor

**Lexington Books**
D.C. Heath and Company
Lexington, Massachusetts
Toronto          London

**Library of Congress Cataloging in Publication Data**

Hazen, William Edward, 1933-
  Middle Eastern subcultures.

  Bibliography: p.
  Includes index.
  1. Arab countries—Politics and government. 2. Elite (Social sciences)—
Arab countries. 3. Social groups. 4. Subculture. I. Mughisuddin, Moham-
med, joint author. II. Title.
DS62.8.H4        301.2'2'09174927        75-21786
ISBN 0-669-00198-8

Published simultaneously in Canada.

Printed in the United States of America.

International Standard Book Number: 0-669-00198-8

Library of Congress Catalog Card Number: 75-21786

To our families

# Contents

# List of Tables

# Preface

This book is predicated on the assumption that action other than that considered to be normal diplomatic intercourse taken by the United States in the Middle East will not be restricted to a single country or limited area. Instead, a rippling effect will take place, by which repercussions will be felt throughout the Middle Eastern region, not necessarily in the same intensity, but still recognizable as reactions. These reactions are the crux of the study since it is believed that certain subcultures found in each Middle Eastern country react in a similar manner. Subculture is defined to mean "any group whose shared, mutually reinforcing sets of expectations have led to stereotyped behavior distinctive enough to warrant separate entries within the literature of the area." Only six subcultures will be discussed, those deemed to be most influential. They are the military, the students, the professionals, the communicators, the bureaucracy, and the Western-educated elites.

Before discussing the subcultures, however, three important factors inherent in the Arab world will be examined. These are regionalism, Islam, and ideologies. These three will then be applied to the various subcultures under discussion—how they are viewed by the subcultures and how the subcultures are, in turn, affected by them.

Because of the number of contributors to this study, there are bound to be divergences in the spellings of names and concepts. To date there is no mandatory system when transliterating Arabic into English. Because the Arabic language has no "e" or "o" in its alphabet, Arabists are trying to eliminate those two letters when transliterating. However, common usage or official spellings of certain names prevents uniformity.

The geographical region described in this study is an area stretching from Morocco to Iran and covers those countries that are normally considered to be Arab. In the study, therefore, Middle East and Arab world have become synonymous, just as North Africa is part of the Middle East and the Arab world.

Much of the material used has been in Arabic, gleaned from literary magazines or articles in newspapers. Then, too, many comments have been made by the authors based on personal observations when in the Middle East. In fact, some of the most serious analytical work undertaken in this book came about as a result of serious discussions with Arabs or Arabists who drew upon their personal knowledge of events and conditions of the region. It must be pointed out, however, that there has been a dearth of material, even in Arabic, regarding certain topics, namely the bureaucracy and Western elites, restricting analysis and a full understanding of the groups. Until reliable field studies have been made, much of what will be said will necessarily be based on personal interviews made *en passant*.

Since the Middle East is constantly undergoing change in its political, economic, and social forces, material published in 1971 could easily be considered out of date, and, therefore, unusable except as historical reference. Changes in regimes—military coups and countercoups—have certainly affected the publication of material in the region. The authoritative stand taken by some regimes, such as Syria and Iraq, has also had a limiting effect on the emanation of good analytical material from the two countries.

Although the bibliography of this paper is extensive, and includes material in French and Arabic, as well as in English, it is still insufficient in some cases for the purposes which the authors wished to achieve. Therefore, this study must not be considered to be definitive on subcultures in the Middle East.

This work owes much in conceptual origin to Dr. Paul Jureidini, who served as project director. Furthermore, the authors wish to express their gratitude to Susan Haseltine for her contributions in providing material used in this work.

A draft of the study on which this book is based was originally sponsored by the Department of the Army under contract DAHC 19-70-C-0015, issued by the U.S. Army Research Office, in accordance with the requirements established by the Office, Deputy Chief of Staff for Military Operations. The conclusions of this study are those of the authors and should not be construed to represent the policies of the United States Government or the views of the American Institutes for Research.

**Part I:**
**A Regional Assessment**

# Introduction to Part I

In undertaking this study, it was thought necessary to give the reader some background of the region, although not primarily of an historical nature. Instead, the reader is asked to examine three factors that are inherent to the area and, at the same time, could be considered unique to the Arab world. These three factors—regionalism, Islam, and ideologies—profoundly affect the internal as well as the international relationships of the area. Similarly, they are involved with unity, or if you will, disunity of the Middle East. Furthermore, they must be considered unique because of their joint interaction.

Dr. Alan Taylor, in the first chapter, *The Dynamics of Arab Regionalism*, has set the scene for the entire study. He defines the various regional arrangements found in the Arab world—geographical locations as well as political motivations— and the key personalities who fostered the regional concepts. He also discusses various existing conditions, many of which contain both positive and negative elements for regionalism. He concludes his paper with a discussion of the future of Arab regionalism by taking into consideration Arab economic schemes, such as the Arab Common Market and the Organization of Arab Petroleum Exporting Countries (OAPEC).

It must be stated that this first chapter is not a definitive study on regionalism in the Arab world but merely serves as an introduction to the area. Furthermore, the concepts of regionalism are ongoing processes. OAPEC's backing of Iraq's recent move to nationalize the holding of the Iraqi Petroleum Company, the meetings held by Presidents Bourguiba of Tunisia and Boume-dienne of Algeria in 1972, and the resultant strongly worded statements for Maghrib unity by the two men are examples of the regional concept and show the usefulness of this study, not only for background reading but also for a basis for development of the various regional schemes.

# 1 The Dynamics of Arab Regionalism

Alan R. Taylor

## Unity and Diversity in the Middle East

Though the Middle East is a loosely defined area with somewhat blurred peripheries, the course of history has given it a distinct identity and a continuity of experience. Stretching across North Africa and eastward to the subcontinent, this geographical entity, which in modern times came to be labelled the "Middle East," has a unique past which binds its peoples through a common heritage. Not only is the area an important staging ground of early civilization, but it has also been the seat of recurring empires which gave it a cohesive character and endowed it with cultural resiliency.

Following the struggle for dominance between ancient Egypt and the contemporary kingdoms in the Fertile Crescent, the Persians established a vast empire that created the first comprehensive political union of the Middle East. This was followed by a millennium of Graeco-Roman rule. And ultimately Islam became the foundation of an even larger imperial structure and of a cultural revolution that proved to be a durable, though intermittent, unifying force. An important aspect of the role of Islam in this regard was the fact that it linked religious commitment to political loyalty, producing a highly charismatic effect that sustained the momentum of empire building.

Countering the impulse to unify, however, is an equally powerful divisive tendency. Despite the binding influence of history and culture, the Middle East is composed of distinct regions separated from each other by geographical barriers, sectional economies, and different languages. The most pronounced division is that between the three major peoples in the area—Arabs, Turks, and Persians. But there are also significant minorities that resist integration, while the Arabs themselves are regionally heterogeneous.

The interplay of these two proclivities has determined the course of Middle Eastern historical development. The passage of time has shown a continuing cycle of unity and diversity—imperial ages separated by periods of fragmentation. Even the Islamic phase itself has recapitulated this pattern in the rise and fall of the Arab and Turkish Empires. The pinnacles of Abbasid and Ottoman achievement were followed by the splintering of Islamic society and the agonizing experience of social and cultural decay.

The flux of fortune has had a direct bearing on the relationship of the Middle

East to other areas, to the West in particular. The Mediterranean has provided a continuing avenue of communications between Europe and the coastlands of the Levant and North Africa, while until relatively recent times, Russia, China, and the Indian subcontinent have been separated from southwest Asia by mountain ranges and vast steppes. The history of the Middle East has therefore been closely tied to that of the West. More specifically, political fragmentation in the Middle East has frequently coincided with empire building in Europe and resulted in Western conquests of the area. Similarly, the Middle Eastern empires themselves have periodically turned the tide and overrun or threatened portions of Europe when decline was apparent there. More recently, Russia has entered the orbit of Middle Eastern politics. The resurgence of Russia under Peter the Great inaugurated a drive to the south that involved Tsarist incursions into Ottoman and Persian territory, and has left a legacy of Russian intervention in the Middle East.

The significance of these contingencies is the relevance of unity and diversity to the fate of the Middle East and their impact on the psychology of the people. The price of division in historical perspective has been the forfeit of sovereignty and territorial integrity, encouraging a will to universalism apparent in the tenacity of Islamic imperialism and the lingering death of the Caliphate as a concept. Yet regional inclinations remain equally forceful, reconditioned by the barriers of geography, race, and cultural differentiation. Though Turks and Persians adhere to Islam, they are also negative in their attitudes toward the Arab world, which is the source of their religious commitment. And the Arabs themselves, despite even closer ties to each other and the currency of Pan-Arab ideals, are regionally oriented in political practice.

An important key to current developments is the fact that a new and essentially different situation came into being after 1918. The demise of the Ottoman Empire was attended by Western attempts at partition and control of the Middle East, setting in motion the traditional pattern of fragmentation and conquest. But in fact the age of imperialism was also in eclipse; and following the immediate success of the Turkish and Persian independence movements, the Arab units systematically established sovereignty in the course of two genera-tions. The achievement of these ends on a regional level suggested the discontinuity of ecumenical programs as the only basis for political viability. The policies of Kemal Ataturk reflect a clear perception of the changed situation and made it possible for an assertive Turkish national state to emerge from the ashes of the Ottoman Empire.

The Arab provinces found it more difficult to develop dynamic regional ideologies, partly in consequence of the administrative fragmentation introduced by the Anglo-French occupation, but also because the appearance of nationalism among the Arabs had generated ecumenical doctrines in a number of instances. Nevertheless, the First World War did become a major threshold in the history of the Middle East. It ended a long period in which the ideal of Pan-Islam had dominated political thought, though it had not always been achieved in practice. At the same time, it led to the introduction of the nation state as the dominant political institution. The structural revolution this set in motion involved not only a pronounced shift in loyalties from the feudal unit to the state, but also a radical revision of traditional political theory, which raised perplexing questions of cultural fidelity and practical applicability.

The divergent forces promoting unity and diversity in the Middle East were therefore thrust into an unprecedented and innovative environment, posing the challenge of modernity. However, it was the Arabs in particular who had to cope with the riddle of their own singularity or plurality. To understand the scope of the problem, it is necessary to look first at the resurgence of the Arabs in recent times.

## The Arab Awakening

The modernist revolution in Arab society developed within the broader context of Ottoman reform. The decline of the Empire after Suliman and the intrusion of foreign powers in the eighteenth and nineteenth centuries led to sporadic and often ineffective attempts to arrest disintegration through changes in structure, methodology, and orientation. The introduction of administrative and technical innovations proved to be superficial, and eventually the cosmopolitan elite turned to the deeper issues of social order and public philosophy. The major products of this endeavor in the nineteenth century were the constitutional and Islamic reform movements.[1] The Turkish participants—known collectively as the Young Ottomans—proposed a variety of substantive changes, ranging from the promulgation of a Western-style constitution to the revival of early Islamic institutions. All were essentially loyal to the empire and were forwarding proposals for its regeneration.

A parallel movement among the Arabs also expressed itself in terms of Islamic reconstruction and Western liberalism.[2] The Muslim reformers, who represented the Arab counterpart of the Young Ottomans, were motivated by a concern for the fate of the empire. The increasing fragmentation of the Ottoman political structure and the threat of Western imperialism impelled them to question the *status quo* and to consider the means of generating a new sense of social solidarity (*'asabiyya*) in the Islamic communities of the Middle East. The consensus of this group was that Islam had lost its resiliency because it was no longer guided by its own principles. It was therefore essential to interpret Islam's confrontation with the modern world by recourse to the faculty of professional judgment (*ijtihad*), which had been dormant for centuries. The contention here was that the ethics and intellectual depth of earlier Islam were the keys to contemporary problems. Consequently this school came to be known as the *Salafiyya* movement, named after *al-salaf al-salih*, the venerable forefathers comprising the first Islamic generation.

The *Salafiyya* movement developed in response to the provocative message of the energetic Persian Pan-Islamist, Jamal al-Din al-Afghani (1839-1897). Al-Afghani settled in Egypt in the 1870s, where he became an influential figure in intellectual and academic circles. The thrust of his argument was that the Middle East was falling under the domination of Europe because Islam had lost its political and cultural resiliency. Though more a political agitator than a systematic or profound thinker, al-Afghani injected a spirit of concern and activism among the younger educated classes of the Arab world and inaugurated a search for means of institutional change. His most illustrious student, Muhammad 'Abduh (1849-1905), became the intellectual leader of the *Salafiyya* movement and developed a comprehensive doctrine of Islamic reform.

Though opposed to innovation (*bid'a*) and arbitrary cultural borrowing from the West, 'Abduh rejected the conservative tradition of accepting established custom without question (*taqlid*). Yet in advocating the revival of *ijtihad* for the purpose of reexamining Islam in the context of modern civilization, he opened the door to innovative political speculation. This was due in part to the fact that Islam regards political solidarity as an aspect of religious fulfillment. But it also stemmed from the opposition to despotic rule which had become an article of faith in the broader movement for Ottoman reform. The intelligentsia recognized that the strength of Western society lay as much in its political cohesiveness as in its technological superiority, and regarded democratic institutions as the key factor. The revisionist attitude toward the *status quo* stimulated a restive spirit that ultimately generated the idea of nationalism and radically transformed the character of political life in the Middle East. Hence, the introduction of philosophical inquiry became the first step in the development of a much broader upheaval which assumed revolutionary proportions.

The disciples of Muhammad 'Abduh moved increasingly in a political direction. One branch, headed by 'Abduh's most talented student, Muhammad Rashid Rida (1865-1935), remained committed to the *Salafiyya* movement and the doctrines of Pan-Islam. Rida looked to the construction of a responsible public philosophy by a new generation of dedicated Arabs and Turks. But the secularism and Turkification policies of the Young Turk junta, which came to power in 1908, led him to a religious Arabism that anticipated a Caliphate in the Arab sector alone. Another Syrian, 'Abd al-Rahman al-Kawakibi (1849-1903), had earlier conceived a predominantly Arab role in the regeneration of Islam, and suggested the formation of secret societies to work toward that end.

Other personalities in the *Salafiyya* tradition veered away from the religious perspectives of Muhammad 'Abduh. This contingent, mainly Egyptian, derived its inspiration from the inherent values of Western civilization and devoted itself to the promotion of secular ideals and the politics of emancipation from British rule. The product of these endeavors was a program of defined regional resistance, culminating in the abortive rebellion of Colonel Urabi and the rise of the National Party under Mustafa Kamil (1874-1908). From this point, a distinctly Egyptian political movement emerged in the context of a reemphasized Nilotic identity. Operating within the framework of secular reform and dedicated to independence from British rule, Egyptian nationalism dominated the politics of the country until 1954, and represents an important development in regional orientation.

Coincident with the rise of religious Arabism and Egyptian nationalism was the appearance of modernist thought among Christian intellectuals in Lebanon. The movement here began in part from a cultural revival encouraged by the educational endeavors of American Protestant missionaries, dating back to the 1830s. The mission schools and colleges became agencies of an intellectual transition involving primarily the rediscovery of the Arab past and the development of written Arabic as a vital and powerful tool of literary expression. These activities were particularly appealing to Christians, who had already turned to literature and history as a means of establishing a more viable and less isolated standard of identity. In effect, they were constructing a secular Arabism, through which they could relate to the larger body of Muslim Arabs.

Prominent among the early Christian Arabists was Butrus al-Bustani (1819-1883), who eventually became associated with the American mission and assisted in editing the Protestant Arabic Bible. Al-Bustani was particularly active in stimulating a new literary tradition, of which the Protestant Bible itself was an important source of inspiration. He was also instrumental in developing the concept of an Arab ethos, which transcended Islam, had played a role in the development of civilization and was now on the threshold of recovering its traditions of science and learning.

In the latter decades of the century, the directions that al-Bustani helped to initiate flowered into a movement of secular reform among the educated Lebanese Christians. The message of this school was put forward in a number of newspapers and periodicals, the most important of which were *Al-Jinan* (1870), *Al-Muqtataf* (1876), and *Al-Hilal* (1892). The major themes that emerged from these publications were the need for change, the importance of intellectual enlightenment, and the validity of a secular approach to political life. No systematic political program was proposed and the writers themselves varied in outlook, some suggesting a broad Arab policy and others a more restricted Syrian or Lebanese nationalism. But there was a common opposition to the status quo and a conviction that the institutions, educational traditions, and social values of Europe should become guidelines for the development of society in the Middle East. With this in view, the various journals concentrated on disseminating knowledge about discoveries of modern science, the implications of political theory, and the interpretation of history.

The impact of the Christian intellectuals on Arab politics in general was twofold. On the one hand they contributed to the idea of Pan-Arabism by reviving the language and history of the Arabs. They also became an important source of regional ideology. The combination of their revisionist attitude toward the Ottoman system, detachment from Islam, and the lack of any clear political commitment suggested a sectional approach to the restructuring of society in the Middle East. Indeed, the political currents in the Fertile Crescent activated by the Young Turk revolution demonstrated the power of regionalism in the area. The separatist organizations that were formed at this time envisioned independence of the Arab east as defined in the Damascus Protocol issued by the Young Arab Society in 1915.[3] And in the ensuing years the idea of an Arab federation in the Fertile Crescent became a dominant political theme.

While these developments were taking place in Egypt and the Arab east, a similar pattern was unfolding in Morocco, Algeria, and Tunisia, known collectively as the Maghrib.[4] Here, too, the advent of European colonialism stimulated a search for political and social change. The French occupation of Algeria in 1830 and of Tunisia in 1881 created a receptivity to the idea of Islamic reform. Muhammad 'Abduh visited Tunisia in 1884 and the concepts of *Salafiyya* revival that he imparted led, a decade later, to the formation of a school designed to develop consciousness of the common problems confronting all Islamic societies. The theory of Arabism was also developed, but in general the Maghribis passed rapidly to regional politics. This was not only because they had the longest experience of foreign occupation, but also because the penetration of European culture had influenced them more than the intellectual currents from the east.[5]

The movement for national independence was in one sense an extension of the resistance to the French occupation of Algeria in 1830. However, it was first systematically developed in Tunisia, which had experienced greater exposure to both European and Arab political thought than either Algeria or Morocco. The Young Tunisian Movement, which began in 1905, initially took the form of an intellectual awakening and then gravitated toward political action. The earlier programs, seeking reform within the context of a continuing protectorate, eventually gave way to a nationalist doctrine of independence championed by the Destour Party. The primary characteristics of this type of political development throughout the Maghrib were the preoccupation with the French presence and the development of national resistance. This not only curtailed interest in the broader question of Arabism, but prevented a comprehensive Maghribi movement as well. Each of the three components was absorbed in its own particular situation, and despite the cultural and historical ties which identify them as regional partners, the struggle for independence remained largely localized. When an interest in Arab affairs developed in the post-independence years, it did not break the pattern of regional orientation, though a specifically Maghribi ideology also failed to gather momentum.

The two most significant peripheral movements in the formative stage were the rise of Wahhabism in Arabia and the Mahdist revolt in the Sudan. The movement of Islamic puritanism inaugurated in the Arabian Peninsula by Muhammad Ibn 'Abd al-Wahhab (1703-1787) should be distinguished from other forms of *Salafiyya* revival. Though also inspired by the example of early

Islam, Wahhabism was not a response to the political and cultural impact of the West; it was the product of self-generated Muslim reformation, reflecting a recurrent theme in Islamic history.[6] When it was established as the state religion in Saudi Arabia, Wahhabism was hardly a vehicle of Arab national sentiment, serving instead to differentiate the Saudis from the rest of Arab society and to perpetuate the regional predispositions of the peninsula.

The Mahdist episode was also an expression of regional disengagement. Ostensibly an Islamic messiah, the self-appointed "Mahdi" really represented the separatist leanings of Sudanese society at a time of resistance to Anglo-Egyptian control.[7] Following the establishment of the Condominium in 1899, unionist and anti-Egyptian parties were formed in the Sudan and the two positions stood as alternative courses of action for several decades. But ultimately, the Sudanese people elected to be independent of Egypt, providing a further example of sectional politics in Arab society.

On the eve of World War I, a pronounced regionalism had taken root throughout the Arab world. The National Party in Egypt and the independence movements in the Maghrib, though following on the heels of Pan-Islamic and Arabist ideologies, were preoccupied with the political future of their own sectors. Similarly, the political societies in the Fertile Crescent were programmed in terms of the Arab east, though the ecumenical doctrines of Arabism had been expressed in earlier years. The more removed areas—especially Arabia and the Sudan—also developed around separatist platforms that precluded participation in a larger Arab polity. Hence, the first manifestations of planned political action were geared to particularism. The underlying cause of this direction, considering the previous interest in Pan-Islam and Arabism, was that while the earlier movements were largely Ottoman-oriented, the political phase anticipated the demise of the empire and the construction of a completely new order in which the immediate challenge was the realization of regional sovereignty. This predisposition was further reinforced by the fact of pluralism in Arab society and the differing immediate problems of the component sectors.

The aftermath of the war encouraged the progress of Arab regionalism. The National Party in Egypt, now reconstituted as the Wafd, became intensely involved in the resistance to continuing British authority.[8] This minimized Egyptian interest in the broader issues of Arab emancipation, though the Palestinian problem (influx of Jewish immigrants and the ensuing unrest between Arab and Jewish populations) became a matter of increasing concern. In general, however, Egypt pursued a predominantly regional policy during the interwar period, as did the Maghrib countries to the west and the new Saudi monarchy in Arabia.

In the Fertile Crescent, the brief period between the end of the war and the imposition of mandatory regimes witnessed the formation of a Syrian Congress, which convened in Damascus in 1919.[9] The resolutions of this assembly called for the independence of the Arab east, the formation of a unitary state in

Greater Syria with close ties to Iraq, and the rejection of Zionist claims to establish a Jewish state in Palestine. This reflected a pragmatic declaration of Syrian nationalism, though devoid of vivid ideological overtones. Later in the interwar period, the Syrian Social National Party (SSNP) developed a doctrinaire approach to regional nationalism in the Fertile Crescent, but the politics of the area in these years revolved primarily around the struggle for independence in the separate fragments created by the mandatory system. In this context, the abortive insurrection in the French-controlled Syrian Mandate, the emergence of a Lebanese national movement, and the conflict between the Arab and Jewish communities in Palestine represent the major political developments in the area.

Two circumstances in particular served to reactivate the resurgence of Arabism in a secular form. Perhaps most important was the drift toward regional oligarchy and diplomatic compromise with the Western powers among the politicians of the interwar period. The generation coming of age in the 1930s felt a deep sense of political frustration, which it attributed to the established leadership's accommodation to the fragmentation of Arab society imposed by the West.[10] Therefore, it seemed that the problems of Arab society originated from its own divisiveness, and that unification was the key to ultimate sovereignty. Also significant was the progress of Zionism in Palestine. This threatened a more permanent fracture of the Syrian region and left unanswered its implications for the Arab world as a whole.

During the 1930s the rebellion against regionalism was expressed in the formation of unionist ideologies and the emergence of organized Pan-Arabism. Sami Shawkat, former Iraqi Director General of Education; Edmond Rabbath of Aleppo; and Amin al-Rihani, the Lebanese poet, were among the first to develop the guidelines of secular Arabism as a political creed. Addressing an audience in 1938, al-Rihani conveyed the central theme of the new doctrine: "The Arabs will remain after Islam and Christianity. Let the Christians realize this, and let the Muslims realize it. Arabism before and above everything."[11]

The earliest inter-Arab assemblies were convened in this period also, largely in response to the deepening threat of Zionism. The first meeting of this type was the Pan-Arab Congress held in Jerusalem in 1931. The Arab Covenant issued by this body rejected the imposition of artificial divisions and colonialism in any form. This established a basis of common outlook, but the congress also set up an executive committee which later mediated the dispute between Saudi Arabia and Yemen. Therefore, at a time when regionalism was still pronounced, the machinery of inter-Arab cooperation was set in motion. The second Pan-Arab Congress was convened in 1937 at Bludan, Syria, to consider the Palestinian problem. The major development of this assembly was the attempt to coordinate the foreign policies of the Arab countries in terms of a mutual commitment to the rights of the Palestinians. The following year the Inter-Parliamentary Congress of Arab and Muslim Countries met in Cairo and established a united front against British policy in Palestine. Both of the latter congresses were called in response to the revolt of the Palestinian Arab community. They represent the attempt to establish an identity of interests and sympathies among the Arab states and to coordinate policies in international affairs.

By the eve of World War II, the Arab world had experienced a disturbing revolution in structure and ideas during the course of more than half a century. In the transition from Ottoman provinces and European colonies to national states, the Arabs had recapitulated in microcosm the timeless engagement of unifying and divisive tendencies in Middle Eastern history. As a predominantly Muslim society, they had participated in the broader movement seeking Islamic revival and solidarity. As subjects of a moribund empire they had become suddenly conscious of the cultural ties that distinguished them from other peoples, suggesting the rise of an Arab polity from the debris of Ottoman fragmentation. Yet the particular circumstances and special attributes of component sectors had encouraged a regional approach to future development that reached its zenith after World War I. However, in response to the frustrations of political evolution in the 1920s and 1930s, they turned again to the concept of Arab union as the vehicle of emancipation and viability. By 1939, Pan-Arabism had emerged as an ideology and a course of action. In the ensuing decades, continuing regionalism provided the framework of a struggle for ascendancy between the forces of unity and diversity. What followed was the intense engagement of both inclinations, providing the background against which the kaleidoscopic events of the past three decades have taken place.

## Regionalism and Federalism in Arab Politics

In May of 1941 the British government announced its readiness to support schemes for unity representing Arab consensus. This elicited a variety of proposals which had the unusual effect of stimulating both regional and ecumenical responses.[12] Emir Abdullah of Transjordan and the powerful Iraqi politician, Nuri al-Sa'id, were the first to react. Abdullah, long eager to enlarge his political role, suggested the formation of a Greater Syrian state under his own crown, a plan he continued to cherish and advertise for some years, despite the negative reaction to it in Syria and Lebanon. Al-Sa'id put forward a much broader proposal for the creation of a Fertile Crescent federation as the core of a wider Arab association. Known as the Blue Book Scheme, it called for an Arab League administered by a Permanent Council designed to coordinate defense, foreign affairs, currency, communications, customs, and the protection of minority rights. It also provided for Jewish autonomy in Palestine and a special status for the Christian community of Lebanon. Though an imaginative combination of regional and federative institutions, the unpopularity of al-Sa'id in Arab leadership circles consigned this plan also to failure, and the initiative passed to Egypt.

Egypt was still a regionally oriented country at this stage, but as the largest and in some ways most prestigious of the Arab states, it was eager to maintain a leadership role in light of the existing drift toward a greater degree of Arab unity. In 1943 the Wafd leader, Nahhas Pasha, announced that Egypt intended to convene an Arab congress in Cairo. This was followed by months of private discussions with various Arab leaders, in which Nahhas promoted his own preference for a loose confederation of Arab states. The value of such a system from his point of view was that it would preserve regional sovereignty while ensuring Egypt's hegemony in the Arab bloc.

The results of Nahhas' efforts were the Alexandria Protocol of 1944, which underwrote his proposal, and the Pact of the Arab League, contracted the following year by Egypt, Syria, Lebanon, Iraq, Transjordan, Saudi Arabia, and Yemen. The Arab League established a political community and an apparatus for cooperation in political, economic, and cultural affairs. But it also stressed the absolute sovereignty of the members, who were not even prohibited from pursuing policies detrimental to their common interests as a group.

The structural weakness of the Arab League served to preserve an aura of solidarity, while it encouraged the emergence of latent rivalries among the participants. The subsequent pattern of inter-Arab relations centered on the emergence of a Hashimite alignment between Transjordan and Iraq in confrontation with an opposing bloc comprised of Egypt and Saudi Arabia. Yemen and Lebanon remained relatively isolated, though clearly opposed to any close relationship with the Hashimite states. This left Syria as the focal point in the balance of power, and later made it the stage of a more complex engagement of competitive interests.

The Arab League's conspicuous failure in preventing the establishment of Israel helped to discredit the organization and the generation that created it in the eyes of the Arab intellectuals coming of age in the 1940s. It was at this time that the Ba'th and similar parties advocating an ideological approach to Arab unity began to formulate fresh doctrines and programs.[13] The basic premise of these groups was that the older nationalists had become obsolete and compromised the integrity and aspirations of Arab society. The aim of the new intelligentsia was to redefine the Arab national ideal as the focus of a common patriotic commitment. The problem confronting this altruistic endeavor was the persistence of traditional institutions and regional perspectives. Despite the sanctity of Arab unity as an article of faith, the established patterns of political behavior precluded either a profound transformation of any given community or a durable union between distinct regions.

At the same time, the doctrine of Pan-Arabism continued to gain increasing support and, with the exception of the Lebanese Christians, few would dare to publicly disclaim it. In Egypt, for example, traditional regionalism began to recede during the 1930s, when the threat of Zionism had become apparent and the Wafd had discredited itself by making a deal with Britain.[14] Finally, two years after the July revolution in 1952, both unity and socialism became the foundations of Egyptian policy.[15] Yet the dichotomy of futuristic idealism and resistance to change produced a developmental paradox that remains a constant factor in Arab politics.

The quarter century following World War II introduced into Arab affairs complications that had been only marginal in the previous three decades. From the proclamation of the Arab Revolt in 1916 to the formation of the Arab League, the problem of independence stood as a dominant and clearly defined issue to be resolved. With the gradual achievement of this goal in the twenty years or so after 1945, the more profound questions of national identity and social progress remained.

At the root of the contemporary crisis in Arab political development is the issue of regionalism, which has played an important role in the course of events. This stems not only from the existence of regional diversity but also from the fact that ideological orientation differs radically from one Arab state to another. The combination of social pluralism and conflicting political philosophies galvanized the latent forces of regional competition against the background of broad general commitment to the theory of unity as the ultimate goal of Arab political endeavor.

The first years after the war witnessed the failure of combined efforts to prevent the establishment of Israel and the emergence of a rudimentary system of rival blocs mentioned above. In 1949, the political situation in Syria attracted the interest of the other Arab states and set in motion an increasingly complex competition among them.[16] Three military coups took place in that year and introduced several important elements into the framework of Arab politics. They served in one sense to announce the appearance and future ascendancy of new political elites drawn from the military and the younger intelligentsia. At the same time they established federalism as a vital issue in inter-Arab relations, challenging the regional status quo institutionalized by the Arab League.

The Syrian crisis became a political field in which the relative strengths of rival blocs were put to the test. Despite the consideration of a possible union with Iraq, the ultimate decision was to maintain cordial relations with Egypt and Saudi Arabia, preserving the structure of the Arab League. This was due in part to Syrian reluctance to develop close ties with the conservative regime of Nuri al-Sa'id in Iraq. But it also reflected the interest of the military in consolidating its power and sustaining the political innovation it had introduced. The last of the coups resulted in a four-year dictatorship under Colonel Adib Shishakli, who preserved Syria's sovereignty while giving lip service to the ideal of Arab unity.

The victory of Egyptian policy in the Syrian episode was further extended by the isolation and eventual subordination of the Hashimite bloc. Abdullah's unilateral annexation of the West Bank at the end of 1948 and his secret negotiations with Israel in the course of the following year completed his alienation from the Arab world.[17] On April 1, 1950, the Arab League adopted a protocol prohibiting the member states from signing a separate peace with Israel. Abdullah acceded to this agreement, but the Arab collective security pact established on June 17, excluded both Jordan and Iraq. Though both of these countries were later brought into the pact, their role in Arab politics had been diminished and Egypt remained the dominant power in the Arab League.

In the 1950s, Arab politics entered a new stage of development involving broader and more complex dimensions. Abdullah passed from the scene with his assassination in July 1951, and was eventually succeeded by his young grandson, Hussein. Of far greater importance, however, was the emergence of a new regime in Egypt a year later. The Revolutionary Command Council, headed first by Muhammad Naguib and later by the real architect of the revolution, Gamal Abd al-Nasser, maintained the regional orientation of Egypt until the conclusion of the new Anglo-Egyptian Treaty in October 1954.

Though the treaty established a terminal date for British presence in Egypt, the revolutionary government was already headed on a collision course with Western policy in the Cold War. The American attempt to establish a Middle East Defense Command in 1951 was sharply rejected by Egypt and other Arab states. A brief rapprochement between Egypt and the U.S. followed the 1952 revolution, but this ultimately collapsed under the pressure of events. Cairo's refusal to participate in the Baghdad Pact opened a breach that became wider as the United States withheld military support and eventually cancelled its offer to assist in building the Aswan Dam. This led to an opening up of Arab relations with the Soviet bloc, and despite President Eisenhower's effectiveness in securing Israel's withdrawal after the Suez crisis, Egypt remained on the neutralist course she had publicly endorsed at the Bandung Conference in 1955.

The international crises of the mid-1950s had a marked influence on Arab politics. On a broad level, they intensified the drift toward more radical and anti-Western policies, sharpening the antagonism between different positions. They also enhanced the prestige of Egypt, which now assumed a role of ideological as well as political leadership. The activist spirit generated by these developments first expressed itself in Syria and then spread to other parts of the Arab world.

Just as Nasser was emerging as the hero of the Arab cause, the situation in Syria was in the process of change.[18] Early in 1954, Shishakli was deposed and the conduct of political affairs reverted to the constitutional system. The established parties were reactivated, but the climate of opinion in the urban centers favored the ascendancy of younger groups, especially the SSNP (Syrian Social National Party) and the Ba'th. The elections in September produced no clear majority, and a government dominated by the conservative People's Party was formed. In the ensuing months the Syrian Nationalists and the Ba'thists sought to strengthen their relative positions within the army with a flurry of recruiting activity. The mounting tension was climaxed by the assassination of Lieutenant-Colonel Adnan Malki in April 1955. Malki, then Deputy Chief of

Staff, was a Pan-Arab enthusiast and had helped to engineer a mutual defense pact with Egypt and Saudi Arabia; his assassin was a sergeant identified with the SSNP. The episode established an ideological conflict that galvanized the latent political predispositions of the country.

The subsequent elimination of the SSNP as a factor in Syrian politics discredited the ideological approach to regionalism championed by the Syrian Nationalists. It also encouraged an active interest in federalism, and the rising influence of the Ba'th became the vehicle of eventual union with Egypt. During 1956 the People's Party lost its control of the government as the Ba'thists took over key posts in the cabinet. This was followed by intense radicalization, involving the ascendancy of Pan-Arab ideology and the intrusion of Communist influence.

The events of 1957 increased the unionist momentum. The Eisenhower Doctrine, which established anticommunism as the major concern of American policy in the Middle East, was interpreted by Arabs as reflecting a basic disinterest in their own problems. Its ultimate effect, therefore, was to encourage the inclination to neutralism and the search for local initiatives. Jordan, which had been a seat of Western influence, became a political issue in this context. Though Hussein had refused to join the Baghdad Pact and dismissed Glubb Pasha as commander of the Arab Legion, his intentions remained uncertain. The Saudi-Syrian-Egyptian military partnership formed in 1955 sought to draw Jordan into its own orbit, and in October 1956 Hussein agreed to the principle of a central Egyptian command in the event of war with Israel. Later he accepted a subsidy from the three adjacent powers to replace the defunct arrangement with Britain.

The pattern of political development, however, favored polarization over general accord among the Arab states. The neutralist and Pan-Arab thrust of Syrian and Egyptian policy not only inclined Jordan to deal with its financial problems through American aid, but also formed the basis of a pronounced ideological rift that drew Saudi Arabia and the more conservative regimes away from the Saudi-Syrian-Egyptian entente. In the latter part of 1957, anti-Americanism reached new proportions in Syria and was to contribute toward impelling the country into the federal relationship with Egypt. This was established on February 1, 1958 and was called the United Arab Republic (UAR).

The United Arab Republic, to which Yemen adhered through a less binding instrument, seemed at the time to represent a major threshold in the quest for Arab unity. Yet ultimately it was more instrumental in reinforcing regional and divisive tendencies than in fostering the federal idea. This was partly because the merger was hastily effected without much thought to the extensive problems a protracted relationship might entail. The Syrian Ba'thists themselves were moved as much by concern over the extent of Communist influence and the threat of Western intervention as they were by commitment to the principle involved.[19]

From the Egyptian side, Nasser had serious reservations about the union in the light of Syria's internal disorder and the lack of substantial preliminary groundwork.[20] Indicative of the underlying weakness of the experiment was the failure of the merger to expand against the background of the dramatic events that followed. The collapse of the monarchy in Iraq and the American and British intervention in Lebanon and Jordan did not produce any changes in the inter-Arab status quo, as might have been expected. Instead, the next three years witnessed only a gradual disintegration of Syrian-Egyptian relations and the escalation of the "Arab Cold War."

The failure of the UAR is a complex phenòmenon, but certain key factors are readily discernible. The disproportion in the size of the two communities and the personal stature of Nasser made the preponderance of Egypt and a corresponding sense of resentment in Syria inevitable. Equally important was the opposition of Syrian Communists and conservatives to the union, establishing a growing spirit of dissent. At the same time, the Ba'thists, who had anticipated a powerful ideological role, were disenchanted by their own eclipse through the abolition of parties and the emergence of internal division within the Ba'th itself. Underlying the breach between the Ba'thists and their erstwhile hero was the emotional and idealistic content of Syrian Pan-Arabism, which stood in contrast to the pragmatic and professional approach to neutralism and Arab politics on the part of Nasser.[21] While the Ba'th sought to project its own political style onto the charismatic image of the Egyptian leader, Nasser himself was disdainful of the Ba'th as a group and questioned Syrian Pan-Arabism as a mature ideology.

The decisive factors in the demise of the UAR were cultural and economic. The regional identities of Egypt and Syria were not changed by the union, and the developing frictions mentioned above helped to magnify the essential differences. Most basic, however, was the economic discrepancy, aggravated as it was by the decline in Syria's relatively higher standard of living and the attempt to amalgamate the two systems under a socialist program. The mounting conflict of interests was resolved through a coup engineered by Syrian army officers on September 28, 1961. This resulted in the reestablishment of Syria's independence, and marked a significant turn of events in the history of contemporary Arab politics.

The 1960s witnessed an increasing complication of inter-Arab relations. Though there was an initial waning of tension with the West, owing in part to the more restrained policies of the Kennedy administration and to the successful outcome of the Algerian revolution, new divisive forces came into play. The civil war which began in Yemen in 1962 became a focus of expanding military rivalry between Egypt and the monarchies of Saudi Arabia and Jordan. Though the war and the participation of contending regimes did not alter the initial victory of the republicans it did serve to deepen the ideological rift between "Arab socialism" and the more conservative political elements, reinforcing regional antagonisms.

Within the socialist camp itself there was further fragmentation. In the early part of 1963, Ba'thist coups took place in Iraq and Syria, ending the separatist regimes in Baghdad and Damascus. This opened the possibility not only of the restoration of the UAR, but of Iraqi participation as well. Hence the Cairo negotiations of March and April between President Nasser and representatives of Syrian and Iraqi Pan-Arabism.[22] Despite the unanimous commitment to the principle of union, the meetings revealed a pronounced disagreement over methods and ideology, as well as a basic personal mistrust between Nasser and the Ba'thists in particular. More specifically, while the visitors expressed a fear of Egyptian disregard for democratic procedure, Nasser was equally suspicious of an arrangement that might put him between "the hammer and the anvil" of a Syrian-Iraqi contrivance. These attitudes reflected not only serious personal frictions, but the traditional regional concerns with which the Fertile Crescent and the Nile Valley had viewed each other for millennia.

The conference, which had from the start assumed a mood of acrimony and recrimination, failed to achieve anything on behalf of a movement toward greater Arab unity. If anything, it magnified the differences rather than the areas of common accord among the participants, and later the purely Ba'thist elements had a general falling out with Nasser. Even the proposal for a Syrian-Iraqi union, to which the Ba'thists of both countries then turned, failed to materialize because of local rivalries and organizational differences.

By the end of 1963, the disintegration of inter-Arab relations had reached an alarming stage, setting in motion an attempt to redress the situation, at least superficially. The Jordan water controversy with Israel became the lever through which Nasser sought to improve Egypt's position in the Arab world. By convening a summit conference in Cairo in 1964, he deflected attention from embittered regional feuds to the common danger of Israel, and effected a more harmonious climate in Arab affairs.[23] Yet the new spirit of amity proved very temporary, owing in part to the continuing Saudi-Egyptian conflict over resolution of the Yemen affair. A further source of renewed friction was the emergence of the Palestine resistance movement, establishing the question of Palestinian rights as an ideological issue with left-right political implications.

The interplay of these initiatives and directions determined the confused course of inter-Arab relations on the eve of the June War in 1967. The war itself became a threshold in the drama of contemporary Arab politics, but before reviewing this most recent phase, attention is drawn briefly to the smaller and peripheral regional movements in the area during the period following the end of World War II.

Lebanon, which had achieved a special status under Ottoman and French rule, continued to maintain its sovereignty and unique identity after 1945. Despite the abortive SSNP coups in 1949 and 1961-1962 and the unsettling events of 1958, the country maintained the delicate balance of interests that had become the key to its independence. Though only a fraction professed a doctrinaire Lebanese nationalism, the principle of separatism commanded the tacit support of most the population and encouraged a highly localized form of regionalism.

Another example of subregionalism is found in the Sudan. Though the Sudan forms part of the Nile Valley complex and has many natural ties with Egypt, it is also drawn to political separatism. As noted above, the Mahdist episode was an expression of this tendency. In the period after World War II, the future of the Sudan remained uncertain, and the unionist and separatist positions were represented by the National Unionist and Umma parties respectively. The ensuing complex political pattern involved a combination of British, Egyptian, and rival local interests and resulted in the proclamation of an independent Sudan on January 1, 1956. Despite the strong Arab orientation of the northern sector, the separatist leanings of the south have served to maintain Sudanese nationalism as a continuing vehicle in the search for reconciliation.[24]

The Maghrib is another site of regional and subregional political development.[25] In general, the Maghrib has been essentially detached from the mainstream of Arab affairs in modern times. Geographically and culturally distinct, the region met the problem of French colonialism in relative isolation. The early nationalists aspired to a program of independence and regional federation, but in practice the liberation movements of the component parts resolved the problem of sovereign status independently, establishing separate and ideologically diverse regimes. This not only precluded the formation of a Maghrib nation, but divided the area with respect to the more general issues of Arab political development. The idea of regional nationalism remains a natural but as yet latent course for the Maghrib states to follow. The impediments stem from the divergence of local ideologies and the general onus on sectional systems not basically committed to the broader concept of Arab unity.

More remote peripheral movements have taken place recently in the Arabian Peninsula. The ebbing British control in Aden gave way first to a South Arabian Federation and then to the formation of the People's Republic of South Yemen. On the eastern shores, a conservative Federation of Arab Emirates tied the Trucial States to each other in a loose political system, but failed to include Qatar, Bahrein, and Oman, which established independent sovereignty. These developments underline the continuity of highly fragmented subregional policies in outlying sectors of the Arab world and do not as yet assume a significant role in the conduct of Arab affairs.

Returning to the situation prevailing after the 1967 June War, the course of Arab politics assumed new dimensions at that point. The elaborate images of Pan-Arabism were gradually overshadowed by more pragmatic approaches to the challenge of viability. In this context, the Ba'thist regimes in Syria and Iraq were consigned to isolation, while the Palestinian movement developed a regional character in the sense that it was openly attacked in Lebanon and Jordan and unofficially downgraded in Cairo. Though all Arab states espoused the rights of the Palestinians, their commandos found themselves increasingly on their own and short of material and moral support. The Khartoum Summit Conference in August 1967 was deferential to the Palestinians in resolving against peace with Israel, but a companion resolution recognized the right of Egypt and Jordan to seek a political solution with respect to occupied territories.[26] The conference also produced a reconciliation between Egypt and the monarchies of Jordan and Saudi Arabia, and an end to the Yemen dispute, marking the subordination of ideological to practical considerations.

The prestige of the Palestinians soared briefly after the successful commando engagement with Israeli forces at Karamah on March 21, 1968. But the clash with other interests was inevitable. The resistance was counting on an overriding Pan-Arab sympathy with their cause, but the immediate problems of Israeli occupation established the priority of regional prerogatives, especially in Jordan and Egypt. Ultimately, Hussein engaged the commandos in open confrontation, beginning with the civil disorder in September 1970 and ending with the virtual termination of Palestinian activity in Jordan during the summer of 1971.

Egypt remained outwardly committed to the Palestinian cause, but actively sought a settlement that would involve recognition of Israel in exchange for return of the occupied territories. The embarrassment caused by this double standard was adroitly offset by Nasser at the Rabat Summit Conference in December 1969. Demanding that the other Arab states share the responsibilities of a future war with Israel, he employed the lack of enthusiastic commitment to abandon the conference and establish Egypt's right to deal with the problem of Israel in its own way.[27]

Later the same month, Nasser laid the foundations of a regional system against Israel with Libya and the Sudan. During 1970, the three states gradually developed the idea of a federation. At the end of November, Syria expressed interest in the scheme, and on September 2, 1971, joined with Egypt and Libya to form the Federation of Arab Republics. The Sudan, still shaken by the internal disorders of the summer—coups and countercoups—delayed participation until a later date. The new organization reflected a combination of Pan-Arab and regional elements. The constitution upheld the principle of a single Arab nationality and specifically rejected regionalism as a policy or a goal.[28] Yet the federation was a regional arrangement, originally an African-Arab project which Syria joined to work its way out of isolation. And though there was a common flag and ambassadors were replaced by "relations officers," the members pledged only to coordinate their activities without surrendering their essential sovereignty. As such, the federation represented a compromise. Increasing antagonism between Nasser's successor, Anwar al-Sadat, and Libya's ruler, Muammar al-Qaddafi, over participation in the internal affairs of each other's country has led to the disintegration and, for all practical purposes, the demise of this attempt at unity.

## The Future of Arab Regionalism

Arab regionalism is the contemporary manifestation of a powerful social force that has played an important role in the history of the Middle East since the dawn of civilization. It stands in juxtaposition to an equally resilient impulse to unity, nourished by a sense of common destiny and a fear of foreign control. Together the two predispositions provide the framework of political conflict in Arab affairs and the source of rivalry and incompatible policies.

Perhaps the most important key to any future resolution of the dilemma lies in reconsideration of structure as an issue in modern development. The existence of divergent inclinations cannot be changed; but the approach to political evolution can be questioned and revised. Traditionally, ecumenical sovereignty was considered the natural form of Islamic cohesion and self-defense in an alien world. But the radical transition in political organization introduced after World War I altered the system of imperial relationships that had prevailed for centuries. The continuance of colonialism under new institutions proved to be a passing institution in the usual sense of administrative control, while the bloc system replaced the obsolete concept of imperial power.

Particular sovereignty in the context of regional organization has taken precedent over the imperial traditions of the past. From an Arab perspective this suggests the viability of intergovernmental arrangements, combining the prerogatives of sectional and broader goals. The major obstructions to such a course of development are the emotional appeal of Pan-Arabism as an ideal and the onus placed on regionalism as a political program. The negative attitude toward regional initiatives stems from the association of statist policies with petty interests or Western machinations. Yet while both continue to play a role in the area, their influence is declining, and the efficacy of multilateral systems, which combine the need for collaboration with respect for separate identities, seems increasingly plausible.

The general sense of malaise that demoralized the Arab world after the June War has set in motion a search for less doctrinaire and more practical avenues of political maturation. The ideological factor, in which Pan-Arabism figures prominently, has been subordinated to the deeper issues of viability. This is not to suggest that moral questions, such as the fundamental rights of the Palestinians, have been discarded, but to point out the increased awareness of pragmatic considerations and the processes of world politics.

In the confusion of untoward international events, which has found the Middle East rather shortchanged in the balance of interests, the Arabs seem in the 1970s to be sifting the grain from the chaff. It is a painful process, involving a reevaluation of regional and ecumenical perspectives. The ultimate outcome will depend upon the degree to which the decisive forces of political decision-making can establish realistic aims in the context of valid aspirations and recognized limitations. Between the unnatural fragmentation imposed by the

West on the Arab world in the course of a century and the compensatory dream of a secular Arab empire, there may yet be a hopeful and promising social reconstruction. This dream, furthermore, has been given substance by the moral victory given the Arabs as a result of the October 1973 war.

One avenue of mutual endeavor likely to play a prominent role in the development of inter-Arab relations is economic cooperation. In recent years the need for an "economic ideology" has been generally recognized, and it is to be anticipated that a variety of regional arrangements will assume an increasingly important role. Within the Arab League there already exist institutions for the promotion of joint development programs and the formation of an Arab common market. These include the Arab Development Bank and the Council for Arab Economic Union.[29] Though both agencies have fallen far short of their full operative capacity, they could provide the functional basis for a new and as yet untested system of Arab interdependency.

The most dramatic experiment in international economic cooperation to affect the Arab world has been the Organization of the Petroleum Exporting Countries (OPEC).[30] Established in 1960 by Venezuela, Saudi Arabia, Kuwait, Iran, and Iraq, OPEC now also includes Indonesia, Libya, Qatar, Abu Dhabi, Algeria, and Nigeria. The original aim of OPEC was "the coordination and unification of the petroleum policies of member countries and the determination of the best means for safeguarding their interests, individually and collectively." More specifically, the participants sought to stabilize prices in international crude oil markets and to insure a steady income for the producing nations.

In practice, OPEC has been successful in minimizing price fluctuation and establishing regular royalty levels. But its role has been expanded by recent developments. Early in 1971, the enhanced bargaining power of OPEC was demonstrated by an agreement to a substantial increase in royalties reached with the companies in Teheran. A year later, the far more significant question of joint ownership—referred to as participation—became the subject of discussion between representatives of the producers and the host countries. The immediate concern of the oil-producing states is to win a 20 percent share in the ownership of companies operating within their borders, but the ultimate objective is to establish effective control through holdings of 51 percent or more.

The leverage that OPEC has been able to exercise, combined with the threat of nationalization most recently apparent in Libya, indicates a profound change in the patterns of international petroleum control. And considering the prominent role played by Arab states in the OPEC system, the attractiveness of this type of regional cooperation is certain to influence the course of inter-Arab policies.

In 1968 a purely Arab oil consortium was formed by Saudi Arabia, Kuwait, and Libya—the Organization of Arab Petroleum Exporting Countries (OAPEC).[31] Algeria, Abu Dhabi, Bahrein, Dubai, and Qatar were admitted to membership in 1970, while Iraq, Syria, and Egypt became members on March 4,

1972. A balance of radical and conservative interests was thereby preserved. But OAPEC remains an essentially incomplete and untested association. As with all other projects of inter-Arab cooperation on the economic level, its ultimate effectiveness will be determined by the degree to which a political accommodation can be achieved. Here again, the interaction of regional and ecumenical inclinations will play a decisive role.

# Introduction to Chapter 2

*In this second chapter, Dr. Atiyeh stresses the importance of Islam to the Arab. Even in a modern world, where the Westerner takes for granted the separation of church from state, Islam continues to hold Arabdom in a tight grip. It is true that certain modernizing innovations have curtailed the all-embracing powers of Islam. However, indications emanating from the Arab world point to the fact that Islam is being used as a means to revitalize the region.*

*Dr. Atiyeh discusses in great detail the various social roles Islam plays in the Arab community. As Dr. Taylor stated in Chapter 1, this chapter, too, shows Islam to foster both unity and disunity. He focuses on Arab society—both its class structure and its religious institutions. He stresses, too, the role Islam has played in stultifying creativeness and innovation among the Arabs, thereby forcing them to face a modern world with unrealistic concepts. He concludes by describing the impact Westernization has had on the Arab world and the response of Islam toward this challenge. This response is seen today in the actions of the leading Arab personages in their rejection of Western ideologies and culture and their adherence to those ideas they consider to have originated in the Arab world.*

# 2 Islam and Its Cultural Aspects

George N. Atiyeh

The main purpose of this chapter is the examination of the role of Islam in the world, in particular the Arab world, as an effective social force in molding the attitudes and behavior of Muslims.

There is no doubt that Islam is a dynamic religion. Dynamic here does not mean solely a manifestation of movement or change but rather the interesting phenomenon of displaying a great variation and contrast in force and intensity, coupled with an undiminished ability to have a strong hold on the great majority of its adherents. In an era when religion is on the defensive and is groping for new directions and goals to readjust to the challenges of our times, Islam does seem to have retained much of its impact, at least to the emotions of its adherents and their sense of belief that they belong to the true religion. This phenomenon may be seen as both a source of strength and of weakness.

In order to understand this phenomenon and how it affects Muslims, the nature and doctrines of Islam must be examined before the cultural aspects of present-day Islam are studied: what are the unifying creeds, rites, duties, and institutions and how did they develop into their present status? The variety of images of Islam as construed by the intellectual class will then be scrutinized, in as much as these are reflections of the attitudes of Muslims towards themselves and towards others. Furthermore, this chapter will attempt to answer the questions: what are the forces of unity and disunity that are operating at present; how are these reflected in the life of the urban and village groups; and finally, how are specific problems dealt with or considered by the educated and the noneducated Arab Muslims?

Needless to say, the content and conclusions of the essay are observational in that they are based on personal knowledge and readings and not on field work.

## Islam as a Community: The Basis for Unity

The preeminent feature of Islam is its social organization as a community (*ummah*) that unites the secular and the religious in one single and interwoven system. The *ummah* is the only true "nation" in which a Muslim has membership. The fact that this community was only briefly a unified political organization is discarded by the true believer. The political states that have

27

arisen inside the body of the community are considered by him to be accidental and irrelevant. Anyone attempting, therefore, to understand Islam as a moving and unifying force must take into account this basic concept and consider the variations that have taken place within its framework. Let us then consider the growth of Islam as a community and look at the unifying and diversifying factors in its structure.

Fourteen centuries ago Islam was founded in Mecca (now in Saudi Arabia). Muhammad, its founder, belonged to the Quraysh clan of the Hashimite tribe. Persecuted in his own city of Mecca after proclaiming that he was a messenger of God, he made a pact with the people of Yathrib (now Medina) to which he fled on July 15, 622. This flight (*Hegira*) is the start of the Muslim calendar as well as the beginning of the Muslim era.

Preaching a monotheistic religion in the name of Allah (the Arabic name for God), Muhammad was soon to build a community (*ummah*) in which the religious and the secular, the spiritual and the material, were fused and interwoven. Before his death in 632 A.D., it became clear that Islam was not simply an amalgam of new and old beliefs. It was instead a new religion involving the establishment of an independent community, with its own system of government, laws, institutions, and above all with a new vision toward history and life.

One of the main social features of Islam (which in Arabic means submission to God) has been the complete integration of religion and state. However, as it developed internally while its atmosphere of political and religious influence was extended from China to the Atlantic, Islam also grew into an integrated culture with one system of values.

Once established in Medina, the distinctions among Islam, Christianity, and Judaism became clear. Friday, instead of Saturday or Sunday, was ordained as the day for congregational prayer. The *Qiblah* (i.e., the direction toward which the Muslim must face for ritual prayer) was transferred from Jerusalem to Mecca. Furthermore, Muhammad declared himself the last of the prophets and, as such, the carrier to mankind of the exact and unadulterated word of God as it was first given to Abraham. Moses and Jesus, among others, were equally messengers chosen by God to carry His word to mankind. However, Jews and Christians have tampered with the original message. The Koran, therefore, is the noblest of the holy books and the last of God-given scriptures to come to mankind. It abrogates all other sacred works that preceded it, and its ordinances are to remain in force till the Day of Resurrection. The Koran was dictated by Gabriel from an archtype in heaven, and, therefore, it is, in a way, a manifestation of God to this world. This miraculous character of the Koran makes it inimitable. Having been revealed in Arabic, its use in religious rites must be limited to that language.

Islam is simply the religion of God. When God created the world, He provided a pattern of living for man and conveyed it through His prophets. But the clear statements of His biddings were corrupted and God in His infinite mercy has now conveyed through Muhammad the true beliefs and practices that would lead mankind into salvation. Islam was not only a restatement of eternal truth; it was also the application of this truth under which society would live.

The doctrines contained in the Koran that the adherents to Islam must accept are: the oneness of God, Muhammad's apostleship, the belief in angels, and the belief in a final day of judgment. In addition to these doctrines, it is incumbent upon Muslims to obey certain divine prescriptions or duties both as individuals and as a community. Designed as the pillars of Islam, these duties are: (1) the confessions of faith, namely believing and stating "There is no deity save Allah: Muhammad is the apostle of Allah"; (2) prayer; (3) almsgiving; (4) fasting during the month of Ramadan; and (5) pilgrimage to Mecca. In the early period of Islam, *jihad* (often translated as "holy war") was also considered a pillar. Today it is advocated as the Muslim community's effort to spread God's rule on earth and to defend the faith.

The accomplishment of these duties will not automatically lead to salvation; they must be accompanied by heart-felt piety and the desire to perform them out of conviction. This devotional aspect of Islam is personal and dependent upon the sincerity and depth of one's faith. Furthermore, the performance of the prescribed duties sets the framework within which Islam as a community is distinguished. In addition to the pillars, the call to prayer from the top of the minarets five times a day, the rhythmical use of the lunar calendar, the interdiction against eating pork meat and the consumption of alcohol, the cemeteries that are not supposed to be transferred or desecrated, and the circumcision of children—all create a picture of what a Muslim community is. The cement that binds the community is the Sacred Law or *Shari'ah* that regulates the relations of man to God and man to man. The prescribed duties covering the religious, political, social, domestic, and private life of Muslims are its basic concerns. In fact, it has been the unifying force in Islamic culture; Islamic social integration has heretofore depended on it. It is because of this particular link between the different aspects of life that Islam must be considered a religion as well as a state. The Sacred Law has produced a community of believers united by the same comprehensive legal system and by the same common principles of social and political organization. The unity of Islam, therefore, resides in the awareness that the Koran and the Sunnah (sayings and actions of Muhammad and his companions which are considered as models of action) are the sources of the Sacred Law. To live according to God's rules is to obey the Sacred Law in all its encompassing details. The Sacred Law's program for man covers the political, social, and economic structure of society and the details of man's everyday chores. All actions, somehow, become religious actions in Islam.

The separation between state and religion to which the West has grown accustomed does not exist in Islam. However, Islam is not simply a theocracy. It is a special kind of theocracy best described in the words of the French scholar Luis Gardet as a "lay theocracy" in that it does not have a priesthood and has displayed all along an egalitarian sense of association. The ideal state as conceived by early Muslim thinkers is one in which conformity to the Sacred Law is dominant, obedience to the ruler complete, righteousness supreme, and justice equally executed.

Given this pervasiveness of religion in Muslim life, it is no wonder that the culture Islam inspired and under whose aegis it grew became intimately connected with religion. In the Muslim countries neither science nor secular literature or art were separated from religion in the way that certain branches of modern humanism were in the West. Radical ideas existed but never prospered.

## The Bases of Disunity

Now we shall take a brief look at the history of Islam, in which the gap between ideals and facts, and between aspiration and fulfillment begin to be clarified. No sooner had Muhammad died than the Muslims began to fight among themselves. The feud between the Caliph 'Ali, cousin and son-in-law of Muhammad, and Mu'awiyah, Ummayad Governor of Syria, led to the first and perhaps the greatest division within Islam. Shi'ism, the competitor to the Sunni or orthodox Islam, appeared and has remained dominant in many regions of the Islamic world, particularly in Iran and southern Iraq. No less than seventy-two more sects were to appear; but except for a very few—mostly offshoots within Shi'ism—these sects did not endure the test of time.

The divisive forces within the state itself began as early as 756. The only remaining member of the Ummayad family (661-750) had wrested from the triumphant Abbasid dynasty (750-1258) the reins of the government of Spain, and declaring it an independent province, established therein a permanent adversary of Baghdad, the new capital of the Abbasid caliphate. After that, it did not take long for other governors throughout the Islamic empire to form their own states and, except for a nominal allegiance to the caliph, to become independent for all practical purposes. Even centuries later after the Turks had taken over the caliphate (1517-1924) and their dominion extended over parts of Europe and most of the Arab world, the Islamic states of Shi'ite Iran, the Indian Empire of the Great Moghols, and Morocco maintained their independence from the main body of Islam. Politically speaking, therefore, the unity that existed in the early Islamic community prior to the triumph of the Abbasids was lost, never to be regained again. In the Arab world a shade of this unity lingered in the form of allegiance to the Ottoman Empire inspired by the deep rooted loyalty to the caliph as the embodiment of the unity of the community. But even this symbolical unity was shattered when the caliphate was eliminated by Kemal Ataturk in 1924 and it was proven that the community does not require the caliphate to give it a political or religious reason for existence. The idea of regionalism and regional loyalty, never absent, grew stronger as nationalism gained strength and became the principal concept among the ranks of the elite. They have come to regard Islamic institutions as political instruments, that are subject to the will of the regional community, which may be abrogated at any time as national interests dictate. In Tunisia, for example, fasting during the month of Ramadan is discouraged because it might interfere with productivity.

The causes for disunity are not difficult to determine. Internally any religion is subject to a variety of interpretations as theological speculation grows. This usually leads to the emergence of different sects. Politically, regional interests in the form of "nationalistic" feelings have always been a strong factor in the creation of new states within the Islamic empire. The attitudes of Muslim Arabs toward the Muslim non-Arabs and the differences and disputes between northern and southern Arabs, has played a major role in the erosion of the unifying power of the Islamic state.

In summary the Islamic faith provided a sense of commonality among Muslims, but it was unable to institutionalize this sense after the early Abbasid period. The diverse regional traditions and feelings that antedated Islam surfaced again and have remained with the Muslims to the present day.

## Islam and the Arabs

In order to understand the forces of unity and diversity in the Muslim community, one has to examine (1) how the Muslims, both Arabs and non-Arabs, conceive of their particular roles within the community, and (2) what are the realities of the present situation.

The Western world has the impression that Islam and Arabism are one and the same, which is not true. However, there is some historical basis for this impression. Given the fact that the Prophet was an Arab, that Arabia was the birthplace of Islam, and that Arabic is the only language authorized for the performance of the liturgy, the Arabs are bound to be given a place of preeminence in the Muslim community.

The Arab image of themselves today is perhaps best described by Dr. Jamal Hamdan who perceives the Islamic world as a radio-concentric system with the Arab lands forming its heart. Islam first appeared in Arabia, and spread throughout most of the Arab world during the first few decades after the Hegira. One hundred million Arab Muslims, comprising one-fifth of the Islamic world's population, congregate mostly in its settled centers. The Christian and Jewish minorities within the Muslim sphere are seen by Dr. Hamdan as small pockets having little numerical importance and living on the periferies of Muslim civilization. The quality of Islam in its heartland (i.e., the Arab world) is the purest. The closer a people is to the core, the greater is its association with Islam.

The Arab world is not only the heart but also the stronghold of Islam. By virtue of its language and history it is the natural guardian of Islam, on whose shoulders rests the responsibility of serving and preserving it. "The Arab world, by necessity, is the great 'school' of Islam; it is a huge 'theological seminary' for the whole Muslim world and in which there are no distinction of classes or races. What we mean, therefore, is that the Arabs are not the lords of Islam, they are simply the keepers of its temple."[1]

The Arabs, among all the Muslim community, feel more intensely the glory of Islam. Their pride in its past achievements has blinded many of them to the realities of the present. Likewise, many Christian Arabs take pride in the great contributions made by medieval Islamic culture to the world of learning. As such, Islam is seen as an expression of the genius of the Arab and a proof of his capacity to create and to contribute to world civilization.

This image the Arabs have of themselves has been expressed in different forms throughout their history, but in spite of the variations in expression it has been consistently preserved, becoming one of the causes of constraint in inter-Muslim relations. The argument of Muslim non-Arabs is as follows: If all believers are equals and brothers, the Arabs should have not more than an honorary place in the community. In the past the Arabs never resolved whether a non-Arab is really a complete Muslim. In early Islam they did not abide by the spirit of universalism and egalitarianism required by their religion. Their old pride in blood and tribal relations clung to them. Instead, it was transferred to the religious sphere. Pride in their preeminent role in Islam was a major cause of the downfall of the Ummayad Dynasty, the purest of all Arab ruling houses in Islam. During the Abbasid period, the *Shu'ubiyyah* movement (i.e., the movement of the non-Arab "peoples" to reassert their own national values) gained importance. Led by the Persians, Arabic lost ground to the Persian language which became the symbol of national pride and the desire for cultural independence.

Whether or not unity does exist in Islam, it is not manifested either in a political or a cultural system. Islam has spread among many nationalities, races, regions, and languages, and diversity seems to be the rule today. The pursuit of unity by Muslims, particularly Sunnis, has been throughout Islamic history a driving force, but in the face of the hard facts of life which heretofore have divided Muslims, unity remains no more than an aspiration. The only tie is an individual inner feeling of membership in one community that has as its base the Koran and the Sacred Law. The ideas of political unity in Islam—whether they be the Pan-Islamism to which the Ottomans subscribed up to the end of World War I, or the Islamic League advocated by the late King Faysal of Saudi Arabia, the Shah of Iran, and the King of Morocco—are only expedient political tools to serve as a temporary political cause, and in the later case, opposition to what is termed "progressive forces."

Culturally speaking, each of the major Islamic political units—the Arab world,

Turkey, Iran, Pakistan, Indonesia, and the Central Asian Republics of the Soviet Union—represents a completely autonomous cultural entity that operates independently from the others.

## Arab Society

Let us now focus our attention on the modern Arab world and examine in some detail its diverse cultural and religious situation. On the surface, the Arab world, made up now of twenty states, shows as much diversity in its internal set-up as the rest of the Islamic world. However, if we, as outside observers, look at the social order, we will find certain similarities, particularly in the classification of the social groups influenced by Islam. Society may be divided into five groups: administrators, army, men of religion, merchants, and the proletariat. The first two belong to the class we may label *governors*; the latter two, to the *governed* class; the men of religion form a class of their own. Intellectuals and professionals fall into several categories, but generally they may be safely classified with the *governors*. Yet if we further scrutinize this society, we shall find that, far from being a harmonious whole, it is a society lacking in integration. Two major obstacles, in this author's opinion, have hindered its growth.

The first deterrent to integration in society originates in the concept that none but Muslims may be full citizens of an Islamic state. Non-Muslims are allowed to enjoy certain rights as spelled out in a specified contract (*dhimmah*) which guarantees their lives and properties. The term most commonly used in Islamic Sacred Law for the fully qualified free citizen is *mukallaf* (one on whom is laid full responsibility for the performance of his religious duties). These at times included *jihad*. Consequently a non-Muslim citizen, by definition, cannot assume the full responsibilities of a Muslim citizen. Needless to say, the armies of most of the Arab states enlist or draft Christians as well as Muslims, but the equality in citizenship, especially in those countries with religious minorities, rests on one's confessionary status. All Arab constitutions guarantee equality of rights and duties to all non-Muslims, but whenever Islam is cited as being the religion of the state (Lebanon excepted), a fundamental contradiction arises: how can one be an equal citizen and still not enjoy full citizenship? In addition, if we consider the deep and entrenched misunderstanding between the different religions, one may understand why the political integration of Arab societies into harmonious political communities has not as yet been achieved. Until now, society in the Arab world is made up of two groups, Muslims (*mukallafs*) and non-Muslims (*dhimmis*), and said in another way, full-citizens and citizens, thereby avoiding the use of the term "second-class citizens."

The second obstacle to full social integration is a result of the existence within the Islamic community of ethnic and religious minorities. Ethnic minorities include Kurds and Berbers, while 'Alawis, Druzes, Zaydis, and

Isma'ilis are among the religious. The historical relationship between these minorities and the Arab Muslim Sunni majority has always been tense and has caused disruption in many Muslim regions.

Even if we consider Arab society from an anthropological point of view, we shall find it to be a conglomeration of urban groups, tribes, and peasant societies. It is no wonder that Carleton Coon saw the Arab world as a "mosaic" of peoples and religions. We may add that the mosaic shows little or no signs of an internal harmonious pattern.

It is of little value for our purposes to examine the social structure of the tribes and villagers. We may say in passing that Islam did not fundamentally change their social or political outlook. Their ways of living have remained almost intact for hundreds of years. In spite of the presence of hundreds of thousands of radio sets, a strong attachment to inherited basic attitudes and modes of behavior and psychology beyond the reach of foreign ideas and influences is actively displayed. Of course some effects of modern life are visible, but on the whole the villagers and tribal members of North Africa, Egypt, Sudan, Iraq, and the Arabian peninsula remain in a backwater existence.

Urban groups have been the leaders of modernization and change. There is a dialectical relationship between their religious traditions and present-day society in the cities and towns of the Arab world.

Under the impact of modernization and evolving internal events, both leadership and institutions have undergone tremendous changes. As a consequence new problems have arisen that demand new solutions. The traditional leadership of the 'Ulama—those versed in religion and the Sacred Law and are also responsible for the performance of some legal duties—is dwindling. The Sufi orders (tariqas) that dominated the religious scene between the twelfth and twentieth centuries have disappeared for all practical purposes. Their influence, however, lingers on in North Africa, Sudan, and parts of Egypt. In the past the Sufi orders provided the Muslim masses with a sense of cohesiveness and belonging, but in the process accumulated superstitions and fostered fatalism and apathy among those masses. Consequently they became the targets of all reformers when the reform movements began to emerge at the end of the nineteenth century.

### The Urban Response to the Challenge of Modernism

The challenge of the West had its greatest response in the urban centers where the elite resided, and resulted initially in intellectual responses. The fact that Wahhabism appeared in the Arabian peninsula in the eighteenth century does not invalidate our thesis since Wahhabism might be considered a great spiritual revival. However, it was certainly oriented towards pristine Islam.

The movement of modernization in the Middle East in general and the Arab world in particular appeared to be an answer to the question "Why are the Muslims backward?" It started as an endeavor to find out and remedy the causes of backwardness and disruption. There were many and varied responses. Some attributed the causes of backwardness to fatalism and complete dependence on the "Unseen." Others saw causes in the passivism generated in the past by the triumph and spread of the mystical philosophy of al-Ghazzali (d. 1111 A.D.), a leading Islamic religious thinker. He advocated spiritualism and exhorted the Muslims to seek piety and to remove themselves, away from the temptations of the world. A corollary to this is the triumph of tradition over reason and the loss of the spirit of adventure and openness that characterized the early periods of Islam.

Others attributed their backwardness, political as well as cultural and religious, to the influence of colonialism and the subsequent adoption of Western values in the nineteenth century. As a result, a trend of thinking opposing everything foreign began to emerge. Enhanced by the growth of nationalism, this trend became the greatest moving force in the Arab world, especially when it was translated into political action. Even those who favored an open society after independence and called for the adoption of Western methodology expressed themselves in anticolonial and anti-Western terms. President Nasser in an address to a congress of Arab writers in 1957 called upon the writers to create an Arabic literature "which is liberated and autonomous, released from foreign domination and influence."[2] In my opinion, this distrust of alien ideas and not the desire for self-assertion is responsible for there being an "Arab" or "Islamic" socialism, rather than a socialism copied *in toto* from the West.

One of the major problems facing modernization in the Arab world has been the inability to reconcile the ideal Islamic view of the community and state with the actual historical evolution in society. Beginning with the 19th century, the military reforms of Selim III in the Ottoman Empire and Muhammad 'Ali in Egypt introduced lasting changes in the traditional system of organization and method that were irreversible. General economic growth, expansion of transport and communication, and the rise in education brought about the breakdown of the old economic and social systems on which religious and social patterns of authority were based.

The Sacred Law (*Shari'ah*) suffered most when the breakdown of the old system occurred. Depending mostly on *taqlid*, literally defined as "imitation" but in reality meaning "lack of creativity," the later medieval jurists had petrified the Sacred Law and had reduced it to a mechanical concern for matters of detail and rigid formulation. Under the impact of modernization and changing internal circumstances, secularization of the Sacred Law began and has continued, until now, unabated. Reformers among the intellectuals, and even among some of the *'Ulamas*, began to question the validity of the Sacred Law for use by modern society. For many, passivity has been replaced by activism, including the formulation and adoption of new interpretations. However, this has remained on a small scale and the submission of the fundamental principles of the *Shari'ah* to rational scrutiny and analysis has not met with great success. Nevertheless, transformation of the *Shari'ah* into national laws modeled upon Western concepts has been encouraged in some countries, while in others (Saudi Arabia, for example), it has remained almost intact. Perhaps out of pragmatic consideration and the use as a guide of "the interest of the community" (*al-maslahah*), jurists in Lebanon and Syria consider it possible to waive temporarily religious injunctions and to adopt those laws that would improve the welfare of the community. They approach this question with the argument that to waive some injunctions certainly does not mean the nullification of the Sacred Law since the basic aim of the *Shari'ah* is the welfare of the community. They further believe it is important to specify in the constitution of the state that the Sacred Law is the source of inspiration for all legislation even though some legislation is contradictory to it. This is how one should understand the article in the constitution of the recently created Federation of Arab Republics in which Islam is stipulated as the religion of the state.

In general, except for laws regulating personal status, the Islamic system of law in the Arab world (Saudi Arabia excepted) has been used to legitimize principles of action on the basis of interest and practicality. Arab Muslims have often successfully rationalized change by citing Koranic verses or traditions in support of new procedures, thereby effecting modernization while working within the framework of Islam. On the other hand, modernists led by Ataturk placed themselves outside this framework by adopting completely Westernized legal systems and methodologies.

The modernization of the Sacred Law was certainly inspired by the desires of the politicians to reform and revitalize the social structure of Islam. The term "human dignity" became the guiding spirit of the new legislators, or so it was stated by the new generation of leaders. However, considering the status of civil rights in Europe and the United States of America, the masses and the minorities in the Arab world as yet have not felt an improvement to their "human dignity." They feel disturbed since the spirit of secularization and the true appreciation of the principles of the natural rights of man have not penetrated into the inner structure of society despite considerable favorable legislation enacted to that effect. At times they wonder whether this will ever happen in the Arab world. On the other hand, the *'Ulama* are profoundly disturbed by the secularization of the Sacred Law. Even the liberals among them look at secularization with dismay. Secularization to them is tantamount to elimination of the Sacred Law and will eventually undermine the very basis of the community.

The other sphere of modernization where Islamic and historical evolution conflict is in the field of education. The governing classes, in order to meet the challenges of modern life, adopted Western education systems without modification. The Muslim masses that have remained loyal to the inherited culture have displayed little enthusiasm for the newly adopted Western culture. Consequently the chasm separating the elite or "the governors" on one hand and the masses on the other has widened. The governing classes were concerned that the traditional schools (*madrasahs*) with their uncreative methods were unable to cope with the new challenges. The minds of the traditionally taught students would be closed to anything outside the range of their religious and philological studies, since subjects, textbooks, and teaching methods were rigidly standardized. Realizing that the traditional schools could not inaugurate the necessary programs to cope with a rapidly changing society, the governors drew upon Western institutions and methodology to educate the much needed new professional classes and military establishment.

The expected reaction of the religious traditionalists soon took place. Opposition was waged on many fronts and it was not until many years later that the al-Azhar, the leading Muslim institution for learning in Egypt, or perhaps in the Islamic world, became more receptive to Western methodology. By introducing some sciences and humanities into their curriculum, the Azharite faculty reflected both the changing attitudes of the Muslims and their feeling of the need to meet the challenges of the modern world. By the same token minor changes in the curriculum reflected their hesitancy to break away from the past.

Although secular, but for the most part state-run, universities are springing up all over the Arab world, it is still not clear how they will bridge the gap between the ideal and reality. The uncertainty shown by the religious scholars and by the intellectuals regarding the position and orientation of religion in society has not, as far as can be ascertained, greatly affected the identity of all Muslims. The feeling of belonging to Islam is perhaps as strong as ever, and actions and attitudes remain molded by inherited culture. Therefore, any questioning of the basic principles governing an outlook on life and the universe has not resulted in a break from the past. Yet if it has occurred, it has been limited to an enlightened few.

## The Status of Religion in Urban Centers

Religion in the urban centers is practiced on a mass level. The main feature of this level is the Friday service at the mosque where all male Muslims congregate to worship and listen to the imam, or religious leader, deliver a sermon, which may deal with any topic. Lately, however, it has served a double function. First it is used as a vehicle of change to make new ideas, institutions, policies, and even inventions such as television, acceptable to the masses. It is usually the educated and somewhat liberal preachers who have undertaken this role. Second, the Friday sermon has served to recruit support for the government and its policies. It has been very effective in arousing the masses to action in times of crisis. Most of the big demonstrations in the large cities usually start from the mosques after a sermon.

Important in influencing the masses of Muslims is al-Azhar. In the absence of a caliph, the rector of al-Azhar assumes a leading role whenever statements on questions of national or international importance need be made by a high religious authority. Locally, the religious leaders are the *muftis* and *qadis*. A *mufti* is a canon lawyer of standing who gives legal opinions in answer to questions submitted to him either by a *qadi* (judge), or by a private individual. On the basis of such an opinion, called a *fatwa*, a *qadi* may decide a case, thereby regulating an individual's personal life. A *mufti* usually wields moral authority and his pronouncements regarding political issues still carry much weight with the masses. In urban centers, thousands of devout but usually illiterate Muslims are still swayed by the pronouncements of the *muftis* as well as by the local leaders (*zu'ama*) of the different urban quarters. The religious leaders usually preside at religious as well as political affairs of their quarters and sometimes act in response to the national leaders' orders. In other words, the dominant force in a city's quarter is not the religious scholars but the religious leaders who in coordination and collaboration with the local leaders drum up the masses for or against a cause or an issue. The masses more often than not respond to a greater degree to their religious leaders than to their national leaders. That is why government heads heretofore have sought the support of the religious and local leaders more than that of the religious scholars, or the secular intellectuals.

But there are signs of change. Labor unions and official political parties seem to be replacing the local religious leaders. The Arab world is undergoing a momentous process of evolution and revolution. Social structure is being transformed. Naturally, in some places the pace of change is slower than others; but the physical and social transformation is apparent everywhere, even in the remotest corners of Oman. The elite that usually establishes the national goals is also changing. The military man from a middle-class family has replaced the feudal or aristocratic lord in many Arab states. He often is a devout Muslim or identifies himself with Islamic traditions, and usually turns to the secular Muslim intellectual or professional for direction and cooperation. How deep the change has penetrated is not clear; but in my estimation, it is only skin deep.

Modern Muslim intellectuals may be classified as being "secular" or "religious" minded. A "secular" Muslim is not a contradiction in terms because as used here, "secular" is relative and refers not only to a subdued religious fervor but also to a positive attitude towards the problems of modernization; it does not mean dissociation from Islam and its doctrines. The "secular" Muslim is usually educated in a Western-style educational system, or has been exposed to Westernized ideas and ways of life. In general, the Muslim intellectual who seems to express himself in favor of a more democratic way of life, social reform, and tolerance of minorities increases or decreases in dialectical response to his geographical location and to his direct exposure to the West. For example, a university professor from Saudi Arabia who has studied in England or the United

States might find himself in agreement on many issues with his counterpart in Algeria or Lebanon, whereas the great majority of the locally educated intellectuals in Saudi Arabia would differ considerably in their attitudes on similar issues. Furthermore, ideologies have created common grounds and common positions in the different states of the Arab world. The attitudes toward Islam or religion in general run a wide gamut from the extreme right to the extreme left, and cut across the different categories and classes of the elite. For example you will find some extremely conservative students studying in the United States or England, such as those who are members of the International Islamic Federation of Student Organizations.

The leftists and especially the Communists are atheists. This sounds prosaic except for the fact that the Communists have chosen to keep their criticism against religion in the Arab world to a minimum, obviously for tactical reasons. They know that the masses are still stubbornly attached to their inherited religion with its accretions of superstitions and resistance to change. Even though they believe religion is the major obstacle to their plans for attracting the masses to their cause, its hold is so strong that if they were to attack it frontally, irreparable disaster would be the result.

The tactics of the small Communist parties are shared by other leftists. When in 1969 a new-leftist Muslim intellectual, Dr. Sadiq Jalal al-'Azm, decided to attack religion and Islam frontally, the immediate outcome was not only a deluge of articles and books against him, but also an arraignment before the courts (he was later acquitted). Dr. al-'Azm was once a professor at the American University of Beirut and the scion of a well-known Muslim family from Damascus. In his book, entitled *The Critique of Religious Thinking*, he attempted to put the blame for the defeat of the Arabs in 1967 on their religious mentality.[3] According to him, all the self-criticism raised after the war, though uncommon among the Arabs, yet still a healthy sign in itself, only superficially touched upon the issue for the debility of Arab society. In his book he asserted that there is a basic undeniable conflict between science and religion that cannot be reconciled. Substantial differences will always remain. The Arabs have been deceiving themselves by using syncretism, rhetoric, self-justification, and far-fetched and arbitrary interpretations that simply do not conform to reality. Muslim intellectuals talk about the "spirit of religion" and how progressive this is. According to these intellectuals the "spirit of Islam" harmonizes perfectly with science. Some of them have even gone so far as to say that the scientific method itself is derived from the Islamic religion. However, when these same intellectuals are faced with the concrete consequences of the scientific method, both in the physical sciences as well as in life in general, they are unwilling to accept the consequences.

Perhaps what is more significant than the criticism of Professor al-Azm is the reactions provoked by his book. Naturally a few articles came out in his defense and in defense of the freedom of thought in general; but if the number of articles and books written against him is any indication of the feeling of the Muslims towards such criticism, there should be no doubt how the great majority of them stand on that issue. On the other hand, it must also be significant that the book was even written by a Muslim, and an avowed Marxist-Leninist at that. Frontal opposition or criticism to Koranic doctrines has happened very infrequently in the Arab world. The last time such a challenge was made by a Muslim scholar to an Islamic doctrine was in 1926 when Taha Husayn, the eminent Egyptian scholar and literateur, published his work on *Pre-Islamic Poetry*. The book doubted the existence of poetry in Arabia before Islam, a supposition that challenges certain statements found in the Koran. Husayn's theory was immediately construed as a challenge to the word of God. His book was banned until he expunged from it the heretical material and changed its title. It is obvious that any attack on Islam as a religion is easily construed as an attack on the identity of every Muslim and his religious beliefs, thereby turning the question of criticism into an emotional question. The intellectuals who usually take a strong critical position of Islam and of religion in general are the Communists and some of the new-leftists. Both envision and work towards a society devoid of religion and accuse religion and the religious leaders as being used, according to each one's situation, by conservative and/or progressive states to help maintain the *status quo*.

A more moderate attitude towards religion is displayed by small groups of nationalists who call for the separation of state and religion. They argue that religion is a personal affair and that religious institutions, because of their intra- and international implications, could easily work against and endanger national interest and national unity. Furthermore, in a state dominated by religious considerations all rights and interests, whether spiritual or material, become the religious rights and interests of the dominant religious group. This annuls the natural equality among all members of a nation. Unless natural equality takes precedence, there will be no equality of obligations or unity of national will. Most of those who hold this view are the followers of Antun Sa'adeh (d. 1949). They are thinly spread all over the Fertile Crescent states, but the majority of them are concentrated in Lebanon. Similar views are heard from various individual writers, but the idea has not found favor because of the special relationship between Islam and Arab nationalism. The laicization of Arab politics is still in the distant future, in spite of the sporadic attempts at secularization. However, these attempts have raised in the consciousness of the Arab masses the following question: What road do we take—the religious or the secular, the native and inefficient, or the efficient but foreign? This kind of questioning has created one of the major uncertainties in the Arab world today.

### The Arabs and the West

The controversy over the nature of Western and Eastern civilizations must be viewed from the knowledge that the concepts of a "state without religion" and the "separation of state and religion" are Western in origin, and that technology is a Western trademark. In particular an examination of the attitudes of Muslim intellectuals regarding the West would be most revealing as to the type of problems that face them as inividuals and as part of a culture.

It is interesting to note that few of these intellectuals have studied the West as a culture in any comprehensive manner. In other words, there are no Arab or Muslim "Occidentalists" as there are Western "Orientalists." There are, for sure, Westernized Arabs, but this is not the same as dedicating one's whole career to an understanding and clarification of another culture. Likewise this may be said of the Muslim scholars who profess a knowledge of Christianity. It is only in the last two decades that a small number of Muslim intellectuals have begun to study Christianity toward understanding it better.

The West is many things to many people, but there are certain basic characteristics that distinguish its culture and identify its personality. The most basic traits are rationalism and its corollary, humanism—the scientific spirit and technology. When the Arabs awoke in the nineteenth century from the slumber of their middle ages and found Europe, once far behind them but now far ahead, it was natural to deplore their own backwardness and to start emulating Europe and the West. They soon realized that the West's progress was due mainly to the above characteristics and that the price of progress and modernization was the adoption of principles foreign to their culture.

Rationalism is the principle of accepting reason as the supreme authority in matters of knowledge and conduct. In theology it means that reason, unaided by revolution, is an adequate or sole guide to all attainable religious truths. Rationalism also implies a concept of nature ruled by immutable laws and not by divine fiat. However, the Islamic concept of nature and natural law does not admit the immutability of laws. The regularity we observe in nature is merely a habit and not a law. The medieval Muslim philosophers and theologians who employed reason to any great extent were considered outside the pale of Islam. Yet since the nineteenth-century awakening, almost all Muslim intellectuals speak of Islam as the "religion of reason." Is this really so? Perhaps, if we understand this in the historical context of Islamic culture. Islam invites man to contemplate the universe, and to build his faith in God on reason (Koran: Surah 24:35). Moreover Islamic culture as we have previously mentioned produced a number of important philosophers and theologians who used logic in their arguments and provided demonstrative or rational proofs of their theories. The early reformers such as Jamal al-Din al-Afghani and Muhammad 'Abduh thought the revival of traditional rationalism would adequately equip the Muslims to meet the West on an equal footing. However, traditional rationalism, unless accompanied by a restructuring of thought, a love for exactness and verification, and reconsideration of what should and should not be done will remain a sterile rationalism. The mind must be organized by training in order to turn rationalism into an effective tool of progress. Unfortunately a great deal of the rationalism displayed by the Muslim intellectuals today suffers from lack of organization, exactitude, and coherence. Indeed some Muslim reformers and modernists when reading into the Koran and the Sunnah ideas that are not there, practice rationalization rather than rationalism. However, I am not proposing to evaluate modern Islamic rationalism, but rather to describe its nature.

Humanism is equally foreign to Islamic culture. In humanism, man is considered as the center of the universe, and as the end of creation. Humanism asserts that man is capable of using his own reason, and emphasizes human values and the importance of the individualism of man. Perhaps secularization of social life is the most striking feature of Western humanism. Of course, there are elements of humanism in Islamic culture since Islam affirms the natural equality of man and his worth as a creature of God for whose benefit he was created. But in order to achieve complete membership in society, man is conditioned by his religious beliefs. It has been the aim of many nationalists to root out sectarianism and organize national life on the basis of open-mindedness and equality. But almost all the constitutions of the Arab states, while guaranteeing religious minorities equality before the law, have not reached a point whereby membership in the nation—and not in a sect—becomes the criterion of equality. Needless to say, some states, such as Saudi Arabia and Libya, are far behind the others in this respect.

The critics of Western humanism argue that Western man is a colonizer and suffers from a great moral crisis. If man is to be the supreme being in creation, and human values the supreme criteria of progress, then peace should have been easily established and equality, justice, and brotherhood should have been triumphant. But if you look at the West now, the critics argue, humanism has led not only to communism and atheism, but also to chaos in the capitalist world. Islam is the only religion that can establish an "integrated" society, a society in which everything and everyone finds its or his natural place.

Regarding the other characteristics of Western culture, namely, the scientific spirit and the advancement in technology, the West offers a greater dilemma to the Arab world. The Arabs realize that Western achievements in science and technology are the most important elements of the West's strength. Therefore, if they ever want to achieve strength, they must emulate the West and adopt its technology. They are aware, furthermore, that a technical mentality based on scientific verification and efficiency is necessary to attain any significant level of technology.

Technology seems to be the least controversial in the Islamic thinkers' concept of modernity. Technology as a pragmatic science of nature and as a procedure to control nature is not in itself evil or good. It deals only with the realm of nature whereas religion deals with the realm of history (i.e., of man and God as makers of history). Consequently, there is no opposition as such between technical advancement and Islam. In fact, the most Islamic of the Arab states, Saudi Arabia and Libya, have opted for industrialization and technical progress.

The criticism raised against technical advancement is that the consequences of technical progress are bound to produce drastic changes in society and in human values. Religious extremists feel that there is a great risk in converting their society into a materialistic one and thus losing their distinctive (Muslim) identity.

All the above subtle points of distinction between the Western and the Islamic Arab worlds have been discussed on various levels by religious thinkers as well as secular intellectuals. Their discussions constitute a whole range of literary, philosophical, sociological, and scientific works. However, one may get a clearer insight into the nature of the image of the West as envisaged by the Muslim intellectuals by referring to special points of reference. This image is certainly not derived from an exhaustive and objective study of the West but is mainly based on reactions to certain events and policies in recent history. A Saudi Arabian intellectual who in 1969 published a book on Palestine entitled *The Battle of Islam* sees the whole question of Palestine as a "struggle between two religious cultures, one Islamic built by the Koran on the basis of faith, moral excellence, and beneficience, and a culture equivocally called Christianity (of which Christ, may peace be with him, is innocent) based on animosity, tyranny, injustice, and corruption."[4] He further sees the battle of Palestine as an extension or a renewal of the battles of Saladin against the Crusaders, and warns that unless the battle is Islamized once more, it will never be solved satisfactorily for the Arabs. The fact that the battle has been changed from an Islamic one in which the faithful, he believes, would fight for the glory of God, into a nationalist or a Socialist-Communist battle, has led to the loss of its sacredness. He further sees both the capitalist as well as the socialist camps in the Western world conniving against the interests of the Islamic community and working to destroy Islam, their common enemy.

A further sample of this extremist image is the one that presents the West as an entity willfully distorting the concepts of Islam either through false interpretations or through the work of Christian missionaries. Abu al-'Ala' al-Maududi speaks in one of his essays on how the *Ifranj* (Westerners) have distorted the meaning of *jihad* by translating it as "Holy War." "Not only that," he further says, "but they (the Westerners) have construed the term to mean viciousness, barbarism, and bloodshed.... Everytime the term *jihad* is used, they visualize a picture of barbaric hoards, drawing their swords to fall on the necks of innocent people, and with fanatic anger, their eyes aglow with the desire to murder and plunder." The surprising thing is that "those who have drawn and exhibited this picture of the Muslims are the ones who have spent centuries in fighting among themselves and who through their unholy wars against weaker nations colonized and enslaved them, and with tanks, airplanes, and huge armies snatched away from the mouths of these poor nations their livelihood and dignity."[5]

Needless to say, the above citations represent an extreme but not uncommon picture among the masses. The more educated intellectuals look at the West, less radically, as the source of materialism, atheism, and moral corruption. They merely accuse the West of bias towards Islam and the Arabs.

There are a few Muslims who admire the West for its achievements and seek a better understanding of its culture. According to them Islam developed in a Mediterranean environment as did Christianity and the West, and as such there are more common denominators between the two than meets the eye. Even they, however, accuse the West of not trying hard enough to understand the East, or of not looking at it with a charitable spirit, the spirit characteristic of true Christianity.

## Conclusion and a Look at the Future

It is highly difficult at this time to break down the Muslim urban population or elite into separate classifications and pigeonhole each one of them into a special category. This needs a more sophisticated field study. One may state, however, and with a measure of certainty, that the tendency for secularization is active in the Arab world, but that it is not strong enough to generate a body politic based on separation of state and religion. Furthermore, the attitudes of the urban elites depend greatly on their exposure to Western ideas, methodology, and on the behavior of the West towards them. Finally, Islam as a religion is very deeprooted in all classes.

The main problem of the elite in the Arab world is a problem of orientation: how much and what kind of religion is necessary for the Arabs to resume their place in world civilization? The impression one gets from distant but continuous observation is that any progress towards deeprooted changes in the mentality and structure of the Muslim community in the Arab world is very slow. The secularizing groups, including many university students, professionals, and intellectuals are all in favor of modernization. However, they limit their actions and will refrain from going too far. The great majority of the Muslims in the rural areas have not yet reached the questioning point. Their faith is spontaneous and genuine and is marred by superstitions and ignorance. In some areas, such as the Sudan and parts of North Africa, the Sufi orders, *tariqas*, are still very influential and their sway over large segments of the population will remain, at least for the near future, a strong force in molding individual and national life.

# Introduction to Chapter 3

*In Chapter 3 Dr. Atiyeh examines the various ideologies that are found today in the Arab world. At first glance one may assume that Western political concepts were incorporated* in toto *into the Arab world to become Middle Eastern ideologies. On closer inspection, though, as Dr. Atiyeh stresses, most political concepts in the region are uniquely Arab.*

*He divides the various ideologies into three categories—those based on religion, on nationalism, and on Marxism—and explains in depth the aspects of each concept, its leadership, and its future. Under nationalist ideologies, the reader will find the concepts of Pan-Arabism and regionalism that link this chapter very closely to both Dr. Taylor's exposition and what is to follow on regional subcultures.*

# 3

# Middle East Ideologies

George N. Atiyeh

We shall attempt here to describe the nature and effectiveness of Middle East ideologies in general and of Arab ideologies in particular. We shall also try to relate them to each other and to consider their sources in the hope of gaining some understanding of the problems facing that part of the world and the ways and means proposed to solve them.

By stretching a little the meaning of the term ideology, we may safely state that the tone of modern politics in the Middle East has been set by ideological aspirations and struggles—the constitutional movements in Egypt, Iran, and the Ottoman Empire; the Turkish and Persian movements after World War I for national preservation and integration; Arab nationalism under the Ottoman Empire; the continuous resistance to Western occupation; the urge for Arab unity; the struggle for Palestine; Arab Socialist nationalism after World War II and the new Arab left after the June War of 1967; the movements of local nationalism, particularly Syrian and Lebanese; and the non-Arab nationalist movements in the Arab countries, particularly of the Kurds and Southern Sudanese.

The above does not mean that the political forces active in the Middle East during the past and the current century were movements continuously inspired by theoretical doctrines of politics, a special philosophy of history, a set of clear cut goals, and a planned strategy to follow. It simply means that the aspirations, first for independence and later for the improvement of life, were used by movements that at times took the form of ideologies and at other times used ideologies to push forward their plans. In the period during which the struggle for independence took place and had primacy over all others, ideologies were sought to reinterpret history, create pride in the past and confidence in the future, or to identify an ethnic group with a geographic region. Later as other aspirations were developed, the desire to improve the quality of life became part of almost all ideologies. The thrust of these new ideologies was to reconstruct society, redefine the relations among social groups, establish new divisions of labor, and assign responsibilities with the ultimate purpose of achieving social cohesion and national solidarity. Moreover, ideology was also concerned with a relief from social tension; the idea of social justice was introduced, and became, in fact, one of the most powerful motives for political action.

The high aims of Middle Eastern ideologies fell short of their objectives and remained, most of the time, impressive schemes of reform, made so mostly by the crisis situations that constantly have existed where they grew. Their main function has been to serve as rallying points for activation of the plans of certain leaders; elite groups; and, rarely, political parties. However, regardless of what we may think of these ideologies, their prominence in the political life of the Middle East and the Arab world is such that one has to take them seriously.

There are three broad categories, depending on the type of solutions offered to the ills of society, that ideologies purported to remedy: religious, political, and technical—the last being the weakest. Only a small minority of visionary scientists and social scientists envisioned a highly technical society. But if considered from the point of view of the problems they seek to solve, ideologies will fall into a greater number of categories because the Middle East faces problems of identity and unity, forms of government, social and economic reform, international relations, and procedures for action.

## General Characteristics of Arab Ideologies

The postindependence period following the Second World War found the Arabs looking for new directions. Unsatisfied with the achievements of the liberal-democratic forms of government established between the two World Wars, unhappy with the West's colonial policies, humiliated by the war with Israel, lagging in economic and technical progress, and precariously situated in international relations, they sought new directions in order to place themselves quickly into a more estimable place in world society. This, ideologically speaking, has led them to assume what might be considered extremist positions, as well as to accentuate in the eyes of others the gap already existing between what they say; what they deliver; and, at times, what they intend or mean.

The gap between aspirations and realities may be explained by the rhetorical propensities of the Arabs, but the truth of the matter is that the Arabs have placed themselves in contradictory positions regarding the two major sources of their ideological struggle: Islam and Arab unity. While they talk a great deal about Islam, their new political community is drifting towards nationalism; and while the great majority of them pay lip service to Arab unity, nobody seems to be ready to put it into practice. Certainly, the indecision and contradictions apparent in their position has its psychological roots, but it stems mainly from the gap between hopes and history, and between aspirations and facts. The Arabs are still searching for an identity. Indeed you cannot be what you are not, even if you wish it very hard in your heart and articulate it elegantly in your literature. In other words, the concept of Arabism might be clear in the minds of the Arab nationalists, but its manifestation in concrete reality is still a far cry. The fact that a good majority of the Arabs answer the question "Who am I?" by stating, "I am an Arab," is contradicted by the undeniable fact of the inability of the Arab states to act as if they were one nation. Furthermore there is still a deeper search going on for the kind of place the Islamic religion should have in a changing society. Should the laws of society be inspired by the traditional laws of Islam, the Sacred Law, or the Western-oriented principles that separate church and state? Finally, the masses who form the great majority of the people have not been brought into the new regimes. Most of the governing bodies belong to the new elite in the military and the intellectual fields.

The currents of thought or political actions that developed in response to the above problems were mostly eclectic in nature except in a few cases which we shall discuss later. These currents that we have broadly classified as religionist, nationalist, and Marxist reflect a variety of aspects and relations hard to unravel because, although they have a Western origin or were responses to Western influx, their substance emanates from and takes place in the Arab Muslim culture.

The eclectic or accommodating nature of these ideologies is clearly evident in the difficulty of drawing a clear-cut line between one ideology and another. One movement might be ultraconservatism yet advocate socialistic ideas in its economic programs. Another might claim to be revolutionary, yet harbor the most conservative principles. Nasserism is a classical example of eclecticism. It combines moderate Islamism with nationalism, socialism, and revolutionism. Arab nationalism, as we shall see, is intrinsically associated with Islam, as Arab socialism is influenced by Arab nationalistic aspirations.

Under the first of the three above categories (religious), one finds the different fundamentalist groups best represented by the Muslim Brethren Association (*al-Ikhwan al-Muslimun*). To this group, pristine or ancestral (*salaf*) Islam should be the only standard for action and the only determinant of change or reform. Under the second category (political), the nationalists show a variety of tendencies: the Pan-Arabists, who form the largest group, would like to establish one state in the whole Arab world; the localists, best represented by the Lebanese Phalangist Party, would maintain the *status quo* and the sovereignty of each state; and, finally, the regionalists would like to unite certain regions such as the Fertile Crescent or the Maghrib into one state. These are best represented by the Syrian Social Nationalist Party in Lebanon and, to a certain degree, by the Istiqlal Party in Morocco. Under the third category (technical), one may place the Communists and the Marxists, including the small new-left groups that have flourished after the June War of 1967.

With varying degrees of intensity the three categories display a wide spectrum of attitudes from extreme conservatism to extreme liberalism. The religionists are naturally on the right and the Marxists on the left while the nationalists fluctuate between the right and the left. Moreover there is a direct relation between the assumed attitude and the question of identity. The religionists, while stressing their Islamic identity, believe in the sufficiency of the Koran and the Sunnah to resolve all the problems of the Arab world. They are wary and often opposed to the West and its Christian heritage but find common ground with it in their stand against atheistic communism. The revolutionaries, especially the Marxists, have kept the question of identity under cover or bypassed it completely; whereas for the nationalists, the question is more urgent and more significant. The Arab nationalists are in fact the group searching most intensely for self-identification and direction. Having gained control of power in most of the Arab states, they must choose between East and West, right and left, conservatism and liberalism, capitalism and socialism, democracy and militarism. As of now, the balance seems to shift in favor of the East, militarism and socialism. Socialism strikes directly at the psychological needs of the Arabs for self-assertion and reform to the extent of acclaiming it as their own. Both Arab nationalism and Islamism have created their own versions of socialism. But deep down in their hearts the Arabs, it would seem to the author, are not certain whether or not the road of socialism is leading them to salvation. Russia and the East might be their models now, but the benefits accrued from the adoption of Western models in economy and technology, their abhorrence of atheism, and their pride stop them from completely embracing communism or socialism as it is understood in the West. Furthermore, for the Muslim Arabs it is still extremely important to maintain a semblance of Islamic legitimization for all their actions; but given the erosion of Islam as a way of life, they resort to seemingly acrobatic maneuvers to accommodate the contradicting realities of traditionalism and modernism and other contradictions inherent in their aspirations.

Judging from what has been previously said, we may state that the most important characteristics of Arab ideologies are indecision and indecisiveness—indecision as to identity, unity, procedures, and aims. The indecisiveness of the ideologies is reflected in the wide gap between aspirations and reality and between the governing elites and the masses of the people. The fact that they now seem to be socialistic in tendency and pro-East is not in itself an indication of their true orientation. The measures taken against communism and the left in general in revolutionary Libya and the Sudan vindicate and substantiate this assumption. Arab society is in a state of flux, and so are its ideologies.

However, there are other aspects of Arab ideologies that should be considered—namely their relation to the West in terms of origin. Being the result of the direct influence of the West, they reflect the tension created between the traditional values of dependence on God and unquestionable obedience to the man in power on one hand, and the modern Western values of humanism, self-sufficiency, and questioning on the other. Many of the Arab Muslim intellectuals consider this tension as being one between spirituality and mundanity. Whatever this may be, a salient aspect of their ideologies has been the endeavor to create pride in the past and confidence in the future. To do so, they have claimed the origins of ideals such as democracy, great scientific achievement, and human dignity.

Another aspect of Arab ideologies has been the lack of inspiring leadership. Except perhaps for Nasser and his charismatic personality, the few leaders who appeared on the ideological scene did not offer genuine and selfless leadership. Nasser, however, did not come to power on the basis of any ideology in particular. He developed one as he grew in power and experience. This is the reason for its eclecticism and pragmatism. He also made use of it to consolidate his power and to implement his reform ideas. In fact, most of the ideologies working at present on the government levels are those the new elites and the hereditary aristocracies in the nonmilitary regimes have found useful for purposes of consolidating their powers. Ideologies are at times tailored to suit the ideas of or to rally support for elite leaders, who as soon as they sense new directions in the wind, try to steer their courses in the same direction. This use to which the ideologies have been put in the Arab world is another of their characteristics. Except in the case of students, all groups including labor, the urban masses, and religious and secular intellectuals have been used to further the cause of official ideologies. Many of the student movements seem to have fallen lately into the same pattern.

Doctrinaire ideologies with their utopian aims might be logically consistent, internally coherent, more nobly inspired, and universally appealing, yet they have not struck deep roots in the Arab world. On the whole, one may conclude that social change in the modern age has brought about a flood of new ideologies, but so far these have had little effect if we consider their final aims. None of the final aims of Arab unity, Islamic rule, social justice, and technological advances have been fully achieved.

We may now ask what are the current forces of political ideologies. In answer to this question we may mention the intellectuals; students; army officers; labor unions; urban masses; and, finally, some political parties. In the following discussion we shall see the contents and operations of the three main currents of ideologies that dominate the Middle East.

## The Religionist Ideologies

All Middle Eastern countries share, to a certain degree, in the ideology of Islam. The burning of the Aqsa Mosque in East Jerusalem in August 1969 brought all of the Muslim heads of government to Rabat, Morocco. The mere fact that they all came to the meeting is very significant in itself, given the political rivalries and divisions existing among them. However, the attachment to Islamism differs in quantity and quality from one country to another. In each country there is a current of fundamentalism that still exerts great influence, no matter how discredited religious extremism might seem to be. The fundamentalist loyalty is usually given to a religious doctrine that is placed above whatever attachment to secular, political, or economic institutions they might have.

At present, after the dissolution of the Muslim Brethren the fundamentalist ideology is not organized into one political party or association, but into widely scattered small groups who hold similar ideals and exert collective pressure at the local level. The number of religious publications in the form of periodicals, journals, pamphlets, and books is overwhelming. Many are published by government agencies or government sponsored organizations. Their cumulative effect is to solidify the fundamentalist trend, although some are more moderate in tone than others. In other words the fundamentalist trend is still strong and manifests itself in forms other than political parties.

The fundamentalist thinking is best represented by the Muslim Brethren Association (*al-Ikhwan al-Muslimun*). Although now defunct as a political organization, their ideals, objectives, and, to a certain extent, methodology are very much alive. Many facets of their history are still unknown since they engaged in secret activities, threatening on several occasions the established regimes in Egypt and Syria.

The founder of the Muslim Brethren Association was Hassan al-Banna, (d. 1949), a school teacher from Isma'iliyah, Egypt, who in the early stages of the association recruited a number of similarly minded persons and commissioned them to preach in mosques and other public places. As their influence spread they began to engage in political activities. The period between 1936 and 1952 saw the *Ikhwan* prestige and power grow, with their organization developing a paramilitary force. After 1943 they had to reckon with the Communists, allied then to the left-wing of the Wafd Party, that like the *Ikhwan* were attempting to arouse the political awareness of the students and the people in general. It is also said that the Free Officers who were to seize power in Egypt in 1952 were on friendly relations with the *Ikhwan*. When they first held the reins of government, the Free Officers had a program resembling, particularly in social matters, that of the *Ikhwan*. This might explain why, when all the other political parties were dissolved, the Free Officers did not dissolve the *Ikhwan* but sought their support and even their collaboration. However, friendly relations did not last long. Nasser who assumed full power in 1954 narrowly escaped an attempt on his life engineered by the *Ikhwan*. The government reacted strongly, arrested their leaders and executed some of them. However, the *Ikhwan* continued to exist, clandestinely in Egypt and openly in several other countries. In 1965 they again tried to assassinate Nasser and again some of their leaders were executed. There is no doubt that until now they have a central organization, but their effectiveness as a group has disappeared.

The essential ideology of the *Ikhwan* begins with their conception of Islam as a *nizam* order (i.e., a religion and a state). They sought to interpret present-day political life accordingly. To them Islam has a "wide meaning and is not adequately defined by that narrow interpretation given to it by many people. We believe that Islam comprises and regulates all human affairs and does not shrink from new problems and necessary reforms. Islam is not restricted to religious and spiritual matters."[1] In one of his basic speeches al-Banna stated that "Islam is dogma and worship, fatherland and nationality, religion and state, spirituality and action, Koran and sword."[2] This total concept of Islam should go beyond the confines of any one class or society.

The *Ikhwan*'s main objective was to create an authentically Muslim state. This ideal was to be achieved through stages until it embraced all the Muslim peoples. It would have at its head a caliph (some members hesitated about this). Until this was achieved a plurality of states was permissible. The leader of the state was to be elected by the community and responsible to it; the community is to act through qualified representatives elected by it; and the *ahl al-Shura* (people of counseling), who elect the leader, have control over his acts, and legislate in cooperation with him. Every person in authority is required to act in consultation with his subordinates, and it is the duty of every citizen to offer his advice to those in authority. The aim of this Islamic state is (1) to see that the laws of Islam are properly observed, (2) to send out and support missionaries who will represent Islam to other nations, and (3) to fight constantly, and with arms, if need be, for justice and the common good of humanity.

God as the Creator and maintainer of the universe has given man a Sacred Law whose sources are the Koran and the Sunnah (Traditions). These should be the only arbiters and it is therefore incumbent upon all Muslims to obey this law and not the positive laws made by man. This can be achieved by having as a model the Prophet and the ancestors (*Salaf*). There is no need for all the later philosophizing and jurisprudence. Simply, the Koran is sufficient for the establishment of this model government. This kind of government is not theocratic because the ruler receives his power from the community and not from God. Neither is it democratic because it is based on religion, nor dictatorial, since the community as the investor of power in the ruler has the right to take it away from him whenever and if he abuses it.

The economic system visualized by the *Ikhwan* is based on the Islamic doctrine of God's ownership. God, having created Heaven and Earth, is naturally the owner. No human being owns anything in reality. All belongs to God. A person may acquire property legally and enjoy its use in accordance with the Sacred Law, but his legal hold on it is not absolute. The community, being the sole representative of God on earth, may confiscate the property and use it when the interest of the general welfare so requires it. Taxes in society shall be the *zakat* (usually translated as almsgiving) provided for by the Sacred Law, and all profit making from money (*riba*) shall be prohibited. Two of the intellectual leaders of the *Ikhwan*, the Syrian Mustafa al-Siba'i and the Egyptian Sayyid Qutb, systematized the *Ikhwan*'s economic doctrine into what was termed as Islamic socialism. While combining the advantages of capitalism and communism, Islamic socialism naturally differed from those two systems in both its nature and its aims. The social and economic programs of the *Ikhwan*, flexible in many ways, stood in sharp contrast to their inflexible religious objectives.

In addition to the principle of God's ownership, the *Ikhwan* exalted the virtues of disinterest, of mutual devotion, and of brotherhood, which, according to Sayyid Qutb in his book *The Struggle of Islam and Capitalism*, existed in the Muslim countries before they were invaded by Western materialism.

A similar attitude towards the West is found in al-Banna's famous 1936 statement addressed to the rulers of the various Muslim countries, in which he indicts Western civilization and advances the excellences of Islam.

This attitude was translated into the primary objective of freeing all Muslim countries from Western domination and ways of life. The *Ikhwan* planned to re-Islamize Egyptian life in all fields including dress, greetings, use of foreign languages, hours of work and rest, the calendar, and recreation, and to abolish the European-based legal codes as well. In this Islamized society they maintained that minorities and foreigners would have equal rights, presumably political, except in religious affairs, so long as they conducted themselves peaceably and loyally toward the Muslims among whom they lived.

Because of its appeal, especially to the oppressed as well as to the fanatically minded, the constituency of the *Ikhwan* was made up mainly of the underprivileged urban masses. At the same time it had sympathizers among the students, professionals, and religious intellectuals. It was said that its peak membership was two million; but because there are no records to substantiate this claim, all that one can state with certainty is that their influence reached tremendous proportions. They had a secret commando-like army (*Fida'iyyin*) and, as the Egyptian government claimed, used it to terrorize and assassinate those in power who did not comply with their wishes and/or struck at their organization. The critics of the *Ikhwan* were the Communists and the secular Muslim intellectuals who had espoused Western culture and were convinced that the future of Islam lies in its spiritual values. When Nasser came forth with a program to undo many of the social injustices, the *Ikhwan* lost many of their arguments. Their attitude to defend Islam and rejuvenate it is shared by many and is not exclusive to them. All countries of the Middle East have their Muslim Brethren Association in one form or another. Some share with the Egyptian *Ikhwan* their zeal, others espouse the return to the ancestral way as an ideal, and still others refuse to see in the Western tradition anything except vice. The physical attack of the Association of Social Reform (*Jam'iyat al-Islah al-Ijtima'i*) on students of the University of Kuwait, which occurred in November 1971 because the students held a seminar on coeducation, is typical of the mentality and behavior of this religious current.

Whatever name the fundamentalists may have, *al-Ikhwan al-Muslimun* as in Egypt or *Fidayin-i-Islam* as in Iran, they all share a similar ideology. They are against nationalism; they believe that the worldly oriented Muslim governments and Western colonialism are the causes of the weakness of Islam; and that unless all aspects of life, political as well as economic, are Islamized, the Muslim world will remain divergent from the straight path.

## The Nationalist Ideologies

At the present time, nationalism is the strongest driving force in the political life of the Middle East. Chronologically speaking nationalism as an ideology is a new phenomenon in the Middle East. The Islamic ideology has deeper roots in history, but the present trend is to exalt nationalism and live by its rules. The three main nationalisms—Arab, Turkish, and Iranian—became articulated under Western influence only during this century. Moved by ideas of nationhood and liberal democracy, many intellectuals saw in them the salvation of their peoples from the tyranny of colonialism or autocracy and from the shackles of Islamic traditionalism.

Unlike Turkey and Iran, which did not suffer for long periods from foreign occupation, the Arab world was under Ottoman and European occupation when winds of nationalism began to blow. Consequently the Arab nationalist movement began as a negative force—to get rid of colonialism. Its first articulations were in the form of a desire to have autonomy within the framework of the Ottoman Empire. In this both Christians and Muslims joined, especially in the Fertile Crescent where the first stirrings of nationalism took place. However, the Christian Arabs envisioned the establishment of a separate secular state in which nationality rather than religion would be the basis of citizenship. The Muslims at first wanted only autonomy and it was not until the First World War that they began to seek complete independence. To the Muslim Arabs, the secular national consciousness of their Arabism appeared to be in conflict with their Islamism. Therefore, they sought to accommodate their concept of nationalism with their concept of religion. Thus, Arabism and Islam became inseparable, although the kind of relationship between the two was seen in different ways. Some saw in Islam the cultural expression of Arabism, others an essential part of it. But some, like Dr. Isma'il Ragi al-Faruqi in his book *On Arabism, 'Urubah and Religion*, have gone as far as considering Arabism to be synonymous and equal to Islamism. Consequently all Muslims are Arabs by spirit if not by blood.

Because of the wide diversity of opinions, the definition of nationalism became essential, and the relation between state and religion crucial. Until socialism emerged as the third basic factor in Arab nationalism, the issues of independence and unity were the two main ones. The multiplicity of definitions propounded by Arab writers and intellectuals reflected the political and cultural conditions in which they found themselves—an Arab world divided into a number of states, and most of it under foreign rule; a changing society whose masses are extremely ignorant; and a leadership based on class and religious distinction.

Arab intellectuals under pressure to define nationalism, and Arab nationalism in particular, offered a series of definitions. The most prominent of which is that of Sati' al-Husri, a Syrian educated in Ottoman Turkey, who spent most of his life in Iraq. Al-Husri stressed in his definition of a nation the unity of language and culture. Unity in these two respects lead to unity of feelings and to the unity of culture. These being the bases of nationhood, he addressed himself to the task of demonstrating that Arabism is based on language and culture; that Egypt, which until recently did not consider itself Arab, is indeed Arab; and that Pan-Arabism neither contradicts nor is inimical to Islam. With this last point, it would seem that he wanted to banish the doubts traditionalists held against nationalism. Islamic unity, he argued, cannot be achieved before Arab unity is achieved. Al-Husri, like all Arab nationalists, was confronted with the problem of where does the loyalty of an Arab Muslim lie. Should he give his first loyalty to Arabism or to Islam? His answer to this question was vague although one easily could feel his leanings towards Arabism. He saw religion as a matter between man and God while the fatherland (*al-Watan*) was the concern of all.

The most coherent answer to this question was given by the Iraqi, 'Abd al-Rahman al-Bazzaz, who asserted that Arab nationalism and Islam went together in every respect. Muhammad is the founder of the Arab nation and Islam itself is the incarnation of the Arab nationalist spirit. This new meaning given to Islam made it easy for non-Muslim Arabs to be considered and to consider themselves Arabs. Islam, being a cultural product of the Arab national genius, may be looked upon simply as a culture, as a creation of man and not as revelation with dogmas and rites to be followed. As a culture it is a manifestation and a fulfillment of the Arabs' contribution to world civilization. As such both Christian and Muslim Arabs may take pride in it. A number of Christian Arab intellectuals—particularly Orthodox Christians—espoused this point of view. Michel Aflaq, founder of the Ba'th Party, and Qustantin Zurayq, once a vice-president of the American University of Beirut, became the greatest exponents of this attitude.

The period after World War II saw a new dimension added to nationalism, namely socialism. This became fashionable, particularly after the July 23, 1952, revolution in Egypt, and the strengthening of the Ba'th Party's hold on the Syrian government. The Iraqi Revolution (1958), the Algerian Revolution (1954-1962), the South Yemen Revolution (1967), the Sudanese Revolution (1969), and the Libyan Revolution (1969) all incorporated socialist ideas or attitudes in their programs.

The term "independence" also underwent a fundamental change, acquiring a Leninist connotation—namely, getting rid of direct as well as indirect colonialist influences or, as it is usually termed, "neocolonialism." The agents of this new colonialism in the Middle East were local governments that gave the Western powers political or military privileges in the form of alliances and/or bases; the capitalists, who owned big businesses, industries, or large areas of land; and the groups or associations who held non-Arab concepts of nationalism, such as Syrian, Egyptian, or Tunisian nationalism. However, the greatest agent of colonialism in symbol as well as in fact is the state of Israel, which is seen as an extension in space and time of Western desires to colonize the Arab world.

Colonialism, many nationalists say, left the Middle East house by the door only to enter it again by the window in the form of a Zionist state.

Independence also became positive neutralism, or nonalignment, a term given prominence after the Bandung Conference in 1955 and the creation of the Baghdad Pact.

Another aspect in the development of Arab nationalism has been the adoption of a new approach to the class struggle. In all the states where the new military regimes took over, the old feudal forces were dethroned and replaced by the new elites of the underprivileged or lower-middle classes, who through the new systems of education were appointed to the army or to important civil service positions. However, the new approach consisted in avoiding the use of the term "proletariat" and using instead the "toiling classes" which include all workers and not only the industrial workers as the term "proletariat" originally indicated.

The many currents within Arab nationalism may be classified as Pan-Arabism, regionalism, and localism. This classification may be criticized on the basis that Arab nationalism is now concerned less with unity and identity and more with social development. However, except in the case of the Marxists, there is a direct relation between the attitude of an ideology towards the problem of unity and identity and the type of social reform practiced or envisioned. Therefore, the classification on the basis of the attitude towards unity is still valid and we shall proceed to use it.

In summary one may say that Arab nationalism is the conviction common among many Arabs that there is an Arab nation. The goals pursued by this nationalism are unity and social and economic progress through a socialism suited to the genius and problems of the Arabs.

The different expressions of this nationalism are mainly manifest in the Pan-Arab sentiment, the attachment to Islam, an attitude of hostility towards or disappointment with the West, a policy of neutrality in international relations, identification with the third World (the Afro-Asian nations), and support for the national liberation movements.

## Pan-Arabism

The ideals of Pan-Arabism are to be found expressed in many documents as well as mentioned daily by the press. You can hardly find a politician who does not avow his allegiance to it although each one differs on how to bring it about—whether immediate or gradually, whether through total unity or a loose unity (i.e., a one state, a federation, or a confederation).

The division of the Arab world into local states (eighteen of them now); the doctrinal divisions between the Socialist states like Syria, Egypt, Iraq, Algeria, and South Yemen, and the traditionalists such as Saudi Arabia, Jordan, and

Morocco; and the rivalry between the U.S. and Russia for gaining access to or control over the strategic locations and oil wealth of the Arab world, plus the vested interests in titles—all make the dream of Arab unity more difficult to achieve although most Arab leaders foresee its coming someday.

The three doctrines that proclaim Pan-Arabism as their ultimate goals and incorporate socialism as a basic ingredient of their ideology are those espoused by the Arab Ba'th (Resurrection) Socialist Party, Nasser's Arab Socialist Union, and the Algerian FLN. All three have common features with small variations. However, unlike Ba'th and Nasserite socialism, the Algerian brand is tailored to the peculiar situation of that nation, and does not seek, as a doctrine, to extend beyond that country's borders. Both Ba'thism and Nasserism exist in one form or another in all the Arab countries—sometimes in an organized branch, but other times in the support public opinion gives them on particular policies or in particular situations.

The Ba'th Party is strongest in Syria and Iraq. The governments of both countries are in that party's hands now. One wing, usually termed as moderate, rules in Iraq; the other wing, the extremists, rules in Syria. The Ba'th Party has organized branches in Kuwait, Oman, Qatar, Bahrain, Saudia Arabia and Lebanon. It has set up a "regional command" in Southern Yemen, but its presence in North Africa is limited to a number of sympathizers, mostly among students and a few intellectuals.

The organizational aspects of Nasserism do not follow the rigid cell system of the Ba'th Party. The Arab Socialist Union (ASU) is not exactly a party; its main function is to channel all political activities and give representation to all popular forces and trends, except feudalism and capitalism. At present the membership in the ASU reaches the five million mark, but in effect it is run by a new elite made up of military, intellectual, and professional groups, with engineers having the highest representation.

Nasserism, it is interesting to note, is a term coined by the enemies of Nasser. Later it was used by Arab nationalists outside of Egypt who supported his policies and upheld his leadership. Nowadays it is used both in Egypt and abroad to denote the totality of doctrines, values, and procedures established by Nasser, particularly in the *Charter of National Action.* It stands for Arab unity, positive neutralism, control over the national economy, development, and a leveling off of social differences.

Nasserites outside Egypt are not united in one centrally organized political group. In fact there is no party machinery for communication between leaders and followers of the movement. However, the strength of Nasserism derives from the popular support it usually receives from the masses. In some countries, Lebanon for example, a number of small groups have organized themselves into a Nasserite Rally (*Wihdat al-Qiwa al-Nasiriyah*, literally, Union of Nasserite Forces). Other movements found in a number of Arab countries, such as the Arab Nationalist Movement (*Harakat al-Qawmiyun al-'Arab*) and The Unionists (*al-Wihdawiyun*), support Nasserism in general but more often than not, each follows a policy of its own. The Arab nationalists in Libya sent a strong protest to the Lebanese government for allowing the Communist Party to hold publicly its Third Congress in Beirut (January 7-10, 1972), while the Arab nationalists of Lebanon were among those who sent a delegation to attend the conference.

The Nasserite approach has been to organize the political forces into nondoctrinaire organizations, allowing for the existence of different ideological trends to be under one umbrella. The Arab Socialist Union has been imitated recently by Libya and the Sudan. Jordan also has set up a similar union—The Nationalist Union—but replaced the "socialist" epithet with "nationalist." The adoption of this approach places most Arab countries into the one-party system. Only Kuwait, Lebanon, and Morocco still have multiparty systems. Saudi Arabia and the Federation of Arab Emirates are ruled by monarchies with little or no disposition to permit political parties to exist.

When the Ba'th Party was first founded in the early 1940s, its founder envisioned for it an educational function—to educate the people to accept and support its principles and platform. However, by 1953, the party had changed its strategy and decided to plunge into the political arena. The circumstances were such that it gained prominence in the Syrian army and later in the government, an unexpected fact that has inflicted factionalism on the party ever since.

The Ba'th's ideology is best set forth in its constitution. It envisions a united Arab society encompassing all Arabs from Morocco to Iraq in which social justice will prevail through distribution of wealth and nationalization of industries, limitation of land, and industrial ownership. The two aspects of Arab nationalism and socialism are inseparable in the ideology of the Ba'th Party, but whereas nationalism is associated with Islam as a culture, socialism is secular. For this reason the Ba'th Party has been described by the religionists as an "enemy of God." The Ba'th's nationalism gives a dominant place to the state which, as events proved, was controlled by a small group backed chiefly by the military. This has left the party without the grassroots support demanded by its program. Moreover, some vestiges of tribalism are manifest in its centers of power since, for the last few years, the 'Alawite officers in Syria have had the upperhand. President Hafiz al-As'ad is an 'Alawite (the 'Alawites are a closed Shi'ite sect predominantly found in the eastern part of Syria). In Iraq a similar situation exists in the government in that many of the people in high positions come from the town of Takrit. One of the first acts of the new regime of President al-As'ad was to try to remedy this basic defect by seeking popular support from non-Ba'thist groups and by forming a national front with other progressive forces. These include the Nasserites, the Arab National-ists (*al-Qawmiyun al-'Arab*), the Unionists (*al-Wihdawiyun*), and the Commu-nists.

The Ba'th Party is opposed to communism as an ideology. According to Michel Aflaq, the founder of the party, communism is unsuited to the Arab world because it does not give weight to the individual, nor does it recognize the right to private property. Furthermore, communism seeks to tie the destiny of the Arabs to the destiny of another nation, which is unacceptable. Communism also is based on the concept of class struggle which Aflaq rejects. However, this ideological opposition did not stop the Ba'thists from cooperating with the Communists, a cooperation that increased or decreased in accordance with what faction in the Ba'th Party happened to be in power—the moderates or the hardliners. The latter, who were in power between 1965 and 1970, were responsible for implementing more socialistic measures in the economy of Syria which reduced the social positions of the rich and feudal families. All major commercial and industrial concerns were nationalized and all education, public or private, was put within a unitary system. More friendly relations with the Socialist camp were established to the point that there is now a complete dependence on that camp for armament.

Nasserism does not really differ much from Ba'thism, ideologically speaking. Like Ba'thism, it believes in Arab unity and socialism and follows a secular approach. There are, however, basic and essential differences on emphasism. Nasser's Arabism is related to his concept of Egypt as being the heart of three circles—the Arab world, Africa, and the Islamic world. Egypt is always first in Nasser's thinking. It is the core of Arab unity. The mild secularism preached and practiced by Nasserism draws criticism from the religionists, but this has not antagonized the religious hierarchy. In fact Nasser drew it to his side and gained its support. Another basic difference between Ba'thism and Nasserism is that the first was born as an intellectual scheme and moved from there into material politics, while Nasserism started as a military coup with the intention of ending corruption and introducing some agrarian reform but moved from there into becoming an intellectual or ideological school. There is also a difference in the methodology of government which was one of the reasons for the conflict between Nasser and the Ba'th Party in the experiment of the United Arab Republic. The Ba'th Party believes in a kind of party democracy in the form of "collective leadership" while Nasserism has been authoritarian—all final decisions were taken by one man, Nasser himself.

After the defeat in June 1967, the criticism leveled against the military elite in Egypt, the student protests, and other manifestations, Nasser moved to strengthen the consultative and participatory processes of the government by promising to place more decision-making responsibilities in the hands of the Arab Socialist Union and the National Assembly once the emergency of the war with Israel is over. After Nasser's death, President al-Sadat moved in that same direction and even went further—by lowering the pressure of authoritarianism in the political, economic, and social fields; by calling for a "return to the rule of law"; and by retouching the socialist structure of the economy with a few strokes of liberalism.

Authoritarianism in Egypt has been a way of life, although one must admit that a few dissenters in the intellectual and political fields have made the pattern uneven. In spite of authoritarianism, or perhaps because of it, Nasserism was able to leave an indelible mark on the new Egypt—an achievement of independence or "Egyptianization" in the government and the economy, an increase in economic and state potential, growth of the working class, the emergence of the technocrats, primacy of the masses and its values in the name of socialism, and a leading role in the Afro-Asian bloc. Naturally, all the above are achievements of a controversial nature and were made at the expense of the upper classes and many minority groups, especially the Lebanese and Greek, who were deprived of their privileges and properties.

*The Charter of National Action* (*al-Mithaq*) proposed by President Nasser to the members of the National Congress of Popular Forces on May 21, 1962, after the withdrawal of Syria from the United Arab Republic, represents in all its aspects the doctrines of Nasserism and marks a turning point in its history. Of the charter's ten sections, only two dealt with Arab unity and foreign policy. The other eight were entirely devoted to domestic affairs, thus confirming the priority of the economic, social, and political aspects inherent in today's Egyptian society.

The charter pays tribute in its first article to the Egyptian people and asserts the legitimate rights of the masses, their will for revolutionary change, and their unshakeable faith in God. It also states the necessity for a revolution to bring about freedom in socialism and unity. Then, a criticism of the "democracy of reaction" is made, which Nasser described as "formal constitutional trappings lacking popular support and progressivism, the two basic qualities of true democracy."[3] Political democracy is inseparable from social democracy in that it is impossible to achieve political democracy where one class dominates all the others. The charter goes further to explain that the class struggle, while it cannot be denied, should be ended peacefully within the framework of national unity and should open the way for democratic interactions between the various elements of the working population—the peasants, the workers, the soldiers, the intellectuals, and national capitalism. This type of harmonious relationship among the members of society, where each "level," not class, has its natural position and function, has been called "integrative society" in which the class struggle is diffused within the framework of national integration.

The charter, although offering socialism as the solution to the problems of progress, specifies that it is a special kind of socialism. Officially it is called cooperativist-democratic socialism while popularly it is known as Arab socialism, thereby underlining the Arabs sensitivity to the question of their independence, and implying that it is an end in itself and not a first step towards communism. There are other qualifications of Arab socialism, namely, the belief in God and the rejection of the economic interpretation of history.

The charter also refers to Arab unity but in terms of the Syrian experience.

The "unity of aims" rather than complete unity is thought to be the first objective of Arab nationalism. Partial unity, which has been lately embodied in the Federation of Arab Republics, is considered an advance toward unity. However, complete unity should not come until the ideology of Arab nationalism had eliminated all others.

## Regionalism and Localism

What are the other ideologies in the Arab world? Reference in *The Charter of National Action*, most likely, is to the Ba'thist and the Communist ideologies, which compete with Nasserism on a Pan-Arab level. However, Nasser might have had in mind the numerous small parties found in each Arab country that reflect a wide gamut of interests and aspirations. These local ideologies usually look at Arab unity and socialism from the point of view of their immediate circumstances. Their effect is usually very limited and their organization, loose.

Regionalism to me is the concept of the Arab world as being made up of four large units, al-Maghrib or Northwest Africa, the Nile Valley, the Fertile Crescent, and the Arabian peninsula. The regionalists believe that each one of these units is a natural unit and that political unity should be limited to said units, each of which constitutes a nation by itself. The localists on the other hand believe that the *status quo* is natural. Therefore, there is no such thing as one Arab "nation." Each Arab country is a nation by itself and owes its first loyalty to itself.

The only organized party in the Arab world that has adopted a regionalist approach and has branches outside its homebase in Lebanon is the Syrian Social Nationalist Party (SSNP). The other groups who believe in the regionalist approach are not organized into a movement that permanently works toward that goal. They reflect an aspiration or a realization that it is more logical to work toward Arab unity through a unification of the basic geographical and cultural units. This aspiration is documented in the constitutions of Tunisia, Algeria, and Morocco; but the clearest expression thereof is in the Tunisian constitution. So far this ideology has had no theoretician. The late Allal al-Fasi of Morocco, leader of the Istiqlal Party, was perhaps the closest to being its spokesman.

The SSNP considers the Fertile Crescent or Greater Syria to be such a national unit and has constantly worked toward its unity, although the party's Arabism in Syria and its acceptance of a Lebanese entity in Lebanon for tactical reasons has been magnified.

The SSNP was founded in Lebanon in 1932 as a clandestine party tightly organized under the leadership of its founder, Antun Sa'adeh. In 1935 the French authorities who held a mandate over Lebanon at this time, uncovered the party and forced it to work in the open. It immediately gained popularity for its opposition to the French mandate and for calling upon the religious sects to unite under the banner of nationalism. However, the party's ideology became more complex over the years. Sa'adeh and other intellectuals of the party developed a total philosophy of nationhood and of life in general. As such they were the first in the Arab world to forge an ideology whose content was derived from the Syrian situation, yet inspired by Western schools of thought. The writings of Sa'adeh, especially his book on *The Rise of Nations*, were indirectly responsible for the great intellectual output by Arab nationalists attempting to elucidate their concepts of nationalism and unity.

The basic ideology of the SSNP is that Syria is for the Syrians, who constitute a complete nation within the region known as the Syrian Fertile Crescent, or Greater Syria (the terms are not interchangeable). According to the party, Greater Syria includes present day Syria, Lebanon, Jordan, Palestine (Israel and the West Bank), Iraq, Kuwait, the Sinai Peninsula, Cyprus, and the District of Alexandretta (now Hatay in Turkey). The unity of the Syrian nation is manifest in the vital interaction between its parts and the interdependence of its parts on each other from economic and social, as well as strategic, considerations.

Furthermore, the party drafted a reform program based on the separation of religion and state. According to this program a politico-religious bond constitutes a serious threat to the existence of nations and their interests. Such a bond denigrates the value of the individual as an integral member of the state. The state, the political expression of the nation, is all embracing. A citizen cannot realize his complete potential being outside the nation. He is an integral part of it and derives his freedom from placing himself at its service. The motto of the party reflecting this ideology became: "freedom, duty, discipline, and force."

The economic reform principles of the party are based on the abolition of feudalism and the organization of the economy on the bases of the principles of production, the protection of the right to work, and the interests of the nation and the state.

Regarding their relations with the rest of the Arab world, the party members called for the creation of an Arab Front led by Greater Syria. They called this "real Arabism" because it is based on what appeared to them as real and feasible. Arab nationalism is "false Arabism" since it is based on an illusion. They added, however, that if the real interests of Syria were to be found in unity, they would not oppose it.

The history of the SSNP is characterized by many ups and downs in the form of persecutions, attempts to gain power by force, internal divisions and a negative popularity. Nonetheless, as the only coherent secularist school of thought, its reasons for opposition to a comprehensive Arab unity had to be considered. As an ideological force against communism, the party was the only movement in Lebanon and Syria to build its membership on nonsectarian bases even though it appealed more to both Christian and Muslim minorities. Furthermore, its economic program seemed at the time of its inception to be both feasible and desirable.

The membership of the party was noted for its complete involvement, thereby giving it a mystique of its own and singling it out as being doctrinaire and inflexible. However, SSNP tactics were mostly flamboyant and by their spontaneity seemed illogical. At times they were most effective, for example, when the party fought on the side of the Lebanese government in 1958 and was instrumental in stopping the pro-Nasser forces of Kamal Jumblat from taking Beirut. Because of their extreme opposition to communism, they became notorious as right-wingers.

Regardless of the ideological strength of the party, its failure to come to power, its lack of popular support, its rightist image, and the popularity of revolutionary thought and socialism, party leaders were forced to undergo self-examination. A congress was held in 1969 in which the party reorganized on a more democratic basis and adopted a leftist label described by some critics as "unbecoming" to the role of the party. The Communist answer to this *apertura alla sinistra* of the party was a biting sarcasm. *Al-Tariq*, the Communist monthly, stated that the rightist nature and history of the SSNP is so much a part of it that no amount of leftist veneer would make it so.

Local ideologies are limited to a few countries, most eminent of which are Lebanon, Egypt, and Tunisia. The common denominator between the SSNP and the localists is rejection of the existence of one Arab nation and of extending the historical roots of nationhood to the pre-Islamic period. Egyptian nationalism bases "Egyptianness" on the ancient, as well as the Islamic, heritage of Egypt, and on the continuity and uniqueness of Egyptian life and history. Lebanese nationalism, best represented by the Phalangist Party (*al-Kata'ib*), stresses the formative role of the Phoenicians and their civilizational role as inventors of the alphabet and carriers of Middle Eastern civilization to many parts of the world, especially Europe. The Phalangist constituency, however, is Maronite Christian and until now pays only lip-service to the principle of separation of state and religion.

A similar trend is found in Tunisia within the ruling Neo-Destour Party. This party's official position is to work towards a Maghrib unity, but it has no clear position as to what its relation to Arab unity should be. Its secularizing approach also lends itself to placing Tunisia under a light different from that of Arab nationalism, which is inseparable from Islamism. In an article entitled "Arabization and Tunisification" published in his periodical *al-Fikr*, Muhammad Mzali, once minister of culture, states: "We understand the Arab nation to be a congregation [confluence] of nations and a cooperation conducive to unity. But since the time of the Prophet [Muhammad]—peace be on him—until today in spite of the unity of belief, the unity of language, there are only countries and regions each having its own specific character. It is important to note that unity is made by diversity and not by the victory of a school over another, neither by exploitation or domination."[4]

There are other trends inspired by the local interests of ethnic minorities such as the Kurds in Iraq who have been intermittently fighting the Iraqi government for several decades in their search for local autonomy and equality. Kurdish nationalism, however, raises its head now and then and clamors for the establishment of a Kurdish state in an area that bestrides Turkey, Iraq, and Iran.

A similar ethnic tendency existed in Morocco. The Popular Movement represented primarily the Berber rural elements. Southern Sudan, where the majority of the people are different from the North ethnically and culturally, is a different case which needs special treatment.

On the whole, regionalism and localism manifest themselves in different ways. They have in common their disavowal of the existence of one Arab nation and therefore each trend seeks self-determination on the merits of its particular situation. Because of Arab nationalism's anti-Western attitude, the localists seem to favor cooperation with the West primarily to defend their own interests. The Arab nationalists refer disparagingly to these trends as *Shu'ubiyah* (other people).

## Marxism and the New Left

Socialist ideas have existed on a minimal scale in the Middle East during the nineteenth and early twentieth centuries. They were rejected mainly because they were linked with irreligious doctrines. Between the two World Wars, a few Communist groups came into existence. After that, Communist literature became more readily available and Communist thinking more familiar. Nevertheless, only in Iraq did intellectuals, influenced by British Fabianism in alliance with some Communists, play a certain role. They became engaged in a military conspiracy in 1936 which took over the government for a short period.

After the triumph of the Allies in World War II, Soviet books and films invaded the Middle East and the small Communist parties began to enjoy certain popularity in Turkey, Iran, Egypt, Syria, and Lebanon until the objectives of the international policy of the USSR clashed with the national interests of the area. In the Arab countries, the decision of the USSR in 1947 in favor of the partition of Palestine debilitated the standing of the Communist Party. On the other hand, the creation of the state of Israel and the support it received from the West increased the anti-Western feeling already existing in Arab nationalism. This was conducive to a search for new political and social systems. Socialism became so popular that, as we have seen, even the religionists laid claim to it, as did the nationalists, who established their own brand of socialism in the forms described above.

Communist ideology in the Middle East has varied from one country to another. Prior to the Moscow-Peking rift, which left the Communists everywhere divided into hardliner Stalinists and moderates who supported coexistence with capitalism, all Communists had followed Russian instructions. The Lebanese

Communist Party is a typical example of this. In its early days the party stressed the original communization of the land and urged the distribution of property and income among the workers in accordance with the amount of work they did. Beginning in the mid-1930s the Lebanese Communists began to shift their emphasis from domestic to international politics. In the process, they were willing to compromise on their socialistic program in exchange for support for the Soviet Union and its allies. So in the party's 1943-1944 Congress, the Communists merely stressed Syrian and Lebanese independence, constitutional and democratic rights, and social reform. In order to achieve this, Western (particularly American) imperialism, they declared, should be combatted and defeated. Once this was accomplished, the Lebanese would freely give up any cooperation with the West and turn instead to the Soviet Union and the Communist bloc. Yet, despite outward appearances to the contrary, the Lebanese Communists never really fought against "imperialism." Their concern all along has been to defend Communist interests as they are viewed at any particular time. Their attitude to Arab unity testifies to this fact. According to them there was no Arab "nation" as such until it suddenly came into being in 1955-1956 after Nasser's arms deal. The Communist's most eminent leader in the Arab world, Khaled Bakdash, concluded in 1939 that there was no Arab nation, since there was no common economic life between the countries of the Arab world. He further proceeded to discredit common language and unity of aims as sufficient elements in the formation of a nation, and concluded by saying that each country in the Arab world had its own national characteristics. This same Bakdash stated later: "the ambition of the Arab countries for unity is not the product of transitory circumstances or the consequences of propaganda spread by a party or a group of people. Rather, it is a reflection of a realistic need and the consequence of historical evolution independent of any sentiments and wills."[5] When negotiations between Syria and Egypt were being conducted in 1958, the Lebanese Communist Party began to champion a federation of an outright union.

The Communist attitude today remains the same although the Communists have begun to downplay the question of the nationality of Lebanon and have allied themselves with other leftist forces: the Arab Nationalist Movement, the Progressive Socialist Party led by the Lebanese deputy Kamal Jumblat, and the Lebanese branch of the Ba'th Party.

From January 7-10, 1972, the Lebanese Communist Party held a public congress to which representatives from other Communist parties were invited. Also attending were representatives of the "progressive parties" in Lebanon and the Palestine Liberation Organization. This was made possible by the new Lebanese government of President Franjieh which ratified a decision taken by the previous president, Charles Hilu, to lift the ban on all prohibited parties, including the Communists and the SSNP. The Third Congress, the first of its kind in the Arab world as a Communist public congress, presages a turning away from secrecy and revolution to a more moderate policy and cooperation within the existing system. It remains to be seen whether this is not another one of the party's chameleonic tactics in order to serve the interests of the Soviets who are at present courting Lebanese friendship and cooperation.

The party's communique at the end of the Third Congress stated that the Communists are working for the triumph of socialism in Lebanon and are hoping to remove the "capitalist band" from their seat of power. Democracy in Lebanon, according to them, is a democracy of the bourgeosie. The party also criticized all the "progressive" Arab regimes but made a scathing attack on the Sudanese government for its persecution of the Communist Party in October 1971. They also criticized the spread of anti-Communist feelings now growing in the ranks of the Fedayeen. Regarding Arab unity, the party's communique came out in its support, and described it as "the product of the real existence of evolution in the Arab world and of the historical ties between its parts."[6]

The Communists are strong in Syria, where they have had representation in the government on several occasions. In Iraq, they enjoyed their peak during the Kassim regime. In Egypt, they are currently strong among the intellectuals. However, the only place they have had labor-union support has been in the Sudan where in spite of their recent persecution they remain a possible source of power. The labor unions in the Arab world included many Communists in their ranks, but on the whole they were not dominated by them nor did they obey union wishes. Of course the Communists tried to make use of labor grievances to further their own political aims.

Except in Lebanon, the Communist parties of the Middle East operate clandestinely or semi-clandestinely. They are tolerated in some countries of the Arab world in order not to displease the Soviet Union; but in the religious-minded states such as Libya and Saudi Arabia, communism is at the present time an anathema. In order to keep their preferential position, the Soviets have acquiesced to the fact that the Arab governments do not accord the Communist parties a legal status. In the event the Soviets stay in the area for an extended period, they most probably will not remain satisfied with this arrangement.

Professor Hisham Sharabi of Georgetown University, in his book *Nationalism and Revolution in the Arab World*, designates the revolutionary and socialistic aspects of Nasserism, Ba'thism, and the Algerian Front of National Liberation as new-leftist. This is true to the extent that they don't consider communism to be the solution to their problems. The three movements also have in common with the new-leftists the use of Marxist terminology and an ideological solidarity with the liberation movements. They differ, on the other hand, on many things, not the least of which is nationalism. The new-leftists orient themselves on the guidelines of scientific socialism only, and are totally opposed to all bourgeois thinking, to the *petite bourgeoisie*, and to all alliances. The small groups of new-leftists that are found now in Lebanon, Morocco, and among the Popular Front for the Liberation of Palestine (PFLP) and its offshoot the Democratic

Popular Front for the Liberation of Palestine (DPFLP) criticize both Ba'thism and Nasserism as being organized forms of national *petit bourgeoisie* and are solely a continuation of the ideology of Islamic modernism and secular nationalism. What Ba'thism and Nasserism did was give the privileges of the capitalists to the *petite bourgeoisie*, whose class members had taken over state apparatus.

Whatever their critics may say, the only political organizations with new-leftist orientations are the two Palestinian resistance movements, the PFLP and DPFLP, whose spectacular activities included hijacking airplanes. All the other new-leftists were limited to the publication of a great number of books and articles showing the dismay of the new-leftist Arab intellectuals at the failure of the Arab nationalist movement to meet the challenges of Israel and to raise the Arab masses from the social and economic misery in which they find themselves. Furthermore, the new-leftists are very critical of the Arab Communist parties, accusing them of deviating from Marxism and serving only the interests of Moscow.

## Conclusion

The numerous ideologies existent in the Middle East in general and the Arab world in particular are still mostly visionary theories, none of which, except for some of the socialistic and economic aspects of Nasserism and Ba'thism have been put in practice. The limited success of these two movements has not been followed by the implementation of the remainder of their lofty ideals. The aims of Arab nationalism as well as those of the religionists are still the greatest driving political forces. However, most have remained in the realm of aspirations. They have been expressed in different forms and have assumed a variety of roles; but as aims for solving the ills of the Arab world, they have been failures. In spite of the formation of the Federation of Arab Republics (Egypt, Syria, and Libya), the future of Arab unity and socialism is still and will remain for some time in the balance. The unity of the Fertile Crescent as envisioned by the SSNP seems impossible to achieve. Similar conclusions must be expressed for the aims of communism.

We have not discussed democracy and liberalism in the Western sense because they have disappeared from the ideological arena of the Middle East. Turkey and Lebanon are closest to being democracies.

**Part II:
Subcultures**

# Introduction to Part II

The core of this study is the subcultures of the Arab world. It is the contention of the authors that there exists in the countries of the Middle East certain groups that have a similar outlook and seem to act in a similar manner. For example, it is seen that the bureaucracies in Morocco, Egypt, and Iraq are conservative, want to maintain a *status quo*, and are generally opposed to socialism. Or, when speaking of the communicators, the journalists of the Middle East want greater freedom to express themselves while the writers are stressing the Palestinian problem.

Initially, there is presented to the reader a chapter entitled *Subcultures in the Arab World*, in which is discussed in general terms various selective groups, as well as the theory and theoretical aspects of subcultures. The authors, Abdul Aziz Said and Mohammed Mughisuddin, have chosen the military, the guerrillas, the students, the Western-educated elites, the bureaucracy, the communicators, and the lawyers of the professional class to be the groups deemed to have the most impact in the region. In the discussions which resulted, the authors found a predominant preoccupation with the Arab-Israeli conflict and the resultant Palestinian problem. Furthermore, the term "revolution" seems to be a word much in vogue in the area. Nevertheless, other national traits emerge which, when analyzed, denote a common action among each group, thereby laying the groundwork for ensuing sections containing in greater detail more information of the specified Middle Eastern subcultures.

# 4

## Subcultures in the Arab World

**Abdul A. Said** and **Mohammed Mughisuddin**

Subcultures is a generally neglected frame of reference for discussions of real national growth. Called "minorities" or "interest groups" by political scientists, and "microsystem" by the new behavioral theoreticians, a subculture is any group whose shared, mutually reinforcing sets of expectations have led to stereotyped behavior distinctive enough to warrant separate entries within the literature. This stereotyped behavior may range from life styles to clothing or language. It must encompass some sense of distinctive group identification.

The function of stereotyped behavior and distinctive subcultures in stable societies is conflict reduction or simple survival. When driving down the highway, the individual driver can make instantaneous probability judgment from such superficially exogenous factors as the date, model, color, and exterior condition of surrounding cars—estimates vital to safe driving. Each distinctive subculture within a society, with its customary behavior patterns and stereotyped sets of expectations, generates its own internal pecking order that minimizes the probability of intergroup clashes—the black militants have more hatred for "Uncle Tom" than for George Wallace. Given this function, it is clear that true social transformation requires the creation of new social stereotypes—the "new man" of Marxist and Falangist literature. The study of subcultures—especially those whose pattern of expectation and vision of the future are changing—is thus a useful starting point for a noneconomic understanding of evolving societies. Newly emerging subcultures are perhaps a real "vanguard" of prospective social change. Identifying characteristics of a particular subculture may tell us more about the future of a society than the beliefs of the current elite or all kinds of silent majorities. By focusing on these groups whose visions and expectations are at significant variance with the national norm of a given society, we wish to draw attention to their critical goal in adaptation; and we are suggesting that social differentiation and the appearance, growth, and expansion of subcultures are, in themselves, better indices of development than the usual standards.

To a great extent, probably because many Arab elites had their advanced

Part of this chapter was published by Abdul A. Said and Bahram Farzanegan 'Subcultures in the Arab World,' in *Protagonists of Change: Subcultures in Development and Revolution*, Abdul A. Said, Editor. © 1971. Reprinted by permission of Prentice-Hall, Inc., Englewood Cliffs, N.J.

education in either the West, the USSR, or other Communist countries, the image of the future has been dominated in the past by the use of only two models of development—the Western model and the Soviet model. During the 1950s and early 1960s the international system was, in fact, viewed as one where the East and the West competed in selling their own prescription for development to emerging nations. With the decline of bipolarity, the rise of China, and the more recent emergence of Japan, the "image" of what development is needs to be reexamined. The new international system in which postindustrial states are reexamining their own basic programs (and in which major actors such as the United States will probably be more interested in domestic affairs) could conceivably affect the role of various nations as "models" of development.

How does a subculture affect the rate of social change? It may do so in a number of ways: by specializing in key occupations, such as the military or the bureaucracy; or by reinterpreting religious and philosophical ideas in such a way that the internal priorities and the vision of the future of the subculture begin to deviate sharply from other subcultures, especially the dominant ones, thereby creating the basis for a new value orientation.[1] Then too, existence of competing subcultures indicates conflict and this becomes the driving dynamic of change. Furthermore, denied access to political power, a subculture may specialize in acquiring wealth and influence through participation in business, banking, transportation, and professional activities.

The Arab world is an ornate mixture of groups, each of which cherishes its distinct sets of expectations as well as a stereotyped behavior. It is a patch work of lifestyles and a diversity of identities. The Arab world is a mosaic of subcultures within subcultures. There are many Arab worlds—no uniquely Arab view of the future, no common dreams, only shared frustrations.

In this chapter, we will examine only seven of the subcultures in the Arab world: the students, the military, the guerrillas, the Western-educated elites, the bureaucracy, the communicators, and the lawyers (professionals). While each of these groups displays a stereotyped behavior distinctive enough to warrant designation as a subculture, none of these subcultures possesses identical characteristics in every Arab state. Accordingly, we will focus upon the common elements of each.

## The Students as a Subculture

Students, for long the vehicle of ideological movements and the backbone of revolutionary rhetoric in the Arab world, now face political emasculation because of reversals in the very process of political relationships that brought them to power. The process began with the defeat in Palestine in 1948, which resulted in the call for Arab nationalism and unity. At that time, the overriding force of the period seemed to be the preservation of the newly won independence and the strengthening of national unities in the most politically conscious countries of Lebanon, Syria, and Jordan.

The Arab defeat in Palestine resulted in the influx of about one million refugees into Lebanon, Syria, and Jordan. This represented a highly political force that proved capable of influencing trends, especially among the students and the youth of the host countries. The alliance of the Palestinian intelligentsia with the political and intellectual circles in Beirut, Damascus, and Amman was inevitable. Both centers of social and political dissent had one inevitable link in common: changing the sociopolitical order from the feudal-aristocratic alliances that had shaped the course of events in these three countries during Ottoman rule and in the post-independence era.

It is this feudal aristocracy that is blamed for the humiliating defeat in Palestine, as well as the moral bankruptcy and underdevelopment of what was once a proud Arab nation that extended from the Atlantic Ocean to the Persian Gulf. The glorious past of Arab history is as much a part of every Arab as is his own being—not an unusual attitude on the part of a people whose pride in and reliance on tradition and heritage seem unequaled by any other people in history.

Thus, it was not difficult for Arab youths and Palestinians to view the succession of military coups in Syria as a natural element in the struggle against a corrupt, self-perpetuating aristocracy whose survival depended upon the commitment of Western powers. Those coups d'etat seemed to be the first and only expression of self-determination; and they were internally inspired, internally carried, and internally supported. This is a significant fact of life in an area where Western embassies had the power of life and death over national governments.

By the mid-1950s, especially with the advent to power of Gamal Abdel Nasser in Egypt, youth movements in the Arab world, especially in Syria, Lebanon, and Jordan, became an inseparable part of any power equation that affected political moves and relationships in the area. This alliance between students and established centers of power contributed in some considerable way to the union of Syria and Egypt in 1958. The military in Syria became so dependent upon ideological and intellectual bases for political survival that inevitably the first communique of any coup d'etat made extensive use of ideological jargon (usually leftist, of course) in order to command a popular base among the restive intellectuals and the politically active Palestinians who were resentful of Western participation in the creation of Israel.

Student-intellectual support for a union between Egypt and Syria made the union viable for over three years, in spite of overwhelming geographical odds and external pressures. Yet the absence of such a power base, in spite of Western and government support, caused the sterility of the Iraqi-Jordanian union, which remained no more than a dream. Contrasted to the Iraqi-Jordanian union, that of Syria and Egypt went so far as to merge government operations and administrative laws. Changes in currency were also underway at the time of the breakup in September 1961. Thus, while the intellectuals and students were powerful enough to help bring about union between Egypt and Syria, they were not powerful enough to preserve it.

The governments in Egypt and Syria, Jordan, Lebanon, and Iraq, tried to retain power without student-intellectual support; and even though this power component was isolated, there was no appreciable decline in the leadership of the established regimes prior to the 1967 Arab-Israeli War.

The Arab defeat in 1967 was to prove beyond any reasonable doubt that more than ideology and intent are needed for a restoration of the Arab dream, let alone the recovery of Palestine. This elusive dream—a progressive, unified Arab world—was at best betrayed by its own apostles and at worst ignored by its converts as unattainable. The Arab defeat drastically altered the power equation that for well over a decade had made it possible for Arab regimes to command significant popular support by socialist slogans and the promise of "unity and liberation." This was true of President Nasser in Egypt as it was of the socialists in Syria, Iraq, and Algeria. It was with the help of such popular support that these regimes, with reliance on the army, could afford to pay lip service to students and the intellectual movements in the Arab world. The war of 1967, however, exposed the shaky basis of Arab programs; and public apathy was the stable diet on which they fed and found their strength.

The emergence of a Palestinian guerrilla movement brought a new factor to the power equation as well as a new element to Arab politics. The movement seemed to be organized along respectable ideological lines, and its ideology could command the brute power from which political power would someday emerge. The Palestinian movement, however, was too divided within itself to satisfy the necessary requirements of cohesion and unity of goal. So far the guerrilla movement has proven inadequate in its efforts to attract wide support from the youth movements in the Arab world, except in the form of sympathy and contributions. But that can hardly provide the basis for the guerrillas to force a course of action on Arab governments that is contrary to their stated policy of seeking a "peaceful settlement" to the Arab-Israeli conflict.

The power vacuum that exists in the Arab world today is an artificial one. It is so because those who hold the instruments of power have not yet relinquished them, and those who are trying to wrest power have not yet decided whether taking over really serves their ends. Any such *status quo* only delays the confrontation necessary for the resolution of such an impasse. Power is relative, and as such is bound to swing one way or another. This seemed to be the case in Jordan in the recent past when the Jordanian army was forced to negotiate a settlement with the ill-prepared, ill-equipped, and ill-trained Palestinian movement.

Given this general picture it is difficult to visualize the role students in the Arab world can play. About the only useful service they have rendered so far has been to act as "factors of rhetoric" for the alleged revolutionary regimes that command power. Given the identity of goals, the guerrilla movement cannot pursue the same course and use students and intellectuals in this manner. A guerrilla movement survives and grows solely on its ability to move and fight, hide and fight, and agitate until its objectives are realized. But this process must be of a progressive, not static or regressive, nature.

Arab students (here one can talk only about those mostly in the Arab East) tend to confuse their goals with their means. This predicament has been the product of events and not muddled thinking. The establishment of a socialist, democratic society can only be made possible, if at all, when a nation diverts its energies to that goal. But the Arabs must first decide whether liberation of Israeli-occupied lands or socialism is what they are after. The policy choice of guns or butter is nowhere more evident than here. It could be that given the true nature of the Arab world, social and political revolutions may have to go hand in hand. This has not been very successfully achieved in the past, but it has been done in at least two recent cases—China and the Soviet Union.

The immobility of Arab students, most of them overeducated and unemployed in a static economy that cannot absorb them in either the military or in the social field, is due to the fact that they have been excluded from the system. About all that the Arab student youth can hope for today is to find a secure job that will repay the heavy investment he has made in pursuit of an education that his country's economy is barely capable of using or absorbing.

Arab society has become too urban for an educated student to engage in a guerrilla movement, and the system has excluded him. What are his options?— force himself into the system, or accept his fate in typical Arab resignation. So far, unfortunately, it seems that the latter form of action has been the rule rather than the exception. Of course, the high percentage of Palestinian college and university graduates filling the ranks of the *Fida'iyyin* movement would seem to deny this. But one must remember the higher percentage of Palestinians determined to liberate Palestine. A yet lower percentage of Arab students in the rest of the Arab countries also seems to have taken the easy way out—to accept their exclusion and go about finding a way to accommodate the *status quo* and therefore their status in it.

Be it modernization, socialism, or liberation, Arab students can only realize their goals if and when they plunge into the debate on what must be done and how to achieve it. Once that is resolved, a course of action would probably flow inevitably. But an unfortunate fact is that the Arab is by nature a romanticist, by heart an adventurer, and by taste a conservative. Are these the characteristics of a revolutionary, someone devoted to and driving for change?

**The Military as a Subculture**

The Arab defeat in Palestine in 1948-1949 dramatized the need for change. Prominent Arab scholars, such as Qustantin Zurayq, Hasan Sa'ab, and others, termed it the great tragedy of modern Arab history. Along with many others they attempted to examine the ills of Arab society and the best means to alleviate them. But their pleas for a rebirth of nationalism and spiritualism, and the adoption of new attitudes to effect modernization, merely served to reveal the moral bankruptcy of the Arab ruling elites, and the ideological power vacuum in the Arab world.

Beginning in the early fifties in the Eastern Arab states and the early sixties in North Africa, a revolutionary wave swept the Arab world. A political complex of norms and values, organization and aspiration, was hastily put together. A spectacular display of radical pronouncements of policy and showpiece projects were exhibited to attract popular support and justify the sacrifices needed to effect development. The Ba'ath party in Syria and Iraq, the Neo-Destour (renamed the Destourian Socialist Party) in Tunisia, the National Liberation Front in Algeria, and the Arab Socialist Union in Egypt all competed for revolutionary leadership.

These Arab revolutionaries failed to focus their strength, let alone rally popular support, among the people. They developed goals of societal change, but failed to mobilize the internal resources, human and physical, to approximate such goals. With the exception of the Destourian Socialist Party in Tunisia, all of these movements turned to the army, the country's sole cohesive force capable of action. The party-army coalition provides a combination of force and intellectual theoretical criticism—the prerequisite for raising a movement to a revolutionary level in the Arab world.

Shifts in balance of the uneasy coalition are commonly recurring because both parties to the coalition are themselves victims of the antagonistic sectional, religious, and minority groupings. Every new shift produces moves for another "revolution," either to redress the imbalance caused by its predecessor or to create new alignments. Each new revolutionary vanguard maintains a set of societal goals, a collection of those promissory notes of rebirth considered long overdue, to justify to the masses—and above all to the army, the main source of support—the concentration of power and the sacrifices called for. Although these revolutionary goals—be they land reform, industrialization, or nationalization of foreign interests—are presented in the form of an ideology that holds little promise of galvanizing or cementing the population, they, nevertheless, become a vehicle for the consolidation and perpetuation of the revolutionary elite. Their realization is indeed secondary; the goals become ends in themselves.

After every coup the Arab revolutionaries endeavor to legitimize their position by exposing the "misdeeds" of the previous regime. Furthermore, the Arab revolutionaries feed the flames of their nationalism with the glories of the Arab past, in contrast to today's Western revolutionaries who question the many myths that assured Western hegemony in the world for so long. Unconsciously seeking diamonds in ashes, the Arab revolutionary reinforces his drive by believing that the fate of his culture will be decided in the battlefield simultaneously with the fate of his aspirations. Therefore, the revolution becomes both an end in itself and a national myth that ensures the "demonization" of the former regime.

The resulting revolutionary doctrine in the national context relies on an eclectic pragmatic borrowing. Militarism, Leninist one-party organizations, long-range economic plans, token agrarian reforms, superficial Western liberalism and fascism are all adapted from this amalgam to perceived local needs. The revolutionary doctrine tries to answer basic questions of social hierarchy and human purpose without providing solutions to the problems these questions raise. In a decade and in a milieu where inherited institutions and customary relationships no longer appear natural, inevitable, or immutable, that which was borrowed assumed an indigenous character for lack of alternatives.

In the search for new institutions and remodeled relationships, hierarchy and control remain as vital as they have been in the past. The complex coordination of human effort needed to meet the promises of the revolutionary leadership is attempted in an economic-demographic set of conditions that predicate pessimistic results. These conditions make it plausible for the few to defy these principles during the democratic socialist experiment. The few must manage and foresee developments. The majority must obey, sacrifice, and endure, as they are important to change or validate the direction of society.

Bound together by their repudiation of the traditional political and social structures, the revolutionaries find themselves even more frustrated in the social aspect of the revolution. At least in the realm of rhetoric, the concept of revolution in the early sixties shifted the focus of ideological attention of the regime in Syria and the Arab Socialist regime in Egypt from political processes to class structure and the economic organization of their respective states. Because parliamentary democracy was frustrated for the lack of a middle class, these regimes developed under army control and without the firm base of a working class.

The quality and quantity of social and economic change in these states, as well as in "revolutionary" states such as Iraq, Libya, and Algeria, will inevitably be the result of the direction and effort embodied in various development programs and the extent to which the masses identify with the goals of radical reform. Such development, it would seem, would not be prejudiced greatly by any ideological conception of a perfect society, no matter how revolutionary. When progress is realized in any given area, it will be justified in ideological jargon, more for external benefit than for anything else. The further these ideals are separated from reality, the more frustrated and explosive will the situation become in societies that must run to maintain a *status quo*.

The manifestation of military regimes in the Arab states reveals that revolutions occur there mainly for military and political considerations and rarely for economic or social reasons. The legitimacy of these regimes is derived from their predecessor's inability to "make good" on their political and military promises: modernization, and the liberation of Palestine. The inability to fulfill promises forms a serious and recurring imbalance in the means-ends relationship of these regimes, whether they are military or civilian. Their recurring imbalance is mainly due not to the lack of means, but rather to Arab inability to deal effectively with practical factors and conditions influencing the flexibility of their means and the priority of their objectives.

In the conventional Arab states ruled by one man, there was no politics. To oppose the ruler was not politics but treason. The army was the traditional source of support for the ruler. Frequent military coups d'etat are the result of attempts to introduce democratic party politics into a system where there has been no traditional foundation for them and where the army has traditionally been employed as much in the internal affairs of the state as in external defense. The cessation of military coups will occur only when some outstanding personality restores one-man rule, the traditional form of Arab government.

The Arab military politicians have no unique single outlook and no uniform ideology. They are divided in their opinions, and their views are more or less identical with those of the civilians. The military politicians are generally unwavering nationalists who favor social reforms. Zealous supporters of the state's independence and prestige, they are indifferent to the values of individual freedom.

The common element in their views is the general "ideology" of Arab nationalism. This ideology, however displayed, is far from being a well-formulated doctrine or system of beliefs and opinions. It glorifies war and struggle against internal and external enemies; it showers praise on the brave who defend the Arab lands; and it emphasizes the historical role of the military but not its absolute supremacy. It does not sanctify war for its own sake.

The army officers who take over their countries hardly ever mention the army itself as a reason for the coup. They announce that the army assumes control to eradicate corruption, prevent anarchy, establish a regime based on freedom and justice, liberate the country from dependence on imperialism, advance the cause of Arab unity—all of these being general social and political goals. They consider themselves the pioneers of national liberation and social reform for the entire nation.

**The Guerrillas as a Subculture**

The defeat of the military in 1967 introduced a new outlook in the Arab world. There could be no excuses and none were accepted as readily as they had been in 1948 and 1956. The prestige of governments reached a new low in the Arab world. The problem was increasingly seen to be not just the liberation of Palestine—a distant goal to which all Arab governments pay lip-service—but also the liberation of the Arab states, revolutionary or otherwise, and the best methods by which to achieve it. The traditional approach has proven to be fallible, and a far more radical alternative is sought. The infatuation of Arabs with the Palestinian liberation movement is in part an appreciation of mass participation as the means to action and goal fulfillment.

Palestinians, aware of this new climate in the Arab world and of the general inability of Arab regimes to restore their rights in Palestine, have moved on their own. For the first time since 1949, the Palestinians have been free and willing to act militantly, independent of their hosts. The success of the Palestinians, however, will depend on whether they can unite into a single revolutionary movement and elicit the participation of the restive Arab intelligentsia. They must also overcome the restraints imposed by Arab regimes and, in some cases, the open hostility of those regimes.

Although the unity of the Palestinian liberation movement is not yet a reality, a radical hegemonic group may yet emerge and move toward the next stage—uniting the Arab intelligentsia. Both Fatah (The Movement for the Liberation of Palestine, and largest guerrilla group) and the Popular Front for the Liberation of Palestine (PFLP) realize their success will depend on their ability to spread the revolution to other Arabs. It is at this stage that they will encounter their greatest challenge. Linking up with other Arabs will require an ideology and the creation of what may be called "parallel organizations" supported by radical means.

Although ideologically uncommitted, Fatah has so far rejected the Marxist-Leninist approach of the PFLP on the grounds that it is part of the traditional revolutionary approach, and thus fails to overcome the impasse in which the Ba'athist and other Arab revolutionary movements have floundered. Fatah has so far relied on a nationalist, anti-imperialist, and anti-Israeli approach. This approach has, until recently, been more successful than that of the PFLP, and its simplicity was made more attractive by the activities of Fatah inside Israeli-occupied territory. It appears that the guerrillas are failing to provide discipline and organization. If this trend continues, they will lose control over other Arabs, and the whole movement may fall prey to "warlordism." On the other hand, the Arab governments, conservative and radicals alike, will view with alarm the development of an organized mass movement that will certainly threaten their continued existence, and will probably not countenance the development of these "parallel organizations."

In refugee camps, Fatah represents the willingness of the Palestinian Arab to seize the initiative in securing what he believes to be his rights. In relation to the rest of the Arab world, it represents a reevaluation, if not an outright rejection, of Arab governments; and the increasing student unrest in the "revolutionary" Arab states must be viewed from this context.

The approach of Fatah has been fashioned according to two propositions suggested by Regis Debray—namely that guerrilla action leads to political action and political structures, and that the former is not dependent on the latter for success. Thus it is only now that Fatah is beginning to come to grips with the cultural inputs to what may become its ideological orientation and platform. Two trends appear: one calls for a reconciliation of Islamic tradition with the requirements of the day through the reform of Islam—reopening the doors of *ijtihad* (religious interpretation and jurisprudence)—while the other suggests a completely secular left-of-center approach.

The prospect of a peaceful settlement may hasten these developments and bring about a major confrontation. There may be an attempt by the Palestinian liberation movements to take a shortcut approach—a direct bid to the masses without the benefit of parallel organizations. They may find themselves stalemated. Although they may be emotionally supported by the masses, the masses, lacking organization, will not be a match for the organized, repressive force of their governments.

The Palestinian cause has potential as a vehicle for a Pan-Arab movement of liberation. The cause of Palestine, many involved Arabs feel, can only be served correctly through a Pan-Arab union. Liberation from without is pushing the agenda for particularistic interests. If and when a union of the PFLP and Fatah takes place, the desire for liberation from demoralizing and repressive regimes will have as much priority as the liberation from Zionism.

## The Western-Educated Elites as a Subculture

Western intellectual penetration and European colonialism succeeded in divorcing the elites from contact with their compatriots; as a result, the elites could find identity only either in the traditional culture that the colonialists had disparaged and repressed, or in total acceptance of foreign values. They became cultural misfits, men without roots or genuine values.

The Arab elites of today are burdened by a conflict of values in their search for identity. One of the most pressing political problems in the Arab states is the establishment of mass support for the leadership groups. Mobilization of the various segments of the population around a systematic framework of national interests is difficult for two reasons: one, a national interest requires commonly held notions of the public good, and such nations have not been crystallized beyond the immediate goal of anticolonialism and anti-Zionism; and two, there are no established means by which a public consensus can be reached by all segments of society.

Colonialism has left behind it a complex legacy of inadequacy. To generate a new and genuine sense of identity, the elite must struggle to transform a negative revolt into a positive affirmation of the self. Many Arab leaders are victims of an upbringing that makes them superficially modern as well as superficially Arabs. The West has implanted within them the notion of utilitarianism, but not the essential spiritual values that have made utilitarian success possible. As a result, they tend to confuse means and ends, and to see their culture in its uncreative, ossified, passive side—the side that allowed the Arab world to be dominated for so long.

The task of leadership of the Arab elites has cast them as the catalyst of progress and modernization. The operational requirements of leadership have included setting up governments, establishing foreign relationships, and implementing policies.

At present, the problems facing Arab leaders arise less from external sources than from basic inadequacies of image and perception. Arab leaders fail to understand or accept either the requirements or the implications of leadership.

There is hardly an Arab state where leader and follower are in agreement over a well-defined common goal. They lack an appreciation of the major environmental factors they face, especially the definition of the problem to which they see themselves responding. There is little or no consensus upon the major elements of an action program. In other words, the problem of who leads and who follows in the Arab countries is directly related to the disagreement regarding where to go. The frameworks of national mission erected by Arab leaders in the preindependence era have outgrown their usefulness. The authoritarianism of present-day Arab leaders may produce surface acquiescence and even some grudging harmonization of policy; but to coerce perpetually one's people is not to lead them.

Inevitably, a perplexing ambivalence is now beginning to complicate the leader-follower relationship in many Arab states. On the one hand, leaders continue to argue that the imminent threat of foreign domination remains as pernicious as ever. From this postulate flows the chorus of ringing appeals for more sacrifices that constitutes much of the Arab leaders' rhetoric. On the other hand, one finds Arab leaders transcending their own argument by discovering a new approach to wealthy nations in a climate of cooperative endeavor. It is doubtful whether the Arab leaders today take seriously the dangers from without; they invoke the psychology of crisis only as a method of perpetuating their own hegemony. Arab leadership is a technique limited in its scope and effect to a situation of crisis or tension. It considers leadership and domination synonymous.

The challenge to Arab leadership is one of combining the massive enterprise of nation-building with a more flexible and many-sided approach on a number of fronts. Such a new attack demands that Arab leaders face some uncomfortable facts and make some hard decisions. They must seriously attempt to balance the rewards of leadership against its costs. They must realize that the added vitality of a national community outweighs the loss of a leader's freedom of choice and action that a close relationship entails. Otherwise, Arabs will be at the mercy of military elites for many years.

The Western-educated Arab elites as leaders will now be fully analyzed. They tend to be organizational rather than issue-oriented in their efforts to reform society. They also seem to place emphasis on establishing new structures and institutions rather than articulating the issues and problems that face the Arab world. This stems mainly from a cultural lag that separates them from their operational milieu. They are still carrying on the political debate popular in the West in the 1940s and 1950s concerning socialism and revolution. The Western-educated elites who expound the virtues of socialism are more impressed by the structural and organizational benefits, which, they believe, would accrue by adopting the system, than by the ideas and ideals of the system.

Notwithstanding their Western liberal education, these elites generally tend to view the individual as subordinate to the collective. They insist that the individual must limit his freedom in the larger interests of the community. Their syncretic amalgam continues to be "guided democracy" as a means of transforming Arab society.

Although what we have said above applies to a very large segment of the Western-educated elites, it would be proper to point out that there are a few who identify themselves with radical approaches to societal change. Those who expound radical ideas are more apt to have had their education in the Anglo-Saxon countries (U.S. or U.K.) or in the institutions supported by them. Radical elites, such as George Habash, a graduate of AUB (The American University of Beirut) would stop at nothing short of complete cultural revolution in their endeavor to transform Arab society. Their ideas and influence, however, have not permeated the stream of present-day Arab perceptions. The Western-educated elites who have been trained in the French-Latin tradition would not, in general, go beyond the evolutionary socialism that has been developed in Western Europe.

The Western-educated elites are severe critics of Western policies in the area; they aver that these official interests are causing a rapid decline in Western prestige and support among the Arabs. They allege that Western policies are instrumental in frustrating Arab efforts at unity, a goal which the Western-educated elites seemingly cherish.

Their experience with Western colonialism has constrained the Western-educated elites to identify parliamentary democracy with the preservation of the traditional bases of power in the monarchial Arab states. Western support to the conservative Arab regimes is considered "counter-revolutionary" by Western-educated Arabs. Had it not been for Western support, they argue, the conservative regimes would have been replaced by progressive forces that, in turn, would have ushered in a progressive era in the Middle East.

For the Western-educated elites, communism has become synonymous with radical negativism which, they contend, seeks to destroy all that is good in Arab society. They reject the basic tenets and assumptions of communism, based on the notion of a continuous class struggle. Pointing to an egalitarian Arab tradition, they consider the notion of class struggle as irrelevant to their milieu.

Inspired by the imperial notion of grandeur and past glories, they seek Arab unity in the name of Arabism, economic and political liberation, progress and self-betterment, which, they hope, will provide strength and deterrence against foreign designs on the Arab world.

The Arab elites educated in the Soviet Union, Eastern Europe, or China have not as yet made a serious impact on the sociopolitical life of the region. The reasons for this are rather obvious. These Arabs received purely technical training in the socialist countries where they were not exposed to the theoretical and social aspects of the system. Generally, their stay in the socialist countries was short; they were usually pressed to finish their programs and return to their jobs back home. Furthermore, with the exception of a small group of young students who recently chose to go to the socialist countries for their higher education, the Arabs sent for training in the socialist countries were already intellectually mature and culturally committed to their own traditions and values. In addition, the language and cultural differences limited the scope of their contacts with the ordinary people of the host countries, thus depriving them of an opportunity to understand the dynamics of the socialist system.

Similarly, the Arab military officers who have been trained in the Soviet Union, East Europe, or China, are far less politicized than their comrades who attended the Command Staff College, and Infantry School in the United States or similar institutions in Britain or France. In the West, the Arab military officers were exposed to both technical and sociopolitical curricula. In the socialist countries, the Arab military officer on the whole only received intensive technical training. Because of the general aversion of the Arab governments toward communism, the Arab military officers, were, by design, not generally exposed to political indoctrination.

This analysis, however, does not apply to the leadership of the Palestinian guerrilla movement whose training in North Vietnam, China, or other socialist countries carried a great deal of political indoctrination. The Palestinian guerrillas have more or less accepted the idea of political indoctrination as part of their training program whereas the regular Arab armies have not. Thus is the difference in the training curricula in the socialist countries.

By virtue of their common educational experiences, the Western-educated elites in Iraq, Egypt, Jordan, and Syria have developed a dialogue (and no more than a dialogue) in an effort to find effective methods for bulding an Arab consensus toward some of the urgent problems facing the Arab world. It is not beyond the realm of possibility that these efforts will bear fruit, provided the Arab elites learn to appreciate the differences between ends and means, between attainable and ideal goals, between a glorious past and a not so glorious present.

## The Bureaucracy as a Subculture

Public bureaucracies in the Arab world may be classified into three distinct categories based on their respective educational background, vision of the future, and their approach to the social and economic problems facing the region.

Several Arab states possess bureaucracies that are Western-oriented primarily because of the educational background of the administrators. Morocco; Algeria; Lebanon; Jordan; and, to a lesser extent, Saudi Arabia and Kuwait fall under this category. Other states, such as Libya, Iraq, Sudan, and the Persian Gulf sheikhdoms, are still under the influence of the traditional elites, who have been trained in local educational institutions, and who continue to follow the model of "traditional authority."

The third category, that of the technocratic elite, is gaining influence in both Egypt and Tunisia and, to a lesser extent, in Syria. The bureaucracies in these countries have also been imbued with the ideological principles of their respective dominant political parties—the Arab Socialist Union, the Destour, and the Ba'ath. Thus, these bureaucracies are burdened with intramural tension between technocrats and politicized administrators.

In general, Arab public bureaucracies tend to be *status quo* oriented and they prefer the evolutionary model of development to that of the revolutionary model, which they consider inapplicable to their needs and circumstances. Because it is a self-perpetuating and self-aggrandizing group, the bureaucracy acts as a stabilizing factor in the Arab world where coups and countercoups would normally create social and economic chaos without the continuous presence of the civil administrators.

Regardless of their location, Arab public bureaucracies are extremely jealous of their independence, feeling threatened by foreign advisers. Arab bureaucrats are committed more to local (parochial) nationalism than to Pan-Arabism. Being generally nonideological and realistic administrators, the Arab bureaucrats look at Pan-Arabism as an ideal to aspire to but not as a political goal to be achieved in the near future. Since the bureaucrats are not directly answerable to the public, they do not see any need to cater to its emotional-psychological needs, as expressed in Pan-Arabism, and Arab socialism.

The Arab bureaucrat's perception of change is similar to that of any other bureaucrat, i.e., that change should be evolutionary rather than revolutionary. He feels at home with time-tested social and political institutions and is unwilling to accept new ones that might constrain him to change his life-style and routine. Furthermore, even if he were willing to accept radical changes in the bureaucratic routine and attitude, his sociopolitical milieu would not be conducive to such changes. His conservatism is a product of Arab conservatism nourished by Islamic traditionalism.

In life-style, the Arab bureaucrat shares with his European counterpart middle class values. Like the European middle class, the Arab bureaucrats seek job security and prestige; they are acquisitive and show propensity towards collecting modern gadgets, such as automobiles and television. They like to travel abroad and prefer to educate their children in Europe or European schools rather than in the local institutions. At the personal level of conversation, the Arab bureaucrats talk more about their "recent" material acquisitions than about political or philosophical ideas.

Notwithstanding their political and social conservatism, the Arab bureaucrats are by and large a secular group. This is especially true at the higher level of the hierarchy. The lower and middle levels have not yet learned to separate religion from politics. This is manifested both in their observance of religious rituals—prayers, fasting, etc.—and in their attitude toward coworkers of different religious faiths—regarding advancements or the lack of it.

Arab civil bureaucracy competes with, as well as supports, the military regimes in their efforts at reforms and economic development. The bureaucrats, however, are generally unimpressed about the self-image of the military as an efficient administrative machinery and an effective vehicle for sociopolitical development in the Arab world. In a number of cases the military regimes have sought coalitions with the bureaucracy in an effort to successfully implement their reforms. It is in this area that the civil bureaucracy has proved to be a moderating influence, even in the so-called radical states in the Arab world. In those states where the military regimes have been unwilling to share power and have endeavored to enforce their dicta without the active cooperation of the bureaucrats, such efforts have usually proved to be counterproductive. These military regimes have been disabled by bureaucratic red tape.

Of the various subcultures discussed here, the bureaucracy is the least ideologically-oriented group. Its members are concerned primarily with day-to-day work and show little inclination towards long-range planning based on ideological guidelines. Vague and undefinable slogans such as "Arab socialism" and "Islamic socialism" are of no practical value in their daily work which requires hard and practical decisions within the limitations imposed by human, material, and technical resources. Marxist ideology, popular among armchair Arab intellectuals, is usually dismissed as "irrelevant to our conditions" by most Arab bureaucrats capable of understanding it.

Although by and large the Arab bureaucrats have remained nonideological and apolitical, important exceptions occur in Tunisia, Egypt, Syria, and Iraq where party stalwarts have been placed in key bureaucratic positions by the national parties. These political-cum-ideological parties—the Destour, ASU, and the Ba'th respectively—made serious efforts at politicizing the bureaucracy in order to more firmly establish their power. Such efforts, however, were only partially successful due to a natural tendency of the parties to oppose the consolidation of power in the hands of a competing group. In areas where political parties have succeeded in politicizing the bureaucracy, the politicized bureaucrats follow the party line and their perceptions are not any different than that of the party in power.

## The Communicators as a Subculture

Modern Arab communicators achieved their preeminence during the nineteenth century reform movements. Then, as now, they played a dual role as communicators and innovators of ideas for reforming society. Convinced of the indispensibility of public support for a successful reform program, many prominent Arab reformers founded and edited their own journals, through which they endeavored to popularize their political, social, and religious ideas. Faced with a massive and unfamiliar problem of transforming a traditional society with its highly developed and well-ingrained institutions, the Arab reformer-communicator elites tended to formulate their ideas in a philosophical and universalistic rather than in a practical and particularistic frame of reference. There were those who defended the traditional institutions yet wished to reform them to meet new needs of the people and there were those who wished to implant among Arabs a wholly Western system of values and institutions.

Even after a century of debate some of the fundamental issues raised in the last century have not yet been satisfactorily resolved. Thus, editorial comments in the contemporary Arab press show that the Arab communicators have not markedly deviated in style or emphasis—they still maintain a philosophical and universalistic approach and they continue to neglect specific issues facing certain segments of society or certain regions of their respective countries. Perceiving their roles as theoreticians and didactics, the Arab journalist elites have, by and large, shown unwillingness to indulge in "parochial" issues. This, however, does not mean that they do not expose incidences of corruption in government or mismanagement of public funds—Arab newspapers are full of such accounts. Rather, what it means is that the Arab communicators have failed to articulate a general strategy or precise program for the future. They express their vision of the future in abstract ideas such as Arab socialism and political and economic democracy. If some of them have tried to effectively define these concepts, their explanations are not readily comprehensible to the masses. They have yet to identify the means by which they hope to achieve Arab unity and establish a democratic system of government in the region.

First the threat and imposition of censorship and later the nationalization (Egyptians call it socialization) of the press by many Arab regimes tended to stifle the creative energies of the Arab communicators. This, however, has not turned them into a group of passive participants in the affairs of the Arab world. Not only Lebanese journalists, who are protected by liberal press laws, but also other Arab communicators continue to show ardent concern about the economic, political, and social conditions prevailing in the region. Within the scope of the *Charter of National Action*, the Egyptian communicators have maintained a high degree of independence of judgment in commenting on external events and in offering factual criticisms on domestic economic and social problems. Since all major Egyptian newspapers are controlled by the government, Egyptian communicators have been prevented from printing public criticism of official policies formulated and sanctioned by the governing party. This self-censorship, however, was challenged editorially by Muhammad Hassanain Haykal, the former editor of al-Ahram, and by university students in the ASU sessions and the national parliament.

Professionally, Arab journalists operate on the assumption that news without views is a wasted effort. Printed and verbal messages are usually charged with resonant opinions, calculated to keep nationalist sentiments in a continuous state of high tension.[2] Their influence on the masses, however, is rather indirect. Messages written for the masses must necessarily pass through educated middle men, such as the *'Ulama* (the learned men of Islam), who interpret and editorialize the news and views during their daily or occaional meetings with villagers.

Educationally, the Arab communicator elites fall into two general categories: Western-educated, and locally educated. Generally, the communicator elites in Lebanon, Egypt, and North Africa are Western-educated; they tend to emphasize Western values and, therefore, hope to modernize their societies along Western models. The locally educated communicators tend to emphasize traditional values of Islam, with the hope of rejuvenating Muslim institutions which, they believe, are more conducive to the needs and circumstances of the people.

Socially, the Arab communicator elites enjoy prestigious positions in the community. Their educational and professional backgrounds and their travel experiences abroad have generally afforded the Arab communicators a position of leadership in the community. A good number of them are privy to the decision-makers and policy-initiators at the highest level, a factor that further enhances their prestige in the eyes of the masses. They see themselves as participants in both political and social processes—both at government and nongovernment levels. They participate in the process of crystallizing the social and political expectations of their own subculture as well as that of the general public. Arab communicators apparently enjoy a status far above that of their American and European counterparts.

Intellectually, the Arab communicator elites are generally considered to be a liberal segment of the society, at par with, if not superior to, such other subcultures as the Western-educated elites, students, and lawyers. Even in such centers of sociopolitical conservatism as Saudi Arabia and Jordan, Arab communicators are receptive to innovative ideas, in the transmission of which they are the most effective channel. In addition to other sources, foreign residents and visitors are an important source of knowledge and innovative ideas for Arab communicators, who meet with them without fear of social stigma or apprehension of governmental reprisals. This is true even during periods of international tension involving the Arab and foreign states.[a] In a sense, Arab communicators enjoy "poetic immunity" traditionally granted to Arab poets by the "prince" who wished to escape their caustic wrath.

---

[a]The much publicized case of Mustafa Amin, sentenced to life imprisonment in 1966 for allegedly giving state secrets to a CIA operative in Cairo, may have temporarily slowed interaction between Egyptian communicators and foreigners in the country.

## The Lawyers

Secular Arab lawyers are an important group within the professional subculture dedicated to creating a more democratic and liberal society through the propagation of the concept of constitutionalism and parliamentarianism. Traditionally, they have been leading actors in the national struggle for independence, defenders of the individual's liberty, and protectors of public interest. As a subculture, the Arab lawyers perceive themselves as innovators and reformers with a "noble mission" for reforming society.

Secular Arab lawyers have been primarily responsible for creating unified judicial systems that accord equality to all citizens. Through their diligent efforts and by maintaining high professional standards Arab lawyers were able to convince European powers and national governments to eliminate mixed courts (those used for foreign nationals), the Shariah courts (religious courts), and millet courts (minority group courts). By unifying the judicial system, Arab lawyers helped in strengthening the spirit of nationalism among the people.

As an organized group, Arab lawyers began their nationalist activities only after World War I. Prior to this, individual lawyers were active in political and reform movements that culminated in national independence and the establishment of parliamentary regimes. For many decades Arab lawyers generally acted as a bulwark against extension of executive authority and were a moderating influence on dictatorial regimes established under martial law. Often they expressed public disapproval of martial law regimes; and as long as they were not deprived of their organizational independence, the Arab lawyers persistently urged military regimes to restore civilian governments. This situation, however, changed when bar associations in Syria and Egypt were forced to accept the official party line.

Although they had been in the forefront of the national struggle and reform movements, Arab lawyers had by the mid-1950s lost much of their influence and support because of their close association with landowning and commercial elements of the upper class. With the nationalization of the large industrial and commercial enterprises, the break up of large estates, and the abolition of private Awqaf (religious foundations), the really lucrative sources of income disappeared. This situation forced a large number of lawyers to seek government employment and thus further reduced their social and political status in reshaping society. (This analysis applies only to such states as Egypt; Syria; Algeria; and, to a certain extent, Tunisia.) This, however, does not mean that Arab lawyers have totally abdicated their traditional role as defenders of the individual's civil rights and as exponents of liberal legal, political, and social concepts. The reality of their influence is manifested in Arab constitutions and other legal documents that guarantee individual and collective rights, at least on paper.

The nature of their profession and educational training have generally

constrained Arab lawyers to reject revolutionary methods of societal change—
they tend to favor a gradual and evolutionary process within the established legal
order. In areas where legal order seems "outmoded," they prefer political action
to reform the system. In their outlook and orientation, Arab lawyers are
generally progressive and Western. Until their disenchantment with Western
policies in the Middle East and the failure of parliamentary regimes to fulfill
their commitments, Arab lawyers had accepted Western models of government
and development. This attitude, however, seems to be changing both for the
above-mentioned reasons and because of a new sociopolitical milieu in which
they find themselves—a milieu where high praise is sung for socialist principles
and achievements.

In the struggle for independence, Arab lawyers played an important if not a
decisive role. Since independence, they have consistently supported the foreign
policies of Arab governments. Two such controversial issues were the nationalization of the Suez Canal and the international status of the Straits of Tiran. By
their advocation, the Arab lawyers sought not only to gain international
recognition and a position of strength for their countries but also to recoup
some of the prestige that should be their due in their own countries.

# Introduction to
# Chapters 5-10

*The next six chapters will be an expansion of the preceding one. In these chapters, W. Hazen and M. Mughisuddin will discuss in detail six of the subcultures previously analyzed—the military, the Western-educated elites, the students, the bureaucracy, the professionals, and the communicators.*

*Although some duplication was inevitable, the authors have attempted to present new material whenever possible, citing examples of certain countries. Unfortunately, for all intents and purposes, two topics, the bureaucracy and the Western-educated elites, have proved to be unexpandable. However, a recapitulation of the material on a less theoretical approach may assist the reader in better understanding the specified subcultures.*

# 5 The Military

In discussing the military of the Arab world as a subculture, it is important to remember that it does not represent, either at the national or the regional level, a cohesive force with clearly defined and articulated goals or political ideologies. Composed of a myriad of ethnic and religious groups, members of Arab armed forces manifest a variety of divergent and occasionally diametrically opposed views on issues such as modernization, Pan-Arabism, Islam, communism, democracy, and capitalism. Specifically, religious, ethnic, and historical diversity and the subsequent lack of consensus on national-regional goals, on priorities, and on the means of achieving them have further kept the Arab armies nationally factionalized and regionally divided. In addition, the colonial legacies and the modes of achieving independence have created serious operational and philosophical barriers among the Arab armies.

Although the Arab army officers do not constitute a separate or distinct class, they do share certain interests, political and economic aspirations, and ambitions—not radically different from their civilian counterparts—that they intend to defend by any available means. These means (materiel and personnel) have, since the end of World War II and especially since the mid-1950s, increased manyfold and so have the armed forces' vested interest and influence in the Arab world. (See Table 5-1.) The degree and quality of expansion, however, is quite uneven between Tunisia, Lebanon, and the Sudan on the one hand and Jordan on the other. With a relatively small beginning in 1956, when the national army was created, the Tunisian armed forces expanded to approximately 16,000 in 1969, to 21,000 in 1971, and to 24,000 in 1974. The Sudan also kept a relatively small army which in 1974 numbered 43,600, after it had been 37,000 in 1971, 18,000 in 1965, and 12,000 in 1958. Compared to its neighbor to the north, Sudan's population is about half (17 million) that of Egypt (36 million) but its army was about one-eighth of the Egyptian army in 1974. After independence, Lebanon increased its armed forces from 4,000 in 1948 to 15,250 in 1974. During the same period the Syrian army increased from 8,000 to 137,500. Compared to Jordan, Lebanon is more populous but its army was one-fifth that of the Jordanian army in 1974. The Jordanian army increased from 8,000 in 1945 to 45,000 in 1965, and expanded again between 1967 and 1974 to the current strength. Similarly, the Iraqi military rapidly expanded after the Palestine war and reached 40,000 in 1954, 80,000 in 1965, 95,000 in 1971, and 112,500 in 1974.

Generally speaking, there are several popular myths about the role of the

**Table 5-1**
**Defense Figures of Selected Arab Countries**

|  | Population | Military Force Strength | Defense Budget | |
|---|---|---|---|---|
| Algeria | 16,350,000 | 63,000 | $ 404,000,000 | (1974) |
| Egypt | 36,600,000 | 323,000 | 3,117,000,000 | (1974-75) |
| Iraq | 10,740,000 | 112,500 | 803,000,000 | (1974-75) |
| Jordan | 2,640,000 | 74,850 | 142,000,000 | (1974) |
| Kuwait | 1,100,000 | 10,200 | 162,000,000 | (1974) |
| Lebanon | 3,140,000 | 15,250 | 133,000,000 | (1974) |
| Libya | 2,240,000 | 32,000 | 402,000,000 | (1974) |
| Morocco | 16,810,000 | 56,000 | 190,000,000 | (1974) |
| Saudi Arabia | 8,670,000 | 43,000 | 1,808,000,000 | (1974-75) |
| Sudan | 17,400,000 | 43,600 | 118,000,000 | (1974-75) |
| Syria | 7,130,000 | 137,500 | 460,000,000 | (1974) |
| Tunisia | 5,650,000 | 24,000 | 43,000,000 | (1974-75) |

Source: International Institute for Strategic Studies, *Military Balance 1974-1975*, London, 1974, pp. 32-38.

military in the developing countries. Among these myths is the notion that military regimes bring stability and social order which, in turn, provide opportunities for economic development. It is also held that military regimes generally and armed forces specifically contribute significantly to the field of education and technical training of their respective nations.[1] In the Arab countries, these notions are valid only for Egypt and Algeria where military regimes did provide stability and did give impetus to educational, technical, and industrial expansion. In most other Arab states, however, where the military came to power—for example, Syria, Iraq, Yemen—the military regimes have been responsible for political and social instability and economic stagnation. Both Syria and Iraq have witnessed a series of coups and countercoups ostensibly effected in the name of progress, Pan-Arabism, socialism, and administrative efficiency. In reality, these coups have generally been staged by individuals whose ideological and political commitment did not transcend the local, ethnic, and religious environs. Yemen has not suffered as many military coups as have the other Arab states in the Fertile Crescent; and the civil war and power struggle among the top military leaders that followed the initial coup d'etat in September 1962 have increasingly come to reflect that country's religious division. We are not suggesting that the Yemeni coup of 1962 was motivated solely by religious factors or that the primary objective of it was to overthrow the Shia Imam of the country. In fact, the Zayedi Imam was overthrown by a coalition of the Zayedi (Shia) and Shaf'i (Sunni) officers of the Yemeni army. After the coup, however, and especially after the Egyptian (Sunni) army arrived to support the Yemeni republican forces, the Yemenis began to resent the high handedness of the Egyptian military and political advisers and used religious differences to discredit the Egyptians in Yemen.

Prior to the 1952 Egyptian social revolution, no military junta in the Arab world was successful in introducing radical politico-economic reforms that would benefit the broad spectrum of the population. Military coups, especially in Iraq, were generally staged to strengthen the political power of the oligarchs. Thus, the Arab armies were generally identified with the established monarchical-oligarchical order. These were primarily "palace coups" which replaced one set of rulers with another. Often the military preferred to stay behind the stage and constrained the "civilian" government to implement the military-dictated policies. So far as their capacity of domestic reforms was concerned, the Egyptian coup and the subsequent reforms implemented by the military junta, however, changed the popular image of the Arab armies. Until recently, the Arab public associated the Arab armies with progress, reform, unity, and socialism. The failure of the Arab armies to meet public expectations has reduced their prestige and credibility. Army power and prestige has been further challenged by the rise of monolithic political parties demanding equality in the decision-making process. This, however, does not mean that the Arab armies have lost their influence and power to effect major changes in the domestic and foreign policies of their respective states. They will continue to enjoy this power for many years to come. Nevertheless, unless the Arab armies show some dramatic results in their confrontation with Israel or in effecting radical changes in the politico-economic systems of the region, it is difficult to foresee how they could regain prestige either at the national or supranational level. With the exception of the Egyptian and Tunisian armies, which are not plagued by ethnic or religious rivalries, most other Arab armies will continue to ingratiate themselves with only those subcultures whose members predominate their respective high commands. In other words the outcome of the power struggle will in most cases be decided by persons with subnational loyalties.

In the country analyses that follow, we will discuss the following factors affecting the military's role in the country's domestic and foreign policies: ethnic, religious, and social background of military groups that have been or currently are influential in the decision-making process, and the military's attitude toward Islam, regionalism, and ideologies.

## Egypt

The Egyptian officers who staged the July 1952 coup were all Sunni Muslims of modest country stock. Their homogeneity reflected that of the Egyptian population which is 90 percent Sunni Muslim and the remainder Copts and other minorities. Members of the Coptic Christian minority rarely, if ever, joined the officer's ranks. This was an important factor in the peaceful teamwork of the ruling junta. Since the coup, the Egyptian military has been recruiting its officers mainly from the middle and lower-middle classes. Before the Egyptian revolution, the two social groups, conspicuous by their absence in the officer class, were the sons of Egyptian aristocracy and the 'Ulama. The landed aristocratic class no longer exists in Egypt, and thus there is no reason to consider them as an actual or potential source for army recruitment. The sons of Muslim religious functionaries, who though still numerous, have not generally been attracted to the armed forces, due mainly to a lack of family tradition in serving the military. Within the Egyptian military, the lack of an adequate representation of the 'Ulama has enabled the military to retain its intellectual cohesion. It should be noted as a comparison that in the Iraqi army the number of officer sons of religious functionaries was, and still is, large.[2] The social strata from which the Egyptian officer class has been recruited are the same as those from which have come the intelligentsia. The fact that the Egyptian officer class was socially homogeneous and reflected the country's population explains the success of the junta in implementing its social and economic reforms without serious challenge to its authority. This was not the case in Syria and Iraq where the bureaucracy strongly challenged some of the socialist views of the ruling military junta. In addition to other reforms, the Egyptian military regime succeeded in secularizing the country's judiciary and in redistributing the landed estates of a handful of absentee landlords who controlled well over half of the country's arable land.

Although there were no open social conflicts among the Egyptian officer class, it faced many challenges from its ideologically motivated members who espoused doctrines of the right or of the left. Ideologically, the military junta endeavored to maintain a middle stance between the ideas of the Muslim Brethren Association on the right and the communists on the left. In this struggle, the military had to dismiss several hundred officers from its ranks. The country has a secular court system but accepts Islam as the official religion. With the sole exception of the 1958 constitution (at the formation of the United Arab Republic, Egypt, appreciating the sentiments of Syrian Christians, agreed not to make Islam the official religion of the new Arab union), all Egyptian constitutions declare Islam as the official religion of the country. In the economic field, the Egyptian military transformed the country's economic system without recourse to ideology. Ideology followed rather than determined events. Economic and political factors constrained the Egyptian military elite to rely heavily on the socialist mode of production and distribution in the country. As a result, nine years after the political revolution in 1952 the Egyptian military elite, with the cooperation of the Arab Socialist Union (ASU) effected a social revolution in the country. The July 1961 decrees of nationalization have had profound effects not only on the domestic affairs of the country but also on its regional Arab neighbors. As one scholar succinctly put it, "until recently the quarrels that divided the Arabs were mainly on the governmental level and were based on dynastic or personal rivalries or, at most, on differing foreign policies. The second Egyptian revolution, of 1960-61, has, however, introduced a far deeper cleavage between different economic and social systems and ideologies."[3]

Even after the purges and dismissals of military officers with allegedly extremist views, the Egyptian military elite has by no means become ideologically monolithical. Newspaper sources indicate that, following the recent release from prison of the MBA's veteran leaders, there is a resurgence of covert MBA activities among the military and the students. Furthermore, if it is true that the Arab youth are once again turning to Islam for inspiration, then it is possible that during the next ten years or so the Egyptian military elites will have a larger number of practicing Muslims—those who will strictly adhere to all precepts and practices of Islam. Such an outcome will, of course, largely depend on the government's policy. Reimposition of repressive measures against the MBA or similar organizations will undoubtedly curtail their activities among the military. On the other hand, acquiescence will produce different results.

Although junior military officers are showing signs of impatience with the military *status quo*, some senior officers, both active and retired, are equally concerned with the political developments in the country. Some would like to see in their country a multiparty system, an uncensored and independent press, free elections, and an end to arbitrary political arrests. Immediately after Nasser's death these views were conveyed to interim President Sadat in a demarche reportedly prepared in concert by Zakaria Mohieddin, Kamal el-Din Hussain, and Abdel Latif el-Boghdady, all charter members of Nasser's Free Officers Movement and all former vice-presidents of the republic.[4] In mid-May 1972, President Sadat was reported to have publicly admitted that he had received critical petitions from his former Revolutionary Command comrades. In reporting the Sadat statement, *The Economist* said *inter alia* that Abdel Latif el-Boghdady seemed to be the leader and spokesman for the group, but Zakaria Mohieddin was potentially more influential. "The group has no power base but the prestige and personal connections of some of its members are considerable."[5]

If the Egyptian military elites utilized ideology as a *post hoc* rationalization of the country's economic conditions, it also tried to harness religious sentiments of the population for the implementation of national goals. During its power struggle with the Muslim Brothers, the military elite tried to acquire legitimacy by establishing their Islamic credentials through public statements and actions designed to show their veneration for Islam. In addition to declaring Islam as the state religion, the Egyptian military regime cofounded, with Saudi Arabia and Pakistan, the Islamic Congress, which was ostensibly created to promote closer links among the Islamic countries. Anwar el-Sadat was elected secretary general of the congress which, however, failed to achieve significant results.

In an endeavor to seek popular support for the socialist decrees of nationalization, members of the military elite interpreted Islam in such a way as to show its compatibility with Arab socialism. Nasser himself took the lead when he distinguished Arab socialism from Marxism and insisted that the former not only was in accord with Islam but in reality was actually derived from it. He maintained that Islam was the first religion to call for socialism, the first to call for equality, and the first to call for an end to domination.[6] Nasser's statements were followed by a formal legal opinion issued by a *mufti* who declared that the Socialist laws of 1961 were sanctioned by Islamic jurisprudence.

The top echelon of the Egyptian military are often seen offering their prayers in the mosques on Fridays and on the occasion of the two annual *Eids* (religious festivals). They reportedly observe other religious rituals that are considered obligatory. Notwithstanding their observance of the basic tenets of their religion, the general approach of the military elite to Islam has been rather modernistic. Both in personal practices and in public affairs, the military officers have endeavored to interpret Islam within the general framework provided by Muhammad 'Abduh. He had urged the *'Ulama* to interpret Islam in such a way as to make it relevant to the current needs and aspirations of the people.

Aware of the deep commitment of the Egyptian people to Islam, President Sadat, in a television broadcast, set the tone for a public discussion on a new constitution for the country. He urged the audience to actively participate in airing their views on the constitution and emphasized that the Egyptian constitution must "be derived from our true nature, and from this land of ours. . . . We have our traditions built up over thousands of years, *and we have, above all else and before all else, our mission of faith.* (emphasis added)."[7] It is not necessary to discuss the ensuing controversy. Suffice it to say that Article Two, Section One, of the 1971 Egyptian Constitution declares Islam as the religion of the state and makes the principles of the Islamic *Shari'ah* the principal source of legislation.

It is interesting to note that all previous Egyptian constitutions adopted since 1952 (exception being the 1958 constitution) had declared Islam as the religion of the state but had not mentioned either its principles or the *Shari'ah* itself as a principal source of legislation, as has been enshrined in the 1971 constitution. In other words, for whatever reasons, the Egyptian military seemed to have felt the necessity to placate public sentiments that had been, by Sadat's encouragement, brought into focus by highly articulate and well-known writers. Given the significant role the Egyptian military plays in the country's decision-making process, it must be assumed that the military wished to see such a constitutional provision added to the new document. What effect, if any, the new provision will have on the country's domestic or foreign policies cannot, however, be accurately predicted at this stage.

Internationally, the Egyptian military elite has tried to utilize Islam to seek political and moral support for its international disputes from many Muslim countries. But the Egyptian military elite has never allowed Islamic ties to override the vital interests of the country. As long as it serves the national interests of Egypt, the Egyptian government emphasizes the Islamic principle of "brotherhood" of the Islamic community. If, however, such ties call for substantial sacrifices, either tangible or intangible, the Egyptian leaders hide behind the veneer of secularism, revolutionism, and modernism. Egyptian leaders have not shown serious interest in any one of the many Islamic conferences convened in recent years. Active participation in such conferences, they contended, would give encouragement to the extremist groups in the country and thus weaken the reform movement ushered in by the 1952 revolution. Another reason, though the Egyptians do not admit it, is that these conferences cannot be dominated by the Egyptians either intellectually or politically—a situation which they do not relish. Nasser was vehemently opposed to an Islamic conference of the heads of Muslim states called by King Faisal in 1966. He referred to its potential participants "reactionary tools' of the "imperialists" and "falsifiers" of the true principles of Islam. To show that he was not against the idea of calling such a meeting and to protect himself against domestic and international criticism, Nasser claimed originality of the idea. In other words, he wished to see an Islamic conference of heads of Muslim states held provided it met under the aegis of Egypt. For similar reasons, Nasser failed to show up at the Rabat conference of the heads of Muslim states meeting in an emergency session to discuss the consequences of Israeli occupation of Jerusalem and the al-Aqsa Mosque fire in 1968.

From the above discussion it should be clear that for the Egyptian military and the ruling elite, Islam is a convenient and sometimes effective tool of foreign policy. Neither in the formulation nor in the implementation of their foreign policies, however, are the Egyptians hampered or tempered by their espousal of Islam. For them, Islamic brotherhood is a oneway street in which it is incumbent on other Muslim states to show compassion and brotherhood without expecting a *quid pro quo.*

As in the case of many other issues facing the nation, the question of Pan-Arabism has been a divisive factor for the Egyptian military elite. Although most high-ranking military officers give high priority to Arab unity as a prerequisite for rapid industrial development and as a strong and effective leverage for dealing with the country's external problems, there are several influential military officers who would place Egypt's interest above all others. Aware of the internal dissension and the complexity of problems faced by every Arab state, the latter group of Egyptian officers wish to focus the country's attention on domestic problems and development. They regard it more important to utilize the nation's resources on alleviating poverty and disease than to dissipate its energies on the elusive concept of Pan-Arabism. In addition, these officers (and their civilian counterparts) do not wish to see Egyptian identity submerged in the sea of Arabism.[8]

Compared to the Arabs of the Fertile Crescent, the Egyptians developed Arab consciousness rather late in the game. Whereas the Syrians, Palestinians, and Iraqis took for granted the idea of Arabism, the Egyptian military regime had to make strenuous efforts to rally the Egyptian mind to the creed of Arab nationalism. Torn by ethnic and religious dissension, the military regimes of Syria and Iraq have considered Arab nationalism as the very means of survival as autonomous national identities. For Egypt, with its homogeneous population, Arab nationalism became a means to dominate other Arab states. An Egyptian statesman and scholar has in the following message candidly described Egyptian goals in the Arab countries:

As an Egyptian, I say that our future is tied to our need of the Arab countries more than to their need of Egypt. . . . It will be almost impossible for Egypt to exist as a military state, a state that guarantees its own military defense first of all and assures its inhabitants of subsistence, without carrying out a thorough industrial revolution. That revolution in itself obliges us to have living space. This living space consists in our brothers, [sic] who understand us and who offer us as advantage in relation to others. On the economic level we need the Arab states, which, as has been demonstrated, possess the richest resources in raw materials essential to our future industry and which at the same time constitute the only market open to our future life. We cannot leave Syria to do whatever she pleases on her own, for she represents our basic strategy. Syria should live in our living space. . . . [9]

Although the above statement does not represent the Egyptian military's point of view, the post-1952 events suggest that the military accepts the basic premises of it. Whenever Egyptian leadership in the Arab world is threatened by the prospects of a union between Iraq and Syria, the Egyptian military endeavors to discourage the prospective partners from consummating it. As the largest and potentially the most powerful Arab state, Egypt is willing to sanction and encourage only those Arab unions that accept its guardianship, a condition other Arab states refuse to accept. This is a recurrent political dilemma that the Arabs are facing.

### Iraq

Since Iraq's independence in 1932, the military has played a decisive role in the political dynamics of the state. It has staged sixteen successful coups primarily effected to protect social and political privileges of certain ethnic or religious subcultures in the country. There are perhaps two exceptions to this—the coup staged in support of Rashid 'Ali al-Gailani in 1941 and the 1958 Abdul Karim Qasim coup which eliminated the Hashimite monarchy in Iraq. The series of coups between 1936 and 1941 achieved nothing worthwhile in the area of political or economic reforms. These coups lacked both political organization and interest articulation. Since the 1958 revolution, however, the Iraqi military coups have become more sophisticated in that the coup leaders have tried either to enlist support from political parties or to effect coups in behalf of the Ba'th Socialist Party. The pre- and postrevolution series of coups differ from each other in another important aspect. While the pre-1958 series was primarily concerned with domestic problems, the post-1958 series was generated by the rivalries between the "unionists" and "antiunionists" supported respectively by the pro-Nasserite and anti-Nasserite groups in the Iraqi military. By eliminating the monarchy that had successfully played the role of a referee in the power struggle between the competing factions, Qasim released centrifugal forces that had laid dormant for a considerable period.

Religiously, Iraq's population is about equally divided between the Sunni and Shia Muslims, with a small sprinkling of Christian and Jewish minorities. Ethnically, the country is divided into two main groups: the Arabs and the Kurds. Although the Sunnis (the sum total of the Sunni Arab and Kurdish population) form only about 50 percent of the total population, their proportion in the military officer corps is much higher. The social origins of the Iraqi officer class fall within three distinct categories—aristocratic families, religious functionaries, and the middle and lower-middle class urban families. Most Iraqi officers, however, are from families whose main source of income is not derived from landed property or invested capital.[10]

After World War II a good number of Iraqi officers were drawn from the lower-middle class and many of them fell under the spell of militant nationalism espoused by the Syrian and Egyptian nationalists during their struggle against European colonial powers. These Iraqi officers perceived the monarchy as the main obstacle in achieving radical social and economic reforms and in uniting Iraq with other Arab states. Such an understanding of the political dynamics of the country proved to be simplistic. They failed to grasp the significance of internal factors that had to be considered in the formation of any new power equation. Proclaiming his ostensible support of Pan-Arab unity, Qasim was successful in marshalling the resources of the pro-Egyptian faction, both in the military and civilian sectors of the population, during the critical postrevolution days of uncertainty and chaos. Once the revolutionary fervor was mitigated by the hard realities of the country's political dynamics—pressure from the Kurds, the Shias, and other anti-Nasserite groups—the Qasim regime made no serious effort to achieve Arab unity. On the contrary, fearing a pro-Egyptian coup by 'Arif and his followers, the new Iraqi government was obliged to purge a large number of "uncooperative" officers from the military, including 'Arif. After three and a half years of conspiracy, 'Arif, however, succeeded in overthrowing Qasim by manipulating the Ba'thists and other anti-Qasim factions in the military. Although an ardent supporter of Arab unity and Nasser, 'Arif failed to rally sufficient forces to consummate a union between Iraq and Egypt. His efforts floundered because the Ba'th leaders and their military supporters refused to accept reduction in their sovereignty. Political expediency eventually constrained him to modify his "unionist" stance and be content with the relatively insignificant steps taken toward unity during his administration.

At this time, the Iraqi military elite was divided into three different groups—those who stressed Arab unity and were sympathetic to Egyptian President Nasser; those who feared reforms that would undermine their social status; and those who were sympathetic to the Communists. Aware of the Egyptian attitude toward communism, the pro-Communist group expressed vehement opposition to the idea of unity with Cairo. Qasim had utilized this group to counter pressure exerted on him by the pro-Egyptian group in the military. To give his antiunionist action an aura of nonpartisanship, Qasim later purged some pro-Communists and the conservative groups from the military. In this process, Qasim retired about two thousand military officers during his dictatorship in Iraq.

Colonel 'Abd al-Salaam 'Arif, who during his brief alliance with Brigadier Qasim was a unionist and was brought to power in 1963 by a coalition of the Michel Aflaq wing of the Iraqi Ba'th and the pro-Nasserite group in the military, also found it difficult to pursue with vigor the plan for union with Egypt. Neither he nor his successor-brother, 'Abd al-Rahman, were able to take a clear and determined attitude toward union with Egypt and the establishment of the socialist system, though 'Abd al-Salaam did try to pattern Iraq's political and economic system after that of Egypt. On July 14, 1964, he banned all political parties and created the Iraqi Arab Socialist Union. In addition, he nationalized all private and foreign banks and about thirty industrial and commercial concerns in the country. Foreign oil companies were excluded from the 'Arif Decree.[a]

The 'Arif Decree was resented by the rich Shia business community whose religious leaders increased their opposition to the regime. It has been suggested that the Socialist decree was actually a cloak for the Sunni bureaucrats and the military elites to dispossess Shia urban businessmen, who had opposed the regime's ostensible efforts at creating an Arab union, of their businesses.[11]

Notwithstanding the numerous charters, treaties, and agreements signed by Iraq, Egypt, and Syria, it is apparent that powerful military groups in the Iraqi, as well as Syrian, armies are not anxious to lose their positions as ruling elites and fall under the domination of Cairo. The successive cabinets that have been formed in Iraq and Syria during the last eight years or so have generally excluded pro-Egyptian elements in the countries. Under President Bakr's regime several hundred pro-Egyptian military officers were purged, transferred to insignificant positions, or retired.

[a]On June 1, 1972, President Ahmad Hasan al-Bakr, a retired colonel who came to power on July 17, 1968, nationalized the Iraqi Petroleum Company (IPC), owned jointly by American, French, and Dutch oil companies. The IPC produced about 88 percent of the country's total oil which was about 10 percent of all Middle East oil. Accusing the United States of collaboration with Israel, the Iraqi government, nationalized, in October 1973, the assets of Exxon and Mobil, the two U.S. companies that had held 23.75 percent shares in the Basrah Petroleum Company.

Although several reform measures have been taken by the military regimes that followed each other in a rapid succession after the 1958 revolution, the Iraqi economy has not shown the kind of vigor one expects from a fertile, oil-rich, and underpopulated country like Iraq. Many soundly conceived agricultural and industrial projects initiated under the monarchy were abandoned by the military regimes in favor of the more spectacular and prestige-oriented projects which have not materially benefited the average Iraqi citizen. About 18 percent of the GNP (estimated at $5.0 billion in 1973) is currently being spent on the military, which has more than doubled its strength to 112,500 during the last nineteen years.

The present Iraqi regime is an ideologically motivated group whose declared goals are to transform the country into a Socialist state. In this endeavor, the regime is supported by the Ba'thists, the pro-Communists, and the federalists.[b] The Iraqi military elite endeavors to interpret "socialism" within the framework of Islamic ideology which, according to the country's constitution, is the state religion and the basis of its laws. Thus, in order to remove the glaring disparity between the Islamic principles—which have traditionally protected the individual's right to private property—and socialism—which seriously curtails such rights—the Iraqi regime has deleted from the Constitution the provision that had declared inviolable public property and private ownership. The Provisional Constitution, which was published in September 1968 and supersedes the Interim Constitution of April 1964, also makes socialism the official model for economic activities. The earlier constitution had merely provided that the economy was guided by a national plan. The Iraqi military elite has endeavored to justify this seemingly anti-*Shari'ah* stance on the ground that "inviolability of private property" does not mean freedom to exploit the masses whose collective welfare, they argue, overrides all other considerations.

## Syria

During the past fifty years or so Syria has experienced long periods of political turbulence and uncertainty. Although occasionally the Syrian military elite serving the foreign rulers was constrained to change its loyalties from one to another foreign competing power, it did not begin to exert its influence on domestic politics until 1949 when Colonel Za'im imposed military rule in the country. Since then the Syrian military has intervened at least fifteen times to impose its will on the country. Successful intervention by the military should not be taken to mean that the Syrian military elite always offered a united front against their civilian counterparts. On the contrary, both the civilian and military

---

[b]In addition to the Communist sympathizers, the Iraq military is politically divided into three major factions: the federalists—those who do not want complete political merger with other Arab states; the unionists—those who want full merger with a strong central government; and the nationalists—those who wish to maintain the country's sovereignty.

elites have shown excessive predisposition toward disunity. This inclination toward disunity stems primarily from the ethnic and religious heterogeneity of the country. In a region where the concept of national loyalty has not yet taken deep roots and is still generally subordinated to religious and ethnic loyalties, such differences play a crucial role in making significant decisions concerning domestic reforms and foreign policies.

With a population a little over seven million, Syria is inhabited by nearly a score of religious, ethnic, and linguistic subcultures.[c] These subcultures vigorously compete with each other for political influence and economic benefits. In this struggle, two of the most powerful subcultures—the 'Alawites and the Druzes—have greatly benefited from the French military policy that endeavored to attract minority groups. Thus, after their departure, the French left behind powerful groups of 'Alawites and Druzes in the Syrian military. Aware of the inequalities and suppression they had suffered as religious minorities under Sunni Ottoman rule, the 'Alawite and Druze military officers were determined to maintain and if possible, increase their political influence in the country. Not only religiously but also sociologically, the 'Alawites and Druze differ from the Sunni majority. While the latter group is an urban, commercial, better educated, and richer subculture, the 'Alawites and the Druze occupy rural farming areas with fewer educational and economic opportunities. Thus, the military, which has been one of the most attractive professions open to the minority groups, has become the most powerful and effective vehicle for the enhancement and protection of their respective interests. It should be noted, however, that although the Druze and the 'Alawite officers have often coordinated their efforts to protect collective interests as religious minorities, occasionally their mutually irreconcilable interests have placed them in opposite camps. Similarly, the 'Alawites have not always presented a united front—within this religious subculture are subgroups that have occasionally engaged in conflicts. (General Salah Jadid's conflicts with General Muhammad Umran and General Hafiz Asad exemplify this situation. While these disputants were 'Alawites, they belonged to two different tribes—General Umran to the Khayyatin tribe and Generals Asad and Jadid to the Haddadun tribe.)

The dominant positions the 'Alawites and the Druze, especially the former, occupy in the military and civilian hierarchies, have enabled them to formulate and implement policies that best serve their parochial interests. To give their regimes the aura of respectability, however, the Syrian military elite, a large

[c]Estimated population figure for 1974 is 7,130,000. Most Syrians are Sunni Muslims with a small number of Isma'ilis and Shi'ites. Among the religious minorities, the 'Alawites are the largest and most powerful subculture with a population of over 400,000; followed by the Greek Orthodox (172,000); the Druzes (117,000); Armenian Orthodox (111,000); and Syrian Orthodox (100,000). Other religious and ethnic subcultures are the: Kurds, Latins, Greek Catholics, Armenian Catholics, Syrian Catholics, Maronites, Protestants, Nestorians, Chaldeans and Yezidis. (*The Middle East and North Africa 1971-72*, London: Europa Publications, Ltd., 1971, p. 592.)

number of whom were Ba'thists, has often collaborated with and acted on behalf of the Ba'th Socialist Party which is dedicated to the popular concepts of Arab nationalism, socialism, and anti-imperialism. Prior to the creation of the United Arab Republic in 1958, the Ba'thists competed among others with the Communists, traditionalists, and the pro-Nasser Pan-Arabists for influence in the military which all factions recognized to be ultimately the decisive factor in the outcome of the power struggle. The Communists seemed to have won the struggle when in 1957 Colonel Afif al-Bizri, a known Communist, was made Chief of Staff with the rank of Brigadier-General. Playing on the fear of traditionalists and on the general delight at the thought of Arab unity favored by the pro-Nasserites, the Ba'th Party and its military members responded by leading the move toward union with Egypt and thus eliminated the challenge posed by Communists who were purged posthaste with the help of the Egyptian administration. This left the Ba'th Party as the unchallenged political-ideological party in the country. The military-Ba'thist collaboration which had brought about the Egypto-Syrian merger also gave birth to the Ba'thist military organization which sought to act as an ideological and political channel for politically minded officers who wished to make their influence felt by the party's decision-making body. Among the original founders of this organization were General Muhammad Umran, General Salah Jadid, and General Hafiz Asad (all 'Alawites). They were later joined by General Amin Hafiz (Sunni). It should be noted that although the Syrian Sunni population generally supported the union, there were, and still are, several Sunni military officers who opposed the union because of Egyptian insensitivity to Syrian historical development. They favored a federal-type arrangement with their Arab neighbors. Although the emergence of the Ba'th military faction as the institutional bridge between its military and civilian elites resulted in increasing usefulness of each to the other and created a relatively stable relationship between the officer corps and the civil bureaucracy, it did not eliminate friction at either level. The two factions have had at least one serious clash on a policy matter. This clash came in September 1970, when, without the prior consent of General Hafiz Asad, the Minister of Defense and Commander of the Air Force, General Salah Jadid, Assistant Secretary General of the Ba'th Party, ordered a Syrian armored brigade, loyal to the civilian faction, to intervene in the Jordanian civil war. Encouraged by the failure of the attempted intervention, General Asad, who had opposed the step, had General Jadid arrested. After holding for several months the offices of Prime Minister and Secretary General of the party, Gen. Asad in February 1971 was elected president for a seven-year term.

The incumbent military members of the Syrian government follow Socialist policies in effecting reforms in the country. They believe that socialism is the panacea for all the maladies from which the country suffers. Although the military, under direct Ba'thist inspiration, introduced Socialist measures in 1964, a lack of competent personnel to manage the economy and refusal of the bourgeoisie Sunni population to cooperate with the 'Alawite-dominated regime sabotaged the government's efforts to quickly socialize the economy. Since February 1966, when the 'Alawites wrested substantial control of the military from their fellow politicized officers, the Syrian government has taken more effective measures to ensure a socialist economy in the country. They have since successfully eliminated serious challenges to the 'Alawites' military power by advertising their espousal of socialism and Arab nationalism. The meanings of the terms "socialism" and "Arab nationalism," however, have been modified to accommodate the sectional and communal feelings of the various subcultures in the country. General Asad's "socialism" is more pragmatic and moderate than the one aspired to by the Ba'th Party during its political apogee in the early 1960s. While the new interpretation of "socialism" still aims at predominance of the state sector of the economy, it also recognizes the private sector and individual initiative as important aspects of the economy. In this effort, the Syrian regime has been given financial and technical help by the Soviet Union, the People's Republic of China, and Libya. Furthermore, the Syrian government has achieved a measure of accommodation with the pro-Nasser faction in the military by joining, in November 1971, the Federation of Arab Republics of Egypt, Libya, and Syria and by placing, two months later, the Syrian military forces under a joint Arab command.

The 'Alawite officers in the Syrian military who presently control the government have been ambivalent toward Islam. In 1964, they issued a provisional constitution that declared Syria a "democratic popular socialist republic" in which Islamic law was the main source of legislation and the religion of the Chief of State had to be Islam. In 1967, however, the military allowed its publication *People's Army Magazine* (Arabic) to attack religion for its "reactionary" effects on the people. In its April 25, 1967 issue, Ibrahim Khlass, a contributor to the magazine, said *inter alia*, that the "only way to build Arab civilization and society is to create the new Arab socialist individual 'who believes that God, religions, feudalism and capital[ism], and all the values which dominated the previous society are only mummified dummies that should be kept in the historical museum.' "[12] Frightened by the strong reaction the article had aroused, the military accused the author of being a CIA collaborator and tried to disassociate itself from these views. Nevertheless, while the Provisional Constitution of 1969, as amended in 1971, still provides that Islamic jurisprudence is to be the main source of legislation, it does not limit the presidency to Muslims.

## North Africa

In North Africa, military subcultures have played important roles in Algeria, Morocco, and Libya. In Tunisia where the size of the military is rather small, the dominant political role is played by the Destourian Socialist Party, the Tunisian political organization which attained independence for its country from France in 1956. Aware of the political ambitions of young military officers and their dissatisfaction with the slow economic progress in the country, President Bourguiba has deliberately kept the strength of the military at the bare minimum level. In his efforts to resolve the country's international conflicts with its Arab neighbors, Bourguiba has been realistic in relying more on his adept diplomats than on the ineffectual forces his country now possesses. See Table 5-1 for figures concerning the military proportions of these countries.

## *Algeria*

Numerically the largest and qualitatively the best equipped organization in North Africa, the Algerian military nevertheless has been plagued by internal dissension and revolts since independence in 1962. Dissension and the lack of cohesion is, however, not unique to the Algerian military establishment. It permeates all institutions and levels of political endeavors in the country which, until the arrival of the French in the early part of the nineteenth century, had never known political unity based on territoriality. With a population of little over sixteen million, Algeria contains within its frontiers about three million Berbers who are divided into four major tribes: the Kabyles, the Shawia, the Tuaregs, and the Mozabites. The Kabyles, who number about two million, are by far the most important Berber group in the country. The Kabyles hold a large number of important positions in the civilian and military sectors as the result of a French policy that sought to play Berbers against Arabs. The war of independence had provided a common rallying point for the divergent ethnic groups in the country. After independence, however, the country began to manifest traditional tribal rivalries and the new political leaders became aware of the problem of welding together into a nation the different groups that comprise its population. Although the problem is serious and difficult, it is not threatening the country's integrity—there are no political or military groups which seek secession of any part of Algeria. Superimposed over the traditional tribal rivalries, is the divisiveness of cultural (French vs. Arab), educational (Western vs. non-Western), and ideological (Marxist-Leninist socialists vs. Islamists) factions which has rendered more difficult the task of achieving national unity and cohesion.

All these, and more, divisions are reflected in the military's high command which, under Colonel Boumedienne's leadership, currently rules the country. Other factors contributing to the restiveness among the military officers are the attitudinal, generational, and professional cleavages that have foiled attempts to integrate the officer class. Serious problems exist among three major nonethnic and nontribal groups in the Algerian military—the guerrilla leaders who became part of the Armee Nationale Populaire (ANP), the postindependence Algerian Army; the officers trained in the French army, 250 of whom were incorporated into the ANP and who do most of the work of the General Staff and appear to be closest to Colonel Boumedienne; and, the young officers trained in Russia, East Europe, and Egypt after independence, who have not yet obtained important positions in the military establishment.

Like so many other emerging nations, Algeria lacks the political infrastructure that would act as an effective means of communications between the masses and the political leadership. The Front de Liberation Nationale (FLN), the Algerian nationalist organization that became the country's official party after independence, soon became dysfunctional because of internal dissension based on personal rivalries and politico-ideological differences. This organizational vacuum left the military as the unchallenged force, requiring national leaders to ally themselves with different factions in the armed forces. During the first three years of independence, the Algerian president, Ben Bella, pursued a policy of equilibrium whereby he attempted on the one hand to divide the military in order to control it, and on the other, to reinforce his own power by establishing cordial relations with the Algerian and French Communist Parties and by making concessions to the Union Generale des Travailleurs Algeriens (UGTA), the Algerian labor federation. Within the military, Ben Bella, without consultations with Houari Boumedienne, now the Defense Minister, appointed Colonel Tahir Zbiri as Chief of the ANP General Staff in the hope of reducing the influence and power of the defense minister. Not content with merely placing his own men in key positions, Ben Bella was alleged to have incited a Captain Bouanane to carry out a coup d'etat against Colonel Boumedienne.[13] For three years, Colonel Boumedienne remained loyal to Ben Bella, in spite of the many anti-Boumedienne maneuvers instigated by the president. Prior to the June 19, 1965, coup, which overthrew Ben Bella, the only serious challenge to the regime, in which a segment of the military was involved, came from Hocine Ait Ahmed, the Kabylia leader who, on September 1963, formed the Front des Forces Socialistes (FFS) to oppose the government. In his opposition to the Ben Bella regime, Ait Ahmed was supported, though for different reasons, by Colonel Mohand ou al-Hadj, the Kabylia commander who resented the government policy of ignoring the guerrilla officers and appointing the "collaborators" (meaning the French trained officers) to high military posts. Although, after minor skirmishes, al-Hadj reached an accommodation with Ben Bella and the military hierarchy, Ait Ahmed continued his sporadic and unsuccessful fight with meager resources allegedly provided by the Moroccan government. On October 17, 1964, after unsuccessful efforts to rally the Kabyles under his banner, Ait Ahmed was captured by the government forces. He was sentenced to death by a three-judge court but his sentence was commuted to life imprisonment.

Perceiving a threat to his position in a cabinet reshuffle, which excluded a

number of his supporters, Colonel Boumedienne, in cooperation with the Ben
Bella appointee, Colonel Zbiri, moved swiftly and efficiently to take over
control of the country by arresting Ben Bella and his supporters on June 19,
1965. Boumedienne criticized Ben Bella on many counts, including his Marxist-
Leninist policies which he believed to be incompatible with Islam. In this,
Boumedienne was fervently supported by al-Qiyam al-Islamiyah, a religio-politi-
cal organization dedicated to strengthening Islamic values and removing foreign
values and ideas from the country. Through the columns of its newspaper,
*Humanisme Musulman* (Arabic and French), al-Qiyam al-Islamiyah had been
critical of Ben Bella's socialism and his alliance with the communists; and in the
fall of Ben Bella the religious organization saw the dawn of a new era. Although
basically not a solicitor of public support or responsive to public pressure and
emotions, Boumedienne welcomed the help given by al-Qiyam al-Islamiyah.[d]
Although not a member of al-Qiyam al-Islamiyah, Boumedienne was in agreement with the basic philosophy of the party in that they both called on the
people to return to "sources of Islam" for inspiration and development of
political institutions.

In addition to being personally a devout Muslim, Boumedienne uses many
traditional Islamic concepts in the daily administration of the country. As a
follower of the reformist movement in Islam, Boumedienne endeavors to use the
traditional Islamic juridical principle of *ijma* (consensus) to reach agreement in
the councils of government. *Ijma*, a decision-making process, though painfully
slow, is considered by its exponents to be more conducive to the needs and
circumstances of Arab and Muslim societies.

The most urgent task which Boumedienne undertook was to create an
efficient and cohesive military organization in the country. The task was not
easy because he had to reorganize under one command such diverse and
mutually hostile forces as the guerrilla commanders, the officers of the
"external" army,[e] the professionals who had been trained in the French
military, and the recently commissioned young officers who had been trained in
the Soviet Union, Eastern Europe, and Egypt. Being essentially a reformist and
an organizer, Boumedienne selected the best and most cooperative elements
available to him. Ignoring pressure from the former guerrilla commanders and
others, Boumedienne integrated into the ANP a large number of French-trained
officers who had been accused of "collaboration" and gave them important
positions in the General Staff.

Boumedienne's firmness with the opposition did not, however, eliminate
dissension either in the military or in the civilian sector of the country. Dissident
groups—the trade unions, student groups, and the far left—began to make

[d]In 1966, the association was abolished for lending support to the Muslim Brethren who
were being persecuted in Egypt.

[e]This army spent most of its time in Morocco and Tunisia during the Algerian Revolution
and was unable to participate in combat.

contacts with regional military commanders and high-ranking officers at the General Headquarters in Algiers. Many and varied reasons have been given for the attempted conspiracies and coups against Boumedienne. For the purposes of this anlaysis, however, it is sufficient to point out that most coups were inspired by either personal ambitions, political differences, or a combination of both. There were no strikingly radical ideological differences between the incumbent and the conspirators. The assassination attempt (on April 25, 1968) and the abortive coup by Colonel Tahir Zbiri (December 14, 1968) were both inspired by personal vendetta and political ambitions of the conspirators.

Since coming to power, Boumedienne has implemented a number of economic and social reforms, including the nationalization of about 60 percent of the nation's oil resources and all of the French-owned farms. In the area of family legislation, however, the Boumedienne government has been unable to effect necessary reforms because of the constant opposition by the *'Ulama*. The military, which is looked upon as a privileged class, continues to absorb a substantial amount of the national budget. The military maintains control over fifty large farms, formerly owned by French citizens, and a number of small industrial enterprises that it had seized during the summer of 1962. Although it has occasionally provided help to civic projects in the rural areas, the Algerian military has not exclusively undertaken a large project for the benefit of the civilians.

The Algerian military elites are fully committed to the concept of Arab unity and they are squarely behind the Palestinians in their struggle against Israel. Although the Algerian coups of 1965 had created tension between Nasser and Boumedienne, the latter stood by the Egyptians during the Arab-Israeli war of June 1967. The Algerian ground and air contingents were the only North African forces to reach the combat zone and to participate in the hostilities. In addition to the military assistance provided during the war, the Algerians also gave financial help to the three main Arab combatants—Egypt, Jordan, and Syria. Furthermore, the Algerians have been providing financial help and military training to the Palestinian guerrillas whose conflict with Jordan has caused friction between Algiers and Amman.

## Morocco

Until the abortive coup of July 1971, the Moroccan military was generally considered to be a loyal ally of the monarchy. The attempted coup, however, exposed this fallacy and brought to the surface the divisive factors in the military. The original components of the Moroccan military were men and officers who had served under the French or Spanish forces. In addition, there were about 10,000 urban guerrillas and mountain fighters who had fought against the French and Spaniards in the Riff Mountains and the Sahara Desert during the "wars of national liberation." Furthermore, the Moroccan military contains a large number of Berber officers and men who differ linguistically and sociologically from their Arab countrymen. One scholar estimates that the Berber enlisted men formed as much as 80 percent of the total military strength and that a high proportion of the officers were from the Berber tribes.[14] Berbers constitute about 35 percent of Morocco's total population.

Cognizant of the ethnic, linguistic, and sociological differences between the Berbers on the one hand, and Arabs and Arabized Berbers on the other, King Hassan II, the head of state in Morocco, has cleverly exploited these differences by balancing one group against the other and preventing either from dominating the military, which is his only effective means to stay in power. Hassan is the supreme commander of the armed forces and he keeps a close and personal contact with the commanders of all major military units in the country. In addition to the regular military forces, Morocco maintains a paramilitary force of over 30,000 men under the command of military officers. These commanders also report directly to Hassan and indirectly through the Ministry of the Interior. Berber officers have generally been so faithful to the monarchy that Hassan, in spite of pressure from politicians, has consistently appointed loyal Berbers as ministers of defense and occasionally as ministers of the interior. Berber officers have also held key jobs in the two ministries and in the provinces. For many years the opposition political parties sought to curtail the king's powers by capturing control of the Ministries of Defense and the Interior. They tried to have General Mohammed Oufkir, the indomitable Berber Minister of Defense and the Interior, fired from the two key positions. In a culture where personal loyalties still take precedence over political and ideological loyalties, it seemed unlikely that Hassan would remove the one man who stood firmly behind him since the days of his princehood in the 1950s. Only General Oufkir's betrayal of his monarch in an attempted coup rid the country of his oppressive hand.

In the aftermath of two attempted coups, the Moroccan military suffered an irreparable loss in the execution of four generals, five colonels, and a major—all accused of conspiracy to overthrow the king. Also, during the skirmishes at the royal summer palace at Skhirat, where the 1971 coup was attempted, the Moroccan military lost about two thirds of its 15 generals and at least 350 soldiers and other officers. Although there is no substantial proof yet available as to the motivations of the conspirators, it has been suggested that they had been unhappy with the monarch's lack of firmness against the corrupt officials and ministers of the government. Other sources have suggested that the abortive coup was a preventive measure by conservative military officers who were opposed to the king's friendly overtures towards "liberal" political figures and parties. If the personal character of General Mohammed Medbouh, the former Minister of the Royal Household who staged the 1971 coup, is any indication of the characters of other alleged military conspirators, then it is to be argued that the most immediate concern of the military generals was to remove corruption, primarily nepotism and graft, from the civilian administration. Oufkir's 1972 attempted coup, however, was for personal gains.

## Libya

Essentially a small frontier force under the monarchy, the Libyan military is being rapidly modernized under Colonel Muammar al-Qadhafi who ousted the aged King Idris on September 1, 1969. With the country's oil wealth, Colonel Qadhafi has purchased several squadrons of French Mirage jets and other highly sophisticated materiel from a variety of foreign sources. The Libyan military exercises absolute power over the country through a twelve-man Revolutionary Command Council (RCC) composed of, in addition to Chairman Qadhafi, five majors, five captains, and a lieutenant. Three of the five majors and Colonel Qadhafi also hold cabinet posts—Colonel Qadhafi is Prime Minister and Minister of Defense; Major Abdul Salam Jalloud holds the portfolios of Finance, Economy, Industry, and Minerals and is Deputy Premier of Production; Education and National Guidance is under Major Bashir al-Saghir Hawady; the Ministry of Communications is headed by Major Mukhtar Abdullah al-Gerway; and Major Al-Khoweildy al-Hamidy is Minister of the Interior. In addition to their cabinet portfolios and membership in the RCC, Majors al-Hamidy and Hawady also are Commander of the Popular Resistance Forces and Chairman of the People's Court respectively. Major Awad Hamsa, who is a member of the Revolutionary Command Council but not a cabinet member, is Controller General of Administration.

Although apparently Colonel Qadhafi is in firm control of the RCC and the military, signs of dissension and conflict in the cabinet have given rise to speculations that his grip on the country is not as secure as it seems. A coup in July 1970 was reported crushed and in the autumn two cabinet ministers resigned. It is believed that the main causes of the conflict had to do with Libya's participation in the then proposed Arab federation of Egypt and Syria and over the lack of political institutions responsive to the needs of the people.

Since its advent in September 1969, the Revolutionary Council has implemented a number of reforms including the nationalization of the Italian-owned farms, and distribution facilities of Shell, Esso, and all of the British Petroleum concessions in the country. The Libyan government has also initiated a number of land-reclamation projects with a view to increasing the country's limited area of arable land.

Colonel Qadhafi and his military supporters are firmly committed to the ideas of Pan-Arabism, socialism, and republicanism. Personally, the colonel is a strong believer in and practitioner of Islamic tenets which he avers are the most effective deterrents against the spread of communism in the Middle East and North Africa. Born in 1942 into a small Berber tribe and educated in a Muslim primary school at Sirte and secondary school at Sibha, Qadhafi's formative-adolescent period coincided with one of the most militant periods of Arab nationalism. President Nasser of Egypt became Qadhafi's idol and model for political action in the later years. After joining the Royal Military Academy at Benghazi in 1961, Qadhafi immediately began to organize a secret society with the aim of overthrowing what he later called the "decadent" monarchy of Libya. On his fellow conspirators, Qadhifi imposed the same strict rules of behavior that he imposed upon himself—that they abstain from alcohol, cigarettes, games of chance, women, and even marriage, and that they performed all obligatory duties required by Islam. In 1966, Qadhafi was sent to England for a six-month training in armored warfare. It was his sole venture outside the Arab world and he was reported to have enjoyed it.

In keeping with his commitment to Islam, Colonel Qadhafi endeavored to support, both financially and politically, the causes of Arabism and socialism. He further provided generous financial and military aid to Egypt, Syria, Sudan, the Palestinian and Eritrean guerrillas, and Pakistan during the Indo-Pakistan war of December 1971. Also, since June 1972 he has provided aid to the Philippine Muslims who are allegedly being harassed by the Philippine Christians and to the outlawed Irish Republican Army.

To defend Libyan and Arab interests, Colonel Qadhafi intends to use every means available to him. In this respect, the most important instrument currently in his hand is oil, which provides Libya an annual income of about four billion dollars. Since 1971, when Qadhafi nationalized British Petroleum in retaliation for the alleged British acquiescence in the Iranian takeover of two Persian Gulf islets claimed by the Arabs, Libya has nationalized more foreign oil companies operating in the country. Sooner or later he intends to nationalize all of Libya's oil resources.

True to his conviction that only a united Arab front could constrain Israel to withdraw from the conquered Arab territories, Qadhafi provided generous military aid to Egypt during the October 1973 war, notwithstanding his annoyance with Sadat for excluding the Libyan leader from the planning stage of the war. According to figures published by the official organ of the armed forces, *al-Fatih*, Libya provided Egypt with over 800 million dollars worth of military aid, which included 70 MIG-21s, 300 modern tanks, 47 armored personnel carriers, 28 self-propelled quad-mounted antiaircraft guns, and an assortment of other military materiel.[15] Although the list provided by the Libyan paper does not mention the Mirage V as part of the country's war assistance, in a post-war statement Sadat conceded the presence of Libyan Mirages in the October hostilities. In this and many other respects, Qadhafi seems to be following the same militant course Nasser followed in the fifties. Some of his most controversial policies have endeared him to Libyan and Arab youth who see him as a defender of the Arab Revolution inaugurated by Nasser.

# 6

# The Western-Educated Elites

One of the least studied subcultures in the Arab world has been the Western-educated. elites. In many respects, this group has had the greatest impact on the region. Through them, the Middle East was opened to Western ideas and concepts. Lebanese Christians, such as Butrus al-Bustani, Faris Nimr, and Shahin Makarius, who were deeply committed to modernization of the Arab world along Western lines, led the way.[1] By becoming the advocates of Western penetration, they not only fostered Western cultural aspects but also the physical presence of European power.

The Western-educated elites were to become the most powerful as well as the most enlightened group in the Middle East. Their officers were trained in Sandhurst or St. Cyr. Their statesmen were as familiar with the European capitals as they were with their own. Their educators spread Western knowledge to a generation of students who envisaged a Middle East made great by means of the tools which had made the Western world so powerful. The American University of Beirut was to produce generations of leaders who had received a Western-type education and who were to become the leading politicians of the region. It has been said, and not untruthfully, that of all the graduates from the American University of Beirut, half is in power and the other half forms the opposition and is waiting in the wings to take over from their opponent colleagues.

Prior to the independence of their countries from foreign rule, the Western-educated elites rose to the top of their society. By using Western ideas such as nationalism and democracy, they showed to the world powers that they were also enlightened and could govern with credibility. Traditional institutions, especially Islam, were attacked: Western law severely limited the *Shari'ah* or Islamic law; parliamentary systems of government replaced the autocratic ruler in several countries; and social institutions were set up to redesign the day-to-day living of the masses.[2]

What the Western-educated elites failed to do, however, was to persuade their own countrymen that they were correct in their beliefs and actions and that Western institutions would work in the Arab world. As each new crisis occurred in the area that involved an Arab defeat, the Western-educated subculture became more discredited. The establishment of Israel, the failure to build the Aswan Dam, the Suez attack, continued arms and monetary grants and credits to Israel, and the 1967 June War—each led to a greater disenchantment with the West and what it stood for. Those who continued to support the actions of the West were labeled imperialists or even traitors.

The Arabs in general continue to admire the West, but reluctantly and only from a technological point of view. The West has much to offer in the field of technology. Its institutions and ideologies, though, failed to achieve the expectations for which they were introduced.[3] Therefore, the modern Arab today is primarily preoccupied with the recovery of his national identity.[4]

Two definite trends have set in as reactions to Western penetration. There is a definite trend to return to the sources of Islamic faith, coupled with a purge of all things decadent in Islamic society. Secondly, stress is being placed on science and rationalism, so that in a forward-looking modern society those traditions and attitudes that do not create obstacles to progress are retained.[5]

But what of the Western-educated elites themselves? How did they react to the actions taken by the West during the past fifteen years? They certainly could not argue in public that what the West did was justifiable.[a] In general terms it can be said that the majority felt themselves betrayed by the action of the West toward the Middle East. They began to look toward their own Arab social origins once more. Some modernists began explaining that Islam was not inferior to the West, that actually Western ideas had their roots in Arab culture.[6] Others, such as Cecil Hourani, said that the Arab defeat in 1967 was a product of their own (Arab) culture. The Arabs have refused to come to terms with themselves, with reality. Braggadocio was no substitute for positive action. Hourani stressed the point that the greatest defeat to the Arabs was not inflicted by the Israelis on the Arab armies but was the defeat the Arab governments inflicted on their own population, causing economic losses, loss of lives, and additional refugees.[7] The need was to criticize themselves, and from this self-excoriation, they would discover what was wrong with their society and correct it.

For many, however, it became impossible to deny their Western acculturation. Those in North Africa could not divorce themselves from French culture. Many Western-educated elites did not even know Arabic. For them, France was their heritage.[b] As the eminent G.E. von Grunebaum so aptly expressed: the Arabs were "... wavering between assimilation and rejection [of European culture] —both equally impossible as total objectives—and groping toward a redefinition of religious and social traditions."[8]

---

[a]Charles Malik, one of the Arab world's greatest living personages, was decried when, following the 1956 Suez war, he had stated that Lebanon must continue to ally itself closely with the West and especially with the United States. President Bourguiba of Tunisia was also severely criticized when he stressed his country's close ties with the West. He had attempted to temper his statement by saying that Tunisia could not deny her allegiance as well to the Muslims and Arab world. This, however, failed to appease his critics. R.K. Ramazani, "Cultural Change and Intellectual Response in Algeria, Tunisia, and Iran," *Comparative Studies in Society and History: An International Quarterly* 6, no. 2 (January 1964): 223.

[b]At the close of the Algerian Revolution in 1962, the representatives of the Algerian National Student Movement were forced to use French since, not only did many of the Arabs not know Arabic but that the Berber representatives rejected outright the use of Arabic as the movement's official language. Willard Beling, "Mobilization of Human Resources in Developing Nations: Algeria, Tunisia, and Egypt," *Maghreb Digest* 5, no. 2 (April-June 1967): 9.

Those who graduated from Western institutions immediately following the era of independence for the Arab countries have the greatest identification problems of all the Western-educated elites. The Western institutions their fathers had established had failed. They themselves were steeped in Western ideology and could not readily accept Arab socialism as it was being propounded by President Nasser. They had been raised to believe in Western laws divorced from the *Shari'ah.* Suddenly they were facing a resurgence in everything Islamic, everything Arab. Many of this generation were and still are bureaucrats. They received abuse because of their lack of enthusiasm for implementing socialist programs, for desiring a *status quo.*

It was as if they have been trying to live in two worlds, but *persona non grata* in either. Because they are under suspicion in their own Arab world, many have migrated to the Western countries. Yet there, they feel a sense of futility since they cannot accept what actions are being taken by the West but are powerless to change these actions. Their alienation is the most complete of all Western-educated elites.

The present generation of the Western-educated subculture is not having to face the alienation that the previous one is facing today. We find a generation that is composed of technicians. They have not absorbed Western culture as deeply. Instead they have only accepted with alacrity Western technology and rationalism. They have faith in their origins and have learned to accommodate Western technology with those precepts and ideas that are basically Arab.

These technocrats are to be found at all levels of the government, from Cabinet Minister, to director of an industrial plant, to field staff worker. Because they are Western-educated, they are not above suspicion by their home governments. Nevertheless, they are dedicated young people who are respected for their learning. It is recognized that they have the expertise to accomplish what is needed for the Arab world and are given the needed support.

Those Arab students being trained in Western institutions are likewise discovering a problem of identification, as did their elders. However, it is not necessarily a question of cultural identification. Instead, the student is faced with three problems. Either he is unable or unwilling to adjust to a lower standard of living than that offered by employment abroad; he is unable to find a suitable position; or the political atmosphere in his country is not conducive to his return.

Lucrative job offers account for a large percentage of the brain drain of the Western-educated elites from the Middle East. The United States is considered to be the greatest "land of opportunity"; and of all the undergraduate Arab students enrolled in foreign universities, approximately one-third are in the United States.[9] Of this number, one-fourth are expected to remain where they matriculated.[c] Developing nations are unprepared to pay high salaries and must depend upon dedicated nationalists or those who have less training. However, the advent of oil money has helped to alleviate this problem.

[c]Lebanon has almost a 50 percent loss of its students to the United States.

For those who do return, the job market may present a major problem. In many instances, positions are unavailable. Students from most developing nations find themselves facing a lack of opportunities for specialists. These nations are not yet ready for the highly specialized skills a Western-educated student may have obtained. Then, too, the Western-educated elite may find that what he was taught is not applicable to his country.[10] His learning, in comparison to that of a locally trained student, took place in a sterile atmosphere totally unrelated to the region.

Politics play a tremendous role in influencing a student's return from his studies abroad. The Middle East has been in a volatile state for the past two decades. Business uncertainty, war, and internal instability have caused many students to have second thoughts about returning to establish themselves in their native countries. Furthermore, in many countries, political motivations may leave the student no other alternative than to remain abroad. Algerians who return from their studies abroad often find themselves taking a mandatory reorientation program sponsored by the government to instill in them a correct national outlook toward Algerian life and politics.[11] For many this is tantamount to brainwashing and, therefore, unacceptable.

The student who studies abroad may not necessarily come from an affluent family. Government or private scholarships are made available to aspirants. Those being sponsored by the home government may stipulate that the recipient return to his country after graduation and serve in some capacity with the government. These conditions necessarily put a strain on the student since he may find himself unwilling to return, yet having the obligation to do so.

The Western-educated elitist in many Arab countries is still considered to be an outstanding person, according to home standards, and is looked upon with awe and admiration.[12] If he is trained in the sciences, his prestige is of even greater rank since the technocrat is the leader of the future in the Middle East. Furthermore, he is more readily accepted in government circles since technology lacks a political connotation. It is recognized, too, that the most advanced technological training comes from the United States.

Those students who do come to the United States for training often find themselves facing a communication dilemma. In the United States, they relish the freedom to speak out and to organize themselves into a political group, something many are not permitted to do in their native countries. They enjoy this political awareness and involvement in public life. At the same time, as an Arab minority in a country that supports Israel, their sense of national loyalty is increased as they find themselves forced to band together and to argue for the Arab cause. This is why there is a high proportion of Arab students (approximately 75 percent) who are strongly in favor of Arab unity, and who also hold strong nationalistic attitudes.[13]

At the annual meeting of the Arab Student Organization of the United States, held in Austin, Texas, in January 1972, this awareness of being Arabs was fully felt by the attending delegates. Although the theme of the meeting was the Palestinian movement and the principal speaker was an author on the history of Palestine, the delegates debated very strongly over the actions taken by Arab governments to persecute popular movements. The final communique condemned the Jordanian government for its actions against the Palestinian movement while calling upon the Palestinians to continue their armed struggle, to clarify their relations with the Arab governments, and to fight against all actions taken by those governments that would lead to curtailment of their activities or eventual surrender.[14]

Since its founding in 1952, this Arab students' organization has established 120 chapters, covering almost every state in the Union.[15] With a yearly average enrollment of over seven thousand, it has sufficient vocal authority to provide some impact. Yet it can be said that their statements go unheeded in their native countries. Unable to speak out at home, the students do so abroad. Their names, however, are known and they become suspect on their return, again stressing the point regarding an unfriendly political atmosphere for the Western-educated elite.

# 7 The Bureaucracy

Little has been published on the bureaucracies of the various states of the Arab world. The only bureaucratic system that has been studied in depth is the Egyptian. Recently, however, several articles have been written and published in Egyptian publications castigating the Cairo bureaucracy. Besides these articles and a few paragraphs on other bureaucratic systems in the Middle East, silence has been maintained.

Nevertheless, some generalities as well as specific items can be discussed. Primarily, the typical bureaucrat is changing. He is now recognized as being a part of the emerging intelligentsia that is supplanting the traditional Middle Eastern elites.[1] As such, he assists in formulating the ideals and values of Arab society. He is required to become a dedicated man and commit himself to improve social conditions. The new bureaucrat, then, wants to become a member of the government so that he can help to bring about good government, which, in turn, will alleviate the wretched conditions in which the poorer classes live. Stephen Longrigg, the noted Middle Eastern scholar, so aptly stated it: "a national [pride] is superseding a merely bureaucratic pride."[2] Because of this change of attitude, one that previously connoted self-service, nepotism, graft, and patronage, a modicum of good will is being extended to the bureaucrat.

The bureaucrat is also considered a more competent person when compared with one who was appointed because he is the son of someone or other. Furthermore, he is a less religious person. Most graduates of religious institutions no longer play an important role in government.[3] Instead it is the technocrat or one who has been trained in Western institutions who is found in prestigious positions. Because of his educational background, coupled with the fact that the bureaucracy is generally a conservative institution, an Arab bureaucrat is more prone to be responsive to Western ideas or even effective sponsors of Western concepts.[4]

This image of the modern bureaucrat is not readily recognized throughout the Arab states. Certain nations retain a more traditional picture of the bureaucracy replete with incompetence, corruption, and patronage. The civil service is either a continuation of, or even inheritance from, a colonial system or else an extension of a tribal system in which the clerk had a particular place in society. Other countries have a burgeoning civil service, and in some instances deliberately imposed in order to incorporate into the governmental system all potential troublemakers so that they can be closely watched and controlled. Still other states are beginning to streamline their bureaucratic structure, eliminating obsolete positions, combining posts, and retiring incompetents.

The attacks made upon the Egyptian bureaucracy during the past few years were sanctioned by the government's leaders. They were designed to instill in the civil service a sense of cooperation. Those in command felt that the bureaucrats were too deeply rooted to the past. They had been inherited by the Revolutionary Council when the monarchy was overthrown. A cumbersome, slow-moving, and highly centralized machine, the Egyptian bureaucracy had out of necessity been kept on, simply because replacements were unavailable.[5]

The Revolutionary Council in the mid-1960s still felt hampered by bureaucratic actions. It felt that the bureaucrats were opposed to socialist programs; that they kept their ranks closed and took care of their own; that those appointed by the government were not delegated authority to perform their work, and, in some cases, were not even permitted to function. Noncooperation could aptly describe the existing situation. Therefore, we find the government originating a campaign to denounce the bureaucracy, thereby hoping to force from them a cooperative attitude through which their programs could be expedited. The Arab Socialist Union was given a key role in examining and exposing the "evils" of the Egyptian bureaucratic system. The Minister of Labor called the bureaucracy a "disease which threatens the whole political system."[6] The bureaucracy has a need for political indoctrination as well as a need to work for the masses.[7] Even when he was chief editor of the newspaper, *Al-Ahram*, Muhammad Hassanain Haykal criticized the bureaucracy for corruption.[8]

The results of this criticism were envisaged to be a bureaucracy embodying the following functions: a government executive; an administrator of large-scale economic operations; an instrument to combat conservatism; and an instrument to fulfill the Egyptian revolution.[9] What has happened instead has been a sharp decline in the status and prestige of the civil service with little change in attitude and action, and much less structure, on the part of the bureaucracy. It has been noted that because of nationalization, the number of civil servants rose from 200,000 in 1955 to 1,150,000 in 1970.[10] Their power, has, therefore, increased proportionately.

Class background continues to play an important role in the Egyptian bureaucratic structure. When reorganized shortly after the British occupation last century, two cadres were created: those who were permanent officials and who were required to have educational qualifications, and those who were hired and paid on a daily basis. What this double standard meant was that the upper classes became the administrators, those in key positions, who made policy and dominated government administration. This same class distinction exists today in Egypt. It has been noted that it takes sons of manual laborers an average of 13.2 years to attain high administrative positions, while for sons of professionals and educated personnel, the average was only 7.5 years. Because of discrepancies and discriminations such as these, the bureaucracy has been charged with being against the socialist revolution and all social programs, and with fostering capitalism and, therefore, Western ideas. There is an allegiance between the middle bourgeoisie from whose members the majority of the administrators come. This allegiance, therefore, extends to the landowning class, which, in turn, had supported the monarchy.

It is known that the bureaucracy has been supporting the single party in Egypt, in which its members maintain a commanding position.[11] Nevertheless, as was stated before, because of the attacks made on it, the bureaucracy is no longer a prestigious subculture. What other effect will come from this campaign to debilitate it can only be speculated upon. It is well-entrenched, powerful, and will serve a government faithfully and with determination so long as its interests remain untouched. It is possible that the attacks made by the government will cause some resignations enabling the more idealistic, socialist-minded technocrat to find room in the structure. It is certain that there can be no clean sweep by the government of those whom it feels are hampering their programs. The process must be evolutionary since there must always be a bureaucracy to maintain a functioning administration.

The attempted coup in Morocco in July 1971 was a warning to those in power that the situation existing in the country could not continue unchanged. Judging by reports emanating from Rabat, one finds a situation similar to that in Egypt just prior to the 1952 coup. Corruption, power, and wealth resting in the hands of an elite few; civil disturbances; and arrests and conviction of communicators and other key personages who had called for a return to political participation by the people were all indications of a general malaise permeating the country.

Within the bureaucracy of the government, a patronage system was creating a tightly controlled, highly centralized civil administration. It was not how much one knew, but who one knew, that qualified a person for a position. Furthermore, in many instances, sums of money were given to the person offering the job by the family of the new employee or by the employee himself. It was understood that eventually the new employee would himself make enough in kickbacks or lucrative deals to pay back the money expended for his position.

Among the lesser ranking members of the bureaucracy, low salaries demanded that every duty performed be "sweetened" by the receiver of the service, even though it be the duty of the public servant to perform such services. For example, if one desired the installation of a telephone, he would pay the person issuing the order for installation some unspecified sum to insure that he would get the telephone and that it would be expedited. For one not paying such a service "fee," it might take months, a year, or even longer for a telephone to be installed.

It can be stated, too, that the bureaucratic process was slow and cumbersome, principally because of the rapid expansion of the bureaucracy. Since independence in 1956, jobs increased six-fold, and, combined with the army, totalled 28 percent of all nonagricultural employment.[12] In comparison to Algeria and Tunisia, where the number of jobs tripled, the rate of increase seems inordinately high.

In describing the upper-echelon Moroccan bureaucrat, certain generalities can be made. First of all, he is either a product of the protectorate system or else has been brought into the civil service by someone connected with this system. He is a part of a clientele group and is allied with this group through the patronage system. He has become a cog in the way of life in which mutual obligations play so great a part.[13] He is not particularly religious, yet observes the proscriptions placed upon him by Islam as long as he is in public. Above all, he is oriented toward the West, principally France, because of that country's former protectorate over Morocco which left a legacy of French culture, administrative and educational systems, and general good will.

What power the bureaucrat has is used to defend his position and his projects. Otherwise, the bureaucrat is content to exist in a *status quo* situation and view bold initiative with repugnance.[14]

Whether or not the bureaucracy will change or be changed as a result of the attempted coups in 1971 is open to speculation. However, most probably the situation will continue to remain the same. A raise in salaries and a shake-up of personnel could result in less corruption and better efficiency. One does see a possible change, though, in the type of personnel. Most college graduates were absorbed into the bureaucracy since the policy of the government was to keep all possible dissidents under close watch.[15] The availability of jobs elsewhere was limited, too, because of the economic conditions found in the country. Today, students no longer docilely accept this situation.[16] They view with distaste the patronage system. Yet, until they are able to acquire more leverage, corruption is reduced, and more jobs become available in an expanding economy, most will have to resign themselves to entering the bureaucracy.

Elsewhere throughout the Arab world, bureaucracy operates in a similar fashion. Only in Tunisia, and to a lesser extent Syria, is the civil service considered to be a highly desirable career to enter.[a] Both tenure and social prestige are acquired in the Tunisian bureaucracy. However, the quality of workers employed has not always been of the highest caliber. Because of the immediate need for personnel following the creation of new positions, incompetent and inexperienced personnel were hired.[17] This is also true in Yemen where there is no properly organized administration for the 17,000 public servants, most of whom lack proper qualifications.[18]

Many Arab bureaucracies had the advantage of colonial training. Where this was not available, the government had to rely on a patronage system, generally corrupt and not highly qualified. Today most bureaucracies are expanding because of the development of their countries. In those states where socialism is being implemented, the strain on the bureaucracy is doubled, not only because

[a]Although it is the goal of many Syrian students to enter into government employment, requirements are such that it is difficult to do so. In many positions a university degree is now mandatory. Tareq Ismael, *Government and Politics of the Contemporary Middle East*, Homewood, Ill.: Dorsey Press, 1970, p. 215.

of an increase in duties but also because socialism is repugnant to the majority of the bureaucrats. In Syria and Iraq, there have occurred disputes of a serious nature, with the regimes generally accusing the bureaucracy of dragging its feet on the implementation of their plans.

The Libyan civil service is probably undergoing the greatest changes of all Arab bureaucracies. Prior to Qadhafi's seizure of power in 1969, the Libyan bureaucracy was organized on an Italian colonial system superimposed over a system inherited from a traditional tribal organization. To show his Arabism, Qadhafi ejected from his country the Italians and other foreigners, some of whom performed duties as administrators in the bureaucracy. Therefore, coupled with his nationalization policies, qualified administrative personnel are under much pressure. They are forced to hire unqualified personnel because the educated are still relatively few in number. In fiscal year 1972, almost 100 million dinars (around $238 million) was spent on government salaries.[19] This figure included military personnel as well. However, the currency expended amounted to over one-third of the entire budget.

A burgeoning bureaucracy is a problem the Arab governments must face. Until more people are educated, the quality of the bureaucratic staff will necessarily be low. Furthermore, there will continue to be conflict between the regimes and the bureaucracies in the progressive states as the latter feels greater impingement on its powers.

# 8     The Students

Since the end of the nineteenth century, Arab students have played an important role in the political dynamics of the region. Prior to independence, they were leaders of freedom movements as well as channels of communication for new ideas inspired by Western education. Since independence, they have become the avant garde of revolutionism, reformism, socialism, nationalism, and Arabism in North Africa and the Middle East. Individual politicians, as well as political parties, have often competed for the allegiance of student groups as a powerful weapon against political adversaries. Such alliances have not, however, been permanent. Impatient with the slowness of change, student groups have often become opponents of the regimes they helped to install in power. Their dynamism, numerical strength, and proclivity to street demonstrations have placed Arab students in almost constant confrontation with many an Arab government. Although revolutionary ideologies are generally sympathetic toward youth, the so-called Arab revolutionary regimes have not taken kindly to student criticism. These "revolutionary" regimes strive to use Arab students merely as a social base to consolidate their administrative control against conservative adults. Once in complete control, these regimes have not hesitated to suppress or contain student activities as a serious challenge to the government's authoritarian policies. Not only the "revolutionary" regimes but also the conservative and moderate governments in the Arab world have been keeping a watchful eye on student organizations which, during the past ten years or so, have generally posed a threat to their existence.

If today Arab students project the image of being revolutionaries of the Maoist or Marxist-Leninist schools, they were not so in the 1940s and the early 1950s. Then, the bulk of politically active Arab students were a conservative-to-moderate group that sought to reform the religious and civil institutions of the Arab countries. During this era, they flocked to such political and-or religious organizations as *al-Ikhwan al-Muslimun* (the Muslim Brethren Association), the Neo-Destour Party, the Istiqlal, the Syrian Nationalist People's Party, and the Ba'th Party. A number of external and domestic variables, however, "conspired" to change the general orientation of Arab students from moderation to extremism as a means of alleviating the socioeconomic conditions of the region. First, it was the reality of independence which Arab students had hoped and believed would bring instantaneous relief from economic poverty and political suppression and usher in an era of Arab unity. Their expectations and hopes, however, were frustrated—they saw little perceptible economic and political change and their dream of Arab unity remained unfulfilled. Failing to understand the deep-rooted causes of economic backwardness and the mitigating factors against Arab unity, Arab students blamed the failures on what they called the "foreign-imposed" political system (parliamentary democracy) and the "reactionary" monarchies; and they rejected both. Secondly, the Arab students confused Western political theories and ideas with the contemporary Western policies in the Middle East and in so doing they not only denounced the latter but rejected the former. By rejecting Western political ideas, Arab students also turned away from those indigenous political parties that expounded the concept of evolutionary and peaceful change. Their domestic frustrations were exacerbated by the establishment of Israel and the subsequent defeat of the Arab armies in Palestine. If these factors were not enough to radicalize the Arab student, the Suez crisis, the Algerian Revolution, the Arab-Israeli war of June 1967, and the activities of the Palestinian guerrillas have certainly transformed him into a protagonist of revolutionary change in the Arab world.

In recent years student relations with the Arab governments have progressively deteriorated due to many and varied reasons. Although student groups were never really closely associated with such conservative regimes as that of Morocco, Jordan, and Saudi Arabia, Arab students have also expressed their disenchantment and disillusionment with the so-called progressive and revolutionary regime because of their failure to rapidly effect basic and fundamental changes in the region. Arab students have been vocal in their criticisms of the domestic and foreign policies of their respective governments which, the students contend, have deviated from the revolutionary paths of socialism, Arabism, and freedom. Student demonstrations, however, have not always been inspired by idealism and political goals. Often Arab students have taken to the streets for such pecuniary reasons as an increase in tuition and lack of jobs after graduation. Frustrated by the domestic and external problems facing the Arab world, an increasingly large number of Arab students have become alienated from the sociopolitical systems of their forefathers. Although compared to their Western counterparts, the number of alienated Arab students is not large; still, according to one survey, they form about 13 percent of the university student population.[1]

Although their life-style, aspirations, goals, and common sense of frustration make Arab students a distinct subculture, there are deep cleavages that keep them divided and prevent them from becoming a truly effective national or regional force. Religious divisions, as well as regional, linguistic, racial, and tribal differences have inhibited the growth of national student movements devoted to societal changes. Like the members of their older generation that hold key decision-making jobs in the government systems of the Arab world, Arab students have failed to arrive at a *consensus juris* within which to compromise their ideological, political, ethnic, and other differences. Many student unions, organized on confessional, ethnic, racial, or geographic bases, tend to compete for the favors of national or foreign Arab governments with whom they identify themselves on the bases of politics, ideologies, or other affinities. As a result of their disunity, the Arab students have been unable to show concrete results in achieving political or economic goals.

Adverse political and economic conditions at home and the prospects of a better life abroad have constrained hundreds of thousands of Arab students to seek employment in the West, especially in the United States, where they have been coming in increasing numbers for higher education. Since the end of World War II, the Arab countries have been rapidly increasing their educational systems with the result in 1971 that there were over 300,000 students receiving more or less free education at the university level as shown in Table 8-1. This number is increasing at an annual rate of 25 percent, which is much higher than the highest annual percentage increase in the GNP of any Arab state. This means that the number of college graduates is rising faster than the economies of the Arab countries can absorb them. Consequently, a large number of Arab graduates and students join the ranks of the unemployed and underemployed labor force which has become a target for spreading extremist ideologies. A good number of these unemployed graduates strive to emigrate to the industrialized countries of

**Table 8-1**
**Student Enrollment in Higher Education**

| Country | Total | Date | Total | Date | 1969 Pop. Est. |
|---|---|---|---|---|---|
| | (*UNESCO Statistical Yearbook 1968*, pp. 185-195) | | (*UN Statistical Yearbook 1970*, pp. 755-775) | | (*UN Statistical Yearbook 1970*, pp. 80-84) |
| Algeria | 8,053 | 1965 | 10,681 | 1968 | 13,349,000 |
| Iraq | 28,410 | 1965 | 41,189 | 1968 | 9,350,000 |
| Israel | 35,878 | 1965 | 44,758 | 1968 | 2,822,000 |
| Jordan | 3,192 | 1965 | 4,077 | 1968 | 2,217,000 |
| Kuwait | 418 | 1966 | 1,320 | 1968 | 570,000 |
| Lebanon | 20,304 | 1965 | 33,587 | 1968 | 2,645,000 |
| Libya | 1,926 | 1965 | 2,215 | 1966 | 1,869,000 |
| Morocco | 8,996 | 1965 | 10,908 | 1968 | 15,050,000 |
| Saudi Arabia | 1,831 | 1965 | 5,352 | 1968 | 7,200,000 |
| Sudan | 7,701 | 1965 | 10,404 | 1967 | 15,186,000 |
| Syria | 32,653 | 1965 | 35,005 | 1968 | 5,866,000 |
| Tunisia | 6,230 | 1965 | 7,336 | 1967 | 5,027,000 |
| UAR | 177,123 | 1965 | 174,614 | 1967 | 32,501,000 |
| Yemen* | – | – | 221 | 1967 | 5,000,000 |
| Yemen, Peoples Republic* | – | – | 294 | 1967 | 1,220,000 |

*Teacher training only.

the West with the prospects for a better and freer life than they enjoy in their native lands. Although there seems to be some disparity in the figures collected by surveyors of Arab student emigration to the West, there is a general agreement that the number of emigrants has been rising at a steady pace. Of course, not all Arab students show the same degree of proclivity toward permanently leaving their homelands in search of a better life. One study shows that during a period of ten years (1956-1966) almost every Egyptian student who went abroad for study decided to remain outside Egypt. In addition to material benefits, this trend may be attributed to the authoritarian milieu then existing in Egypt. The same study indicates that about 80 percent of all Jordanian students never return home. (At least 50 percent of these were most probably Palestinians holding Jordanian passports.) Compared to the high percentage of Egyptian and Jordanian emigrees, Lebanon loses only about 50 percent of its students to foreign countries.[2]

Another study, undertaken by Halim Barakat, a teacher at AUB, indicates that approximately 5,000 to 7,000 skilled Arabs emigrate from their countries each year and that the United States alone attracted about 3,500 skilled Arabs during the five-year period ending in 1970. The author of this report bemoans the fact that the economic, social, and educational systems of the Arab countries have not been strong enough to retain these highly qualified and urgently needed experts on whose education and training the Arab countries spend hundreds of millions of dollars each year. He contends that the cost of training one scientist is about $20,000, which amount is permanently lost when the scientist decides to emigrate.[3]

Although Arab universities are considered to be responsible for politicization of Arab students and are therefore centers for radical elements, the great portion of students remain apolitical during their period of study. One survey indicates that in one of the universities in Lebanon only 8 percent of the students participated in political activities "persistently" and that a mere 6 percent were active members of political parties such as the Ba'th and the SSNP.[4] The Barakat study concludes that there was a direct correlation between the intensity of student participation in political activities and the degree of their alienation from the religious and political institutions of the Arab countries—the more alienated a student was, the more active in politics he became and more fervently he supported such militant movements as the Palestinian guerrillas, Pan-Arabism, and revolutionism. Another survey indicated that citizenship, national identity, and religious affiliations were also highly important and significant factors in determining attitudes towards such movements.[5]

Politicization in the Arab world begins at a fairly early stage of education. From the primary school to the university, Arab students read a glorified version of Arab history which tends to "burden" them with emotionalism, a sense of false pride, and illusions of power and strength. Arab students are instilled with the ideas of Arab nationalism and absolute righteousness of their cause—be it

Palestine, Algeria, or the Greater and Lesser Tombs. This political socialization process has been greatly strengthened by the thousands of Egyptian and Palestinian pedagogues teaching throughout the Arab world. Palestinian teachers who more or less have a monopoly in Kuwait and Jordan have been partially responsible for instilling in the minds of their pupils a greater urge for Arab unity than is manifested, for example, by Saudi Arabian students. Similarly, Sudanese and Libyan students show a high incidence of Pan-Arabism partially because of the presence of a large number of Egyptian teachers in these states. There are, of course, other variables that influence student attitudes in the Arab countries. Among these is the social, religious, and cultural background of the student. The Lebanese student who is exposed early to communal or confessional education tends to be more of a nationalist than a Pan-Arabist. The Egyptian student who comes from a rich urban family tends to be more liberal and shows more attachment to such values as personal freedom and a competitive economic system than his classmate from the lower classes who favors a socialist system, government ownership of means of production, control of the press, and regulation of the relations between employer and employee.[6]

## Egypt

Since the early part of the nineteenth century, when the Ottoman governor of Egypt, Mohammed Ali Pasha, introduced Western education into the country, the student population and their participation in the political affairs of Egypt have been on the rise. Quantitatively, this rise has taken quantum jumps since the Eyptian Revolution in 1952. Even before that year, however, the student population had become so "inordinately vast" that their unions and organizations had already become a target for political propaganda and recruitment by political parties subscribing to all shades of extremism, reformism, nationalism, and Pan-Arabism. An eminent scholar of Middle East affairs, P.J. Vatikiotis, has observed that by 1952 Egyptian students had become an "identifiable community—al-talaba—the student body—with a student-anschaung characterized by a bitter enmity against all well-to-do Egyptians and foreigners, and against the West in general; ready to be recruited into militant movements which purported neat and easy formulae of salvation (e.g., the Muslim Brethren, Young Egypt Association, and the Communist Party)."[7]

Aware of the dirth of dedicated and trained personnel for carrying forward the "revolutionary" movement they had inaugurated, the Free Officers attempted in 1953 a radical reorganization of the entire educational system which until then had been geared to producing the personnel and manpower needs of a feudal society. The new regime was interested not only in the eradication of illiteracy but also in the Egyptianization of education. Educational reforms, Nasser's spectacular rise in the international system, and efficient police methods of the Egyptian regime against its opponents all contrived to maintain an alliance of convenience between the military regime and the students. Students who belonged to the outlawed Muslim Brotherhood did not, however, support the Nasser regime and continued to engage in covert activities against the government. With the exception of participating in some minor, government-inspired demonstrations against foreign countries, the bulk of Egyptian students did not independently engage in the political activities of the country. These political doldrums apparently ended in 1968 when Egyptian university students once again strove to reassert themselves in the political equations of the country. In that year, Egyptian students, frustrated by the Arab-Israeli impasse and angered by the incompetency of the military leaders, as disclosed in the trials of several military officers, began to question the government's domestic and foreign policies. Undaunted by the government's threat of reprisals, the students defied the ban on political demonstrations by holding meetings in several Egyptian towns. During these demonstrations, the students expressed their contempt of the military hierarchy by demanding a stiff punishment for the officers accused of dereliction of duty. These demonstrations, though seemingly directed against a handful of scapegoats, were in reality a manifestation of the students' disillusionment with and rejection of Nasser's policies. For fifteen years, Nasser had been supported fervently by members of his own generation and by the one that was in school at the time of his spectacular successes in breaking the Western arms embargo and the nationalization of the Suez Canal. Since then a new generation of students had entered the scene and had been given less, if any, reasons to be captivated by Nasser's charisma. The new generation had witnessed nothing but a series of setbacks and failures of Egyptian policies in Syria, Iraq, Yemen, and finally the humiliating fiasco in June 1967. Domestically, economic conditions had not improved perceptibly and the unemployment rate showed no signs of abating. Furthermore, the spectacle of small Arab states giving financial aid to sustain the Egyptian economy did not enhance the prestige of the government in the eyes of the youth. All these factors seemingly combined to exacerbate the feeling of disillusionment among the Egyptian students with the government. It should be noted that both the Communists and the MBA were reported to have actively participated in these demonstrations. The significance of their participation may be summarized by stating that in spite of a legal ban on their activities, both extremist organizations have been able to continue their activities. In the case of the Communists, their participation also indicated their determination to weaken the Egyptian regime, with whom they had ostensibly "promised" to cooperate through the Arab Socialist Union (ASU). In the case of the Muslim Brotherhood, their participation in the demonstrations showed their tenacity to survive under the regime's extreme repressive measures and manifested their implacable opposition to the Nasser government which had persecuted them for fifteen years. Although the 1968 student demonstrations and riots were quickly contained by a series of expedient measures by the government, the students were not totally mollified, as evidenced by the more recent anti-government demonstrations that took place in early 1972. That the students had not been appeased and their demands not fully met was also obvious from the identical demands they presented to the government in 1968 and again in 1972. In 1968, President Nasser tried to appease the students and the rest of the population by democratizing the ASU. However, he would not alter the status of the National Assembly, which the students would have preferred. This step brought temporary peace to university campuses and enabled the government to disregard the more militant demands of the students. These demands included: one, that all plans for reaching a settlement with Israel be repudiated and that the country be immediately mobilized for a new confrontation; two, that the military training facilities available to the students be expanded and improved; three, that the censorship of the press and other media be lifted; and four, that Egypt sever "once and for all time" its contacts with the United States.[8]

In 1972, Egyptian students made similar demands of Nasser's successor, Anwar el-Sadat who, soon after his accession, had begun to liberalize the country's political system. As a response to student demands, President Sadat announced on January 17, 1972, the formation of his "confrontation" cabinet and gave it the responsibility of placing the Egyptian economy on a "war footing." In addition, President Sadat eased control over the news and other media, imposed "war taxes" on Egyptian landowners, and gave indications that his dialogue with the United States would soon end. It should be noted that although these steps were announced in the wake of student demonstrations and riots, indications are that most of them had been long in preparation.

To the question as to how much influence Egyptian students have in the country's politics, one might conclude by saying that as a united force they are able to wield a great deal of power to prod the government into reformist actions. Although they have adopted many revolutionary slogans, denoting that many may even be sincere in their revolutionary pronouncements, the Egyptian students alone are incapable of bringing about a revolutionary movement to fruition. In order to succeed in bringing about revolutionary changes in the country's policies, the students have to depend on military support and popular pressure, a condition that does not seem to be currently present in Egypt. Not only do they lack this support, the Egyptian students are not even a united force. With the exception of their common opposition to Israel and common support for the Palestinian guerrillas, Egyptian students are divided on most other issues considered vital to the nation. This division became evident during the student demonstrations in Cairo in the early part of 1972 when the University of Alexandria students, in opposition to the student body at the University of Cairo, sent messages of support to President Sadat.

Since the early 1950s, Egyptian students have remained fervent advocates of Pan-Arabism. They have supported every move for unity which would place

Egypt at the head of a union. Although expounding the concepts of republicanism and revolutionism, it mattered little to the students whether the unity was between divergent political systems such as Egypt, Syria, and Yemen in 1958 or between complementary systems such as Egypt, Syria, and Libya. Aware of their country's potential to become a "superpower" of the Arab world, the Egyptian students wish to bring under Egyptian influence as many Arab states as would be willing to accept a junior partnership in a future Arab nation.

## North Africa

North African students began to organize themselves into a union in 1927 when a small number of North African students in Paris founded the North African Muslim Students Association (AEMNA) for the purpose of conducting organized political activities in France. The limited resources at the disposal of the AEMNA, however, prevented it from making a serious impact on the decision-makers in France. Five years after the end of World War II, the AEMNA established a permanent secretariat to draw plans for a unified North African union; but political events in Morocco, Tunisia, and Algeria hindered their realization. With the increase in the tempo of nationalist activities in the 1950s, North African students began to organize themselves into separate national groups representing Morocco, Algeria, and Tunisia. With the support of the Neo-Destour Party, the Tunisian students in 1953 were the first to organize themselves into a national union, the General Union of Tunisian Students (UGET). Their example was followed by the Algerians who, with the support of the FLN, founded the General Union of Algerian Muslim Students (UGEMA) shortly after the outbreak of the Algerian Revolution in 1954. While the Tunisian and the Algerian students organized themselves during their struggle for independence, the Moroccan students formed their union after independence in 1956. Like their Tunisian and Algerian counterparts, the Moroccan students were also supported by the dominant political party, the Istiqlal, in organizing the National Union of Moroccan Students (UNEM). Whereas by participating in their struggles for independence, both the Algerian and Tunisian students unions became highly politicized, the Moroccan union remained temporarily "weak and very much dependent upon Mehdi Ben Barka, the Istiqlal organizer, for animation and direction."[9] Two years after Algeria's independence, North African students once again turned their attention toward establishing an all-Maghrib union and in 1964 formed the Confederation of Maghrib Students, composed of the student unions of Morocco, Algeria, and Tunisia. The confederation has been given the task of finding the means and methods to unify the educational systems of the three North African states, and to strive for an all-Maghrib university, with the national universities agreeing to specialize in different faculties. Due to political disagreements among the national governments, which control educational facilities in their respective states, no substantial progress has been made in this direction. At the time of its establishment, the Confederation of Maghrib Students made laudatory comments on the socialization measures adopted by Algeria and Tunisia while condemning Morocco and Libya for their repressive rules.[10]

## Morocco

Although the last to organize into a national union, Moroccan students have formed the most strident protest movement in North Africa, primarily because they have found an easy and visible target in the person of King Hassan II, whom they consider to be feudalistic and oppressive in his domestic policies. One reason that Moroccan students were left behind in organizing themselves was that in the preindependence period most Moroccan students came from the upper classes and from families of the traditional elite who were not amenable to radical social changes. With the expansion of educational facilities after independence, however, children of all social and professional classes began to enter schools and colleges where they learned the concepts of liberty, equality, democracy, and other modern political precepts. Having had no organizational experience, the Moroccan students accepted Mehdi Ben Barka's guidance in articulating their political and educational goals. Initially a supporter of the Istiqlal Party, the UNEM joined the rest of the Moroccan left in support of the newly formed Union Nationale des Forces Populaires (UNFP), a splintered radical faction of the Istiqlal Party. Since social restratification is absent in Morocco and students without contracts in the hierarchy are unable to obtain responsible jobs in the inner circle of the government, they continue to show a pronounced tendency toward radicalism and revolutionism.

Expression of radical and revolutionary ideas has often brought the students in conflict with the monarchy and its major instrument of power, the military. Moroccan students show little respect toward their national military forces whom they contemptuously call a "parade" army. Since 1963, when the student-supported leadership of the UNFP was arrested for an alleged plot to overthrow the monarchy, the National Union of Moroccan Students has been calling for the overthrow of the regime that the UNEM accuses of being responsible for all the economic and political crises the country has suffered since independence. During the year 1963-1964, the UNEM held twenty student strikes and took responsibility for six "occupations" of the Moroccan embassies abroad. Angered by such tactics, the Moroccan government cut off the union's subsidies and unsuccessfully tried to outlaw the UNEM on technical grounds. Having failed to intimidate the students, who maintained their pressure by staging an increasing number of strikes in the following years, the Moroccan government began to apply selectively a new law instituting universal conscription. Refusing to give deferments to students, as provided for in the law, the government drafted all but one of the UNEM's Executive Committee on the eve of its Eleventh Congress in July 1966. These steps have solved nothing. Neither the student strikes nor the actions of the government have changed conditions substantially. The students have maintained an adamant stance toward the government and 14,000 of them have been on strike since February 1972, ostensibly to alter the curricula of the universities, but in reality to apply pressure on the government to change its domestic policies. The Moroccan government is unable and unwilling to compromise with the UNEM because of the latter's vow to overthrow the monarchy. And on its part, the UNEM is unwilling and unable to compromise because by doing so it would lose its *raison d'être*.

The National Union of Moroccan Students has not only been critical of the government's domestic policies but also of its foreign policies. In addition to being critical of Morocco's close ties with the West, the UNEM had been highly critical of Morocco's policies toward Algeria since the two North African neighbors engaged in border skirmishes a few months after Algeria became independent in July 1962. During these initial border incidents, the UNEM president expressed solidarity with Algeria's socialist government and condemned Morocco's "imperialist" claims over Algerian territory. It should be noted that in this question, the UNEM did not reflect the popular sentiments that seemed favorable to the government's action.

*Algeria*

The violent struggle between the Algerians and the French that began on November 1, 1954, gave birth to the General Union of Algerian Students (UGEMA). (After independence, the UGEMA was changed into the UNEA—National Union of Algerian Students.) By the time the first shot had been fired at Batna and other places throughout Algeria, it was clear that the forces of moderation had been overshadowed by the forces of militancy, and that the struggle for Algerian independence would be decided by force of arms rather than by negotiations. Although, with the possible exception of Hocine Ait Ahmed, who was one of the nine founders of the FLN, Algerian students were not the initiators of the conflict, they soon became an intimate part of it.[11] Throughout the eight years of conflict, Algerian students and their union, the UGEMA, remained solidly behind the FLN and its goals. The UGEMA was not only a staunch supporter of the nationalist cause in Algeria but the union also enhanced FLN prestige in foreign countries by disseminating Algerian nationalists' views to the host countries. As the conflict intensified and finally moved toward a solution in 1962, the UGEMA's statements on domestic and foreign policy issues began to show a more leftist orientation than that of the Provisional Government of the Republic of Algeria (GPRA), founded in September 1958.

Unlike the Moroccan student union (UNEM) or the Tunisian student union (UGET) which became subordinate adjuncts of their countries' respective dominant political parties, the Algerian student union successfully maintained a fair degree of autonomy until shortly before the fall of Ben Bella in 1965. Under the leadership of Houri Mouffok, a student who had attended an East German university and was a sympathizer of the outlawed Algerian Communist Party, the Algerian student union supported Ben Bella's socialist policies. Colonel Boumedienne's coup against Ben Bella brought to the streets the UNEA and its Communist sympathizers who demanded the immediate release of the former president of the country. The Revolutionary Council answered the students' demand by placing under arrest three of the union's top leaders. Since the coup, Algerian students have had many occasions to organize street demonstrations over a number of events, primarily concerning foreign issues. Starting with the Mehdi Ben Barka affair in the fall of 1965, Algerian students organized several strikes and demonstrations in 1966 and during the Arab-Israeli war in 1967.[a] This conflict, ironically, provided the government with an opportunity to weaken the student movement by inducting about 5,000 students into the army for six weeks, for the ostensible purpose of improving the country's military strength against Israel.

Although many Algerian student leaders expound revolutionary concepts, the bulk of Algerian students are not prone to radicalism. None of the foreign ideologies have made many converts from the Algerians. Under the Boumedienne regime, religious education has become an essential part of the school curricula. Furthermore, the Algerian government has embarked upon a program of Arabization and Algerianization of the educational system of the country. Evidently, these steps have instilled in the minds of the students a sense of cultural pride, restored in them a feeling of cultural identity with the Arab and Islamic past, and immunized them against extremist ideologies.

Like other Arab students, Algerian students subscribe to the concepts of Pan-Arabism and to the idea of regional unity in North Africa (the Maghrib). Neither the Algerians nor their neighbors, however, seem overenthusiastic about creating a political union between Algeria, Morocco, and Tunisia. North African students may be able to forge closer ties with each other by strengthening such Magribian organizations as the Confederation of Students but their design for regional unity will remain frustrated so long as there exists political and economic disagreements between the three governments of the Maghrib.

---

[a]Ben Barka was killed in France by Moroccans, allegedly carried out by Oufkii. Therefore, it had to be government-ordered. France protested violently.

*Tunisia*

Backed by the Neo-Destour Party then seeking independence from France, Tunisian students in Paris founded, at a clandestine meeting, the General Union of Tunisian Students (UGET) in July 1953. For the next ten years or so, the UGET and the Neo-Destour Party remained closely associated with each other's activities—an association that created a credibility gap between the union members and its leadership. By the early 1960s, in the eyes of a large number of students the union had become nothing but a mouthpiece of the Neo-Destour Party whose policies were being seriously questioned by the Tunisian intelligentsia. Prior to the split which occurred between the Neo-Destour Party and the UGET on the one hand and autonomy-minded students on the other, a large number of Tunisian students shared with the leadership of the Neo-Destour Party a common geographic region, the Sahil, which is a coastal strip south of the capital city of Tunis. A survey shows that as much as 25 percent of the student population in 1960 and the majority of the ruling elites of the country came from the Sahil. In as much as the Tunisians are inclined to identify themselves more with regional groups than with social classes, a common Sahili background appears to have provided a temporary stable working arrangement between the two groups.[12] In addition to regional loyalties, student-government rapport was also based on utilitarian grounds—a large number of students were being annually absorbed into the political system until the early 1960s when the economy reached a saturation point and ceased to provide employment opportunities to a large number of university graduates. Although the process of restratification continued to operate, the economic conditions of the country created a large pool of dissatisfied and unemployed students and former students, some of whom have manifested a tendency to accept radicalism to alleviate economic conditions in the country.

Only seven years after independence, it had become apparent that a group of activist students would no longer acquiesce to the Neo-Destour Party's continued unchallenged hegemony over the country. In the meantime, the UGET, following the party line, began to deny executive positions to members of the "autonomist" student group which sought to dissociate the student union from the Neo-Destour Party. As student opposition became more serious, both the UGET and the Neo-Destour Party cracked down on the autonomists, accusing them of being Communists, Trotskyites, irresponsibles, and parasites. By 1967 even "loyal student members of the party were dissatisfied with the way the party was running the nominations for union office. Students from the Sahil had a disproportionate share of union positions and clans or groups of individuals within the party were using their union influence against other groups. Party control and personal opportunism had discredited the union in the eyes of most students."[13] Generational, regional, and political conflicts, which had remained dormant for almost ten years, were laid bare when in 1966 Tunisian students staged an unprecedented strike designed to demonstrate their antagonism and opposition toward the Neo-Destour Party and the government of the country. It was a student revolt against the party's and the government's efforts to impose and maintain student leadership on the UGET.

Having failed to change the political *status quo* by peaceful means, Tunisian students staged antigovernment riots in the spring of 1968. Although it played down the episode, these riots were serious enough to cause the government to issue a "white paper" giving its version of the problem. The student riots seem to have sufficiently unnerved the Bourguiba regime for it to use repressive measures against the activists. In that year, a specially convened state security court awarded stiff sentences to a large number of student leaders and lecturers accused of subversive activities, controvention of press laws, and plotting to overthrow the Bourguiba regime. One student leader, Ben Djennet was sentenced to twenty years hard labor for participating in the student strike. The harshness of the sentences, the suggestions that torture had been used in the Tunisian police interrogation cells, and the less than judiciary process obtained in the court, were highly criticized by both Tunisian students and a number of French observers.[14]

After an apparent calm of approximately three years, Tunisian students once again began to protest against the government's foreign and domestic policies. In February 1972, a large number of college and high school students demonstrated against President Bourguiba's "40 years of tyranny and oppression."[15] Following this demonstration, the Tunisian government closed Tunis University's law and arts schools until September 1972. In criticizing the students for their behavior, Premier Hedi Nouira told the National Assembly that the demonstrators were "inspired by leftist agitators from a Ba'thist country in the Middle East."[16]

Elsewhere in the Arab world, students have occasionally manifested restiveness and impatience with the policies of their respective countries. In Syria and Jordan, students had been involved in political demonstrations and anti-government riots in the 1950s and early 1960s. To a certain extent, it was due to student demonstrations that Jordan was prevented from joining the Baghdad Pact in 1955. Sentiments in favor of the Palestinian guerrillas are fairly high among Syrian, Jordanian, and Lebanese students who are often engaged in political and fund-raising activities for the Palestinians. It may be surmised that although antigovernment student bodies exist in Jordan, Syria, Saudi Arabia, and Kuwait the repressive nature of these regimes has probably prevented the students from expanding their activities.

Under a confessional-democratic system of government, students in Lebanon enjoy a high degree of latitude in expressing their sentiments on domestic and foreign policies of the government. Not only Lebanese but also students from other Arab and foreign countries enjoy freedom of speech and expression. Many Arab students who are denied in their own countries the right to criticize their governments find a haven in Lebanon where they are often engaged in political activities against their national governments.

From Marxism to Pan-Arabism, Lebanese students, as well as other Arab students in the country, support a variety of ideological and political movements. A product of confessionalism, most Lebanese students, however, tend to show a pronounced spirit of territorial nationalism. They are sharply divided on such critical issues as the Palestinian guerrilla movement and Lebanon's role in the Arab-Israeli conflict. During the Jordanian civil war (1971), pro- and antiguerrilla students in Lebanon fought pitched battles in the street in which several students were reported injured. During the same period, students at the American University of Beirut went on strike after the university administration announced an increase in the tuition. A small group of students temporarily occupied a number of administrative buildings and caused the administration to close the university for the remainder of the academic year. Incidents of street clashes were also reported between the opponents and exponents of the strike.

# 9  The Professionals

Diversity of profession becomes a significant factor when discussing the associational groups. Heretofore, the members of the other subcultures have belonged to groups professing a common career or common background. The subculture of the professionals contains many varied types of personnel; of organizations; of careers and backgrounds; and, if taken separately, each could readily be classified as a distinct subculture in itself. However, for the purpose of simplification to the reader, all associational groups will be discussed as one entity.

Within this subculture, one finds members of the intelligentsia elite. One also finds laborers and farmers. Represented are doctors, lawyers, teachers, and engineers, as well as blue collar workers, and day laborers. Normally, those students who belong to student union organizations would also fall under this category. However, they have been discussed previously in their own subcultural group.

When researching the various groups comprised by the professional class, except for labor unions, little material has come to light. The primary reason for the lack of information is the ineffectiveness of the professional associations. In the United States and other Western countries, many professionals have formed powerful lobbying organizations. The American Medical Association, the American Bar Association, and the National Education Association are all spokesmen for their professional members. Their names appear daily in newspapers, in the records of Congress, or on programs of local community halls. In contrast, one rarely sees mentioned the names of their Arab counterparts.

The reasons for the ineffectiveness of the professional groups are many. Of first consequence, except for labor unions, is the relatively small number in each professional association. In several countries, especially those of North Africa, a majority of the professionals were of European origin. Individual Arab professionals gained prominence only after the independence of their countries. Then, too, because of their association with Western institutions, some professional groups, such as lawyers, suffered an eclipse in the Socialist countries. They were recognized as being part of the *ancien régime*. It was further recognized that they remained fragmented, even though organized.[1]

The establishment of one-party systems in several countries of the Arab world has not helped the professional associations. Instead of being permitted to function as a separate entity, most associations have been brought under the aegis of the national parties.[a] It is the contention of those govern-ments with a single-party system that professional groups are fostered by belonging to a larger organization since the party would be able to furnish the necessary organizational trappings. Furthermore, by having control of the asso-ciational organizations, these interest groups would be able to assist the party in educating the people in the national development of their country.[2]

Instead of abetting the interest groups, what has occurred can only be described as a stifling of all initiatives. As an entity they have lost identity, and as a voice they have been stilled. They follow the dictates of the party without opposition.

Each associational group does attempt to foster their own aims under the controls imposed upon them. Statements do appear in the journals of their organizations or in the papers that cover the congresses held by the associations. From these, one is able to discern that the interests of the party and/or state must come first. Delegates attending the Arab Engineers Congress in March 1972 voted affirmatively on a resolution calling for solidarity to face the "imperialist" aggressors who are threatening the Arab homeland; internal national unity; nationalization or national control over all foreign interests, especially oil and mining resources; and material and spiritual support for the Palestinian move-ment.[3 b] These are statements of principal. Nowhere was there made mention of recommendation of a more substantive nature. Because of such grandiose statements, the delegates were severely criticized by some newspapers. They were accused of accomplishing little toward fulfilling their promises. It was necessary for them to stand united and committed. If not, they would continue to remain ineffectual.

The only professional group that can be credited with even a moderate amount of constructive action is the lawyers. Products of Western tutelage, secular Arab lawyers used the law introduced into the Arab lands by the West to further their countries' status among the nations of the world. Lawyers were

[a]Using Tunisia as an example, the Destourian Socialist Party has attached to it the following principal associational interest groups:

> Workers—Union Genérale Tunisienne du Travail
> Alumni—Association des Professeurs et Etudiants de la Grande Mosqueé
> Businessmen—Union Tunisienne des Industriels, Commerçants et Artisans
> Youth—Les Jeunesses Destouriennes (girls)
>       Association des Jeunes Musulmans (boys)
> Students—Union Genérale des Etudiants de Tunisie
> Women—Union Nationale des Femmes Tunisiennes
> Farmers—Union Genérale des Agriculteurs Tunisiens

Practically every group having some importance is represented.

[b]Two years previously, at the Congress of the Arab Engineers, the delegates stressed again the question of Palestine. Here their ideas were more concrete in that they offered their services to rebuild the town of al-Karameh where the Palestinians first engaged the Israelis in actual combat, and to design shelters for the Palestinian refugees. *Majallat al-Muhandiseen* [*The Engineers Magazine*] 21, no. 2 (March 1969): 16-17.

among the forefront in striving for the independence of their states. They helped to draft the constitutions and build the governing institutions. Above all, many became parliamentarians and became a part of the governing elite. Their foremost labor has been the codification of the laws of the various states in the Arab Middle East. Where conflicting statutes arose, they were able, in most cases, to resolve these discrepancies so that uniformity could be achieved. It could be said of them that their activities made them dedicated Pan-Arabists although they must be considered nationalists first.

When the military juntas began toppling the parliamentary governments in the Arab world, lawyers lost their position of preeminence. Their powers were usurped and their livelihood taken from them. In Egypt, especially, where all the foremost parliamentarians of the day were lawyers, they were forced to find other work. It is only recently that their eclipse seems to be subsiding. A new generation of lawyers has emerged—those who have been trained to deal with the Arab Socialist systems.

Although their lost prestige will probably never be fully regained, lawyers, at least, continue to strive for the rights of the common man. Their statements are tinged with Socialist jargon, but the meanings remain clear—defense of civil liberties, condemnation of torture, freedom for the masses, guarantees for individual freedom, and exhortation for all citizens to fight against those laws antithetical to their liberties.[4] Nevertheless, the lawyers have learned to adhere to the policies of their governments. The resolutions emanating from the various meetings of the members of the Arab Lawyers Union clearly indicate an acceptance of Pan-Arabism (the Arab nation is indivisible in the East and in the West), support for the Palestinian movement ("The Arab Lawyers Union—which sees in the Palestine revolution the noblest phenomenon in the modern history of our nation . . ."),[5] and anti-Americanism (the United States must be boycotted politically, culturally, and economically).[6] Judging also by the statements read at the meetings, the union seems to be dominated by those countries who favor socialism and who are opposed to the traditional states. Morocco is condemned for violation of civil liberties as well as for permitting American bases on Moroccan soil. Saudi Arabia is chastized for torturing political prisoners. Jordan is denounced for fighting the Palestinian *Fida'iyyin.*[7] The fact, too, that lawyers from the traditional states refused to attend the latest meetings, indicate a subjugation of the union by the "progressive" states.

Trade unions, as shown in Appendix 9A, comprise the best organized and most powerful of all the professional groups.[c] They have played in the past a

---

[c]Theoretically, farmer's organizations should play the most important role of all associational groups since two-thirds of the population of the Middle East is engaged in agricultural pursuits. Even though there are farm groups located in several countries, they have acquiesced to the dictates of the single party or the government, whichever one controls the activities of the professional subcultural groups. Charles Issawi, *Modernization of the Arab World*, edited by Jack Thompson and Robert Reischauer, Princeton: Van Nostrand, 1966, p. 143.

significant role in the political development of some Middle Eastern countries. During the colonial era, when political parties were frowned upon and either forbidden permit to form, forcefully disbanded, or severely curtailed, labor unions became the outlet for political expression. In many instances, trade unions were formed by the political parties, thereby ensuring a growing and active constituency.

As stated in the preambles of most of the trade unions in the Middle East, the unions' principle objectives, as defined in the bylaws, were to be the "defense, protection, or promotion of the occupational interests of their members."[8] The politicization of the unions at their inception, however, has affected greatly the fulfillment of these objectives. Much energy has been expended on politics. Because of this, the governments expect the unions to continue to play politics, thereby making it necessary to closely supervise the unions, while at the same time, ensuring that they remain weak.

With the introduction of the one party system to the more progressive states, labor unions have found themselves closely integrated into the party organization. In those countries that do not have the single-party system, trade unions are closely watched by the government for signs of a subversive nature. In both cases, the unions' power is curtailed and they have been relegated to playing a relatively minor role in power politics.[9]

Although a product of Western culture, the trade unions became a battleground for opposing theological concepts. Because Communist influence was strong in the European trade unions during the 1930s, communism was carried over into the fledgling unions of the Arab world where it was to spread and become the dominant force in several labor organizations. The Sudanese labor unions were successfully penetrated by the Communists who controlled the labor scene for several decades. Although those Sudanese labor unions that were Communist-led were dissolved, they were able to retain their power and were active in the abortive coup that took place in 1971 against the incumbent regime.

A Communist labor hierarchy also gained eminence in Algeria and Iraq. Being in control of the unions, the Communists were able to ally their organizations with the World Federation of Trade Unions (WFTU), a Communist-dominated worldwide trade organization whose policies are directed by the Soviet Union.[d] Nevertheless, in both Iraq and Algeria, Communist influence has ebbed, even though those two nations remain on friendly terms with Russia. Suspicions of Communist motives remain very strong in Iraq where it took a bloody coup to oust Qasim and his Communist supporters.

In opposition to the Communists, other trade unions were established and

---

[d]The Tunisian Labor Organization was at one time affiliated with the WFTU. However, because its leaders were unable to speak freely within the framework of the Communist organization, it withdrew. Willard Beling, *Modernization and African Labor; a Tunisian Case Study*, New York: Praeger, 1965, p. 80.

based on labor principles used in the United States and Great Britain. They affiliated themselves with the International Confederation of Free Trade Unions (ICFTU) which had been established purposely to oppose the WFTU and to give to those unions who did not desire to belong to a Communist-inspired organization a voice in world labor relations.

This ideological struggle has produced both a negative attitude toward world labor organizations and a desire to remain aloof from the conflict. Arab labor unions have, in fact, established their own trade organization, the International Confederation of Arab Trade Unions (ICATU). Because most labor unions are government controlled, they have begun to opt for those ideas their governments decree to be Arab—Arabism, Arab unity, and Arab socialism. Nevertheless, trade unions continue to act as a medium for Western penetration in those traditional countries that are now experiencing rapid economic growth, especially in the oil sector. Kuwait's first labor unions were not organized until 1964.[10] Saudi Arabia now employs over 300,000 foreign workers, the majority of whom belong to petroleum cooperative societies.[e] Unfortunately for the Saudi regime, some workers will not only listen to ideas expounded upon by their labor union, but they will also adhere to the teachings of more subversive personnel whose sole aim is to overthrow the traditional rulers and establish revolutionary governments. Heretofore, dissidents were readily controlled. However, with a highly trained core and an organized mass, a potential threat to the traditional rulers could possibly develop.

Trade unions in the Middle East were first begun in Egypt in the 1890s.[11] However, it was not until 1942 that workers in Egypt were given, by law, the right to organize. This law was an attempt by the government to maintain order and security, and to harness the activities and energy of the labor mass by channeling it into controllable outlets. Heretofore, the labor mass was a mob, easily dominated by political parties whose intent was to demoralize its opposition. According to the 1942 law, union members had to register. At the same time, political activities were denied them.[12] Nevertheless, labor unions were given a legal status.

Even though restricted legally from participation in politics, labor unions continued to foment political unrest. The labor demonstrations in 1954 that helped Nasser consolidate his position was a political ploy staged by his followers.[13] The strikes and demonstrations in February 1968 were again of a political nature since their purpose was to protest the light sentences meted out to those officials blamed for Egypt's defeat in 1967.[14]

Labor is organized in Egypt under the auspices of the Arab Socialist Union (ASU). The charter of the ASU glorifies the worker and places the condition that one half the members of the ASU must be either workers or farmers.[15]

---

[e]Labor unions are still prohibited in Saudi Arabia and the other countries of the Arabian peninsula. Nevertheless, labor has been permitted to form cooperatives, which, for all intents and purposes, are trade unions.

Nevertheless, the ASU places strict control on labor. It undertakes all bargaining activities, sets wages, permits no strikes, and in general stifles initiative and incentive on the part of the unions. Since the nationalization of most industries in Egypt, union membership numbers approximately one-and-a-half million.[16] Even though in recent years labor has flexed its muscles by demonstrating and causing riots, labor is considered to be weak. Laborers still work a forty-two-hour work week (six days a week, seven hours a day). Minimum wages for unskilled labor are still approximately fifty cents a day. During the strikes in 1968 and again in 1971 when the workers protested their working conditions, troops were sent to quell the strikers.[17f] What must be remembered, though, is that the unions did attempt to force the government to take action in their favor, a feat that is a rarity in the Arab world.

The only other Arab country whose labor unions have shown an independence of action is Morocco. The Union Marocaine du Travail (Moroccan Trade Union—UMT) dominates the labor sector of the country. Its membership numbers approximately 700,000 while most of the other smaller unions are affiliated with it. Because of its tenacious adherence to an independent policy, the leadership of the union has refused a ministerial chair.[18] To accept would be to put the organization under an obligation to the throne. As it is, the union is a close supporter of the government—supporting its development programs. Nevertheless, its criticism of specific government activities, or lack of it, has caused some of the leaders to be imprisoned. What must be stressed is that the UMT is a national organization and, as such, stresses Moroccan nationalism. Its policies are directed toward the Moroccan laborer, since unemployment is approximately 30 to 40 percent. By championing the labor class, the organization retains a power that could make it a worthy opponent to the government. However, in acquiescing to the imprisonment of its leaders, without demonstrations or strikes, one is given the impression that the government has nothing to fear from organized labor in Morocco.

The other leading trade union is the Union Generale des Travaileurs du Maroc (General Union of Moroccan Laborers—UGTM). This body is closely allied to the Istiqlal Party and was, in fact, founded by that party in opposition to the UMT, which had refused to join the Istiqlal Party as an affiliate. Its policies, therefore, are not of an independent nature and are dictated by the Istiqlal Party. Although the former leader of the party, Allal al-Fasi, considered himself to be in opposition to the palace, he, nevertheless, accepted the monarchy and was therefore, considered a loyal opponent. His successor follows this same practice. The UGTM has come out in favor of the Palestinians, a united Maghrib, irredentism over Mauritania, and limited socialism—policies that have been advocated by the Istaqlal Party.[19]

---

fThe strike itself was called an "aggression against the interests of workers and the peoples' property." John Cooley, "UAR Labor Strikes at Iron, Steel Center," *The Christian Science Monitor*, August 31, 1971, p. 2.

There have been strikes and demonstrations over unemployment.[20] Labor has also gone on strike in sympathy with students who were demonstrating ostensibly for administrative reforms in the schools and universities. The security forces, however, were able to suppress the demonstrators with ease.

The other states of North Africa—Algeria, Tunisia, and Libya—have labor unions dominated either by the single party or the government. The unions are deeply aware of the economic conditions existing in their countries yet feel that only through cooperation with their respective governments will anything be accomplished.[21]

There have been reported periods of disagreement between the unions and the government in Tunisia. The cause of tension has usually been over who should defend the workers' interests.[22] However, the General Tunisian Labor Union (Union Generale Tunisienne du Travail—UGTT), is too closely allied to the government to remain in disagreement for a lengthy period of time. Approximately 21 percent of organized labor in Tunisia works for the government. Furthermore, its ranks are replete with Destourian Socialist Party cadres.

Since the takeover by the military in Libya in 1970, very little information has become available to the researcher. It was known that, prior to the coup d'etat, the labor sector was organized under one union, the National Trade Unions Federation, with a membership of approximately 30,000. It was affiliated with both the ICFTU and its Arab counterpart, the ICATU. Its president, Salim Shita, was elected to both the Libyan parliament and to the presidency of the ICATU.

Closely watched by the monarchy, the labor union was careful not to antagonize the government.[23] This close scrutiny was necessitated by the influx of workers from other North African countries seeking employment in the burgeoning oil industry.[g] Almost xenophobic in outlook, the Libyan government was highly fearful of the penetration of subversive ideas emanating at this time from Egypt and Algeria.[24]

With the nationalization of certain oil industries and the ouster of Italian and other foreign communities, the labor sector must be undergoing some change. It is conceivable that additional Egyptian and Palestinian technicians have had to be brought in to replace those foreigners who were required to leave. Nevertheless, it is certain that the government retains close supervision of its primary source of income, the oil industry.

Algerian labor was at one time the most powerful of all labor movements in North Africa. Affiliated with the French unions since its beginning in 1932, it was not until 1956 that Algerian labor became an independent entity. Then it

---

[g]Approximately 2,500 foreign technicians were employed in the oil industries, 1,600 of whom were from the Arab states. Of this number, the majority came from Egypt. In addition, 10,000 day laborers entered Libya from Algeria and Tunisia. Richard Ward, "The Long Run Employment Prospects for Middle East Labor," *Middle East Journal* 24, no. 2 (Spring 1970): 154.

was used specifically by the nationalists to further the cause of independence and the revolution. Since independence the unions have been under the direct control of the Front de Liberation Nationale (FLN) and have little say in the running of their organizations. However, it must be remembered that the Algerian revolution disrupted the economy of the state. The majority of the French who controlled the nation's economic sector returned to metropolitan France, leaving behind much chaos. Since 1962, with the help of the oil and gas industries, Algeria has made remarkable strides in its development. Nevertheless, although the number of members in the trade unions has swelled to over half a million, labor organizations remain in a weakened state, guided by the government through the auspices of the FLN.

Elsewhere in the Arab world, trade unions either do not exist or remain untried and in a weakened state. The area as a whole is only now being developed. Unemployment will be a serious problem for some time to come.[25] Many workers, especially in North Africa, will be forced to find work in Europe. The Palestinian refugees will continue to be a disruptive force, not only for Jordan, but also for Lebanon and Syria. These problems, coupled with the present repressive actions taken by the Arab governments, will continue to ensure debilitated labor organizations in the region. However, there are signs pointing to a rise in the effectiveness of the trade unions. There is a trend in Lebanon to support the unions. They are being credited with "raising the workers' social and economic standards. . . ."[26] Strikes in Morocco, Egypt, and Bahrain denote not only a strength to challenge the government but also the ability to demand publicly their desires in a time honored (Western) tradition. As more and more development capital is expended, it is expected that labor unions will expand. This expansion will be helped, too, by the nationalization policies of the "progressive" states. It is hoped that, in time, an increase in the size of the labor memberships will result in better governing policies for the unions.

# Appendix 9-A:
## Principle Trade Unions

### Algeria

*Union Generale des Travailleurs Algerians—UGTA:* f. 1956; 300,000 members
Affiliated with the UGTA are the:
*Federation des Travailleurs de l'Alimentation et du Commerce* (Federation of
Food and Commerce Workers): f. 1965; 14,000 members.
*Federation du Bois, du Batiment, des Travaux Publics et des Activités
Annexés* (Federation of Building Trades Workers): f. 1964; 17,000
members.
*Federation des Travailleurs de l'Education et de la Culture—FTEC* (Federa-
tion of Teachers): f. 1962; 13,000 members.
*Federation Nationale des Cheminots* (National Federation of Railwaymen).
*Federation Nationale de l'Energie Electrique et du Gas d'Algerie—FNEEGA*
(National Federation of Utility Workers): f. 1963; 5,000 members.
*Federation des Travailleurs des Mines et Carrières* (Federation of Mine and
Quarry Workers): f. 1965.
*Federation des Travailleurs Municipaux d'Algerie* (Federation of Municipal
Employees): 15,000 members.
*Federation des Travailleurs du Petrole, du Gaz et Assimiles* (Federation of Oil
and Gas Workers): f. 1964; 8,000 members.
*Federation des Ports, Docks et Aeroports* (Federation of Dock and Airport
Workers): f. 1964; 2,500 members.
*Federation des Postes et Telecommunications* (Federation of Postal and
Telecommunications Workers): f. 1964; 6,000 members.
*Federation Nationale de la Santé* (Federation of Hospital Workers): f. 1962;
15,000 members.
*Federation Nationale des Travailleurs de la Terre—FNTT* (Federation of Farm
Workers): f. 1964.

### Iraq

*General Federation of Iraqi Trade Unions:* f. 1964; 19 unions, 250,000 mem-
bers.
*Union of Teachers.*
*Union of Palestinian Workers in Iraq.*

### Jordan

*The General Federation of Jordanian Trade Unions:* f. 1954; 15,000 members.
There are also a number of independent unions, including:

*Drivers' Union.*
*Union of Petroleum Workers and Employees.*


## Libya

*National Trade Unions' Federation:* (affiliated to ICFTU); f. 1952; 30,000 members.
*Union of Petroleum Workers of Libya.*


## Morocco

*Union Marocaine du Travail (U.M.T.):* 700,000 members.
*Union Générale des Travailleurs du Maroc (U.G.T.M.):* supported by unions not affiliated to U.M.T.
*Syndicat National Libre:* f. 1958; 69,000 members.
*Union Marocaine de l'Agriculture (U.M.A.).*


## The Sudan

*Federations*

*Federations of Sudanese Workers' Unions (F.S.W.U.):* f. 1963; includes 135 affiliates totalling 450,000 members; affiliated to the International Confederation of Trade Union Federations and the All-African Trade Union Federation.
*Federation of Workers' Trade Unions of the Private Sector:* f. 1965.
*Federation of Workers' Trade Unions of the Public Sector:* f. 1965.


*Principal Unions*

*Central Electricity and Water Administration Trade Union:* 3,000 members.
*Department of Agriculture Trade Union:* 1,170 members.
*Egyptian Irrigation Department Trade Union:* 1,210 members.
*Forestry Department Trade Union:* f. 1961; 2,510 members.
*Gezira Board Non-Agricultural Workers' Union:* f. 1961; 6,600 members.
*Khartoum Municipality Trade Union:* 891 members.
*Khartoum University Trade Union:* f. 1947; 1,400 members.
*Mechanical Transport Department Trade Union:* 2,593 members.
*Ministry of Education Trade Union:* 679 members.

*Ministry of Health Trade Union:* 3,592 members.
*Ministry of Irrigation and Hydro-Electric Power Trade Union:* 15,815 members.
*Ministry of Works Trade Union:* 607 members.
*Posts and Telegraphs Trade Union:* 700 members.
*Sudan Textile Industry Employees Trade Union:* f. 1968; 3,750 members.
*Sudan Railway Workers' Union (S.R.W.U.):* f. 1961; 28,000 members.


## Tunisia

*Union Générale Tunisienne du Travail (U.G.T.T.):* f. 1946 by Farhat Hached;
   affiliated to ICFTU; 150,000 members in 23 affiliated unions.
*Union Générale des Etudiants de Tunisie (U.G.E.T.):* f. 1953; 600 members.
*Union Nationale des Femmes de Tunisie (U.N.F.T.):* f. 1956; 37,000 members.


## United Arab Republic

*U.A.R. Federation of Labour (U.A.R.F.L.):* f. 1957; 27 affiliated unions; 1.5
   million members; affiliated to the International Confederation of Arab Trade
   Unions and to the All-African Trade Union Federation.
*Arab Federation of Food Workers (AFFW):* 500,000 members.
*Federation of Arab Engineers.*
*General Trade Union of Agriculture:* 350,000 members.
*General Trade Union of Banking and Insurance:* 32,000 members.
*General Trade Union of Building Industries:* 46,000 members.
*General Trade Union of Business and Management Services:* 46,000 members.
*General Trade Union of the Chemical Industries:* 60,000 members.
*General Trade Union of Engineering, Electrical and Metal Industries:* 70,000
   members.


## People's Democratic Republic of Yemen

*General Confederation of Workers of the People's Republic of Southern Yemen:*
   f. 1956; affiliated to W.F.T.U. and I.C.A.T.U.; 35,000 members.
   There are fifteen Registered Trade Unions, including the following:
*General and Port Workers' Union.*
*Forces and Associated Organizations Local Employees' Union.*
*Government and Local Government Employees' Union.*
*General Union of Petroleum Workers.*
*Miscellaneous Industries Employees' Union.*
*Aden Port Trust Employees' Union.*

*Civil Aviation Employees' Union.*

*Banks Local Staff Union.*

Source: *The Middle East and North Africa 1971-72*, London: Europa Publications, Ltd., 1971, *passim.*

# 10 The Communicators

The communicators, as a subculture group, have the greatest potential power to influence others. Their number includes journalists, editors of newspapers, magazine and publishing houses, cinema directors, television and radio personnel, writers, playwrights, and poets. They have the facilities to reach the public—with newspapers, books, magazines, movies, and broadcasting stations. By means of these media, the communicators' political, social, and economic ideas should stimulate a society and, therefore, should produce some reaction.

When speaking of the Middle East, the preceding paragraph becomes conjecture or its contents weakened by mitigating circumstances occurring in the region. The communicators in almost all the countries of the region are handicapped by laws limiting their potential. Except for Lebanon and Kuwait, and to a lesser extent Morocco, the governments either control or own the communication media. What is disseminated must first be approved by the regime in power. It follows, then, that change or even the maintenance of the *status quo* is dependent on the policies of those in power.

Then too, the audience in general in the Middle East is not receptive to messages put forth by the communicators, and therefore, further limits their impact. One study, undertaken in Egypt in 1966, pointed out that the majority of the readers of *Al-Ahram* newspaper read first a serialized version of Tarzan, followed by the sections entitled "Morning News" (having to do with local news stories) and "Your Fortune Today." Editorials and science news items were those sections least read by the public.[1]

Nonreceptivity by the reading public was again pointed out when field work in Egypt was undertaken by a doctoral candidate who wanted to prove or disprove whether the communicators were successful in putting across their message to the general public. The author learned from his sample questionnaire that the attitudes of the majority of those polled remained unchanged. The communicators failed in their campaign to alter their audiences' disposition toward the status of women, superstition, and other traditional values. He found that the fatalistic attitude toward life in general, fostered by Islamic precepts and religious teachers, was too well entrenched to penetrate.[2]

Middle Eastern communicators also fail to reach their public because of the presentation of their ideas. Rhetoric plays a great part in the written word of the Arab, so much so that meaning or emphasis takes second place to stylized structure and verbosity. Furthermore, many of the tools with which the communicators work are relatively new to the user. It is only in the last decade that television has made some advancement in the region. In most areas outside the urban centers, television is still unknown, and the caliber of locally produced shows is of relatively poorer quality than those produced in the countries where the media industries have been established for a longer time.

Furthermore, almost all modern Arab writers are engaged in political activities. They tend to neglect the cultural contributions they could make toward society.[3]

The art of journalism in the Middle East was begun in the second half of the nineteenth century. Generally speaking, advocate journalism was the rule. Newspapers were initiated as personal organs of political parties or of politicians. The main function was the propagation of the party's or owner's point of view rather than the dissemination of information. This same function holds true today for many of the newspapers published in the region. Lebanon, for example, has approximately ninety-six newspapers, the majority of which advocate the wishes of their sponsors. The numbers of publications the Lebanese public must read to grasp all sides of an issue is therefore staggering, and makes it virtually an impossible feat to accomplish. The result must be confusion for the reader.

### The Press

There are in the Arab world approximately three hundred dailies, two hundred weeklies, and more than five hundred periodicals. These numbers include government agency publications as well as scholarly and specialized journals. Circulation varies in number. However, except for the Egyptian papers, *Al-Ahram, Akhbar al-Yom*, and *Al-Akhbar*, which circulate more than 250,000 copies daily, few other newspapers sell over 20,000 per issue.[4]

Longevity of a newspaper has been generally short, a few years at the most. The reasons for this have been the size of circulation, lack of advertisement, and demise or failure of the political backer. Since most of the publications are now government-owned or controlled, the precariousness of the private publishing industry has become greater. However, government control could also bring stability and respite to some publishers, depending upon their strict adherence to the laws. Those papers under government control will probably be dependent upon how long a regime remains in power.

There are, however, a few newspapers that have survived the numerous coups and revolutions that have taken place in the Arab world since their founding. Among these are: *Al-Ahram*, the oldest in the region, founded in 1877; *Al-Hilal*, the oldest monthly, 1892; *Al-Musawwar*, a weekly, 1924; and *Al-Nahar*, a daily, 1934. All the above are Egyptian except the last which is Lebanese.

In Egypt, the press is only semi-autonomous. All major papers have been placed under the control of the Arab Socialist Union, while journalists are required to obtain licenses (work permits) in order to ply their trade. Nevertheless, there is a great deal of freedom permitted when journalists write on domestic affairs. However, when writing on foreign relations, the governments' official line must be followed.

Of all the newspapers in the Arab world, the Egyptian dailies are considered to be the most important. Not only are they sold widely within the country, but they also have a large circulation throughout the region, where permitted, of course. Because of the wide coverage of Egypt's most important paper, *Al-Ahram*, its former editor-in-chief, Muhammad Hassanain Haykal, is well known worldwide and is considered to be an important Arab personage. His father, Muhammad Husayn Haykal, was considered to be one of the leading writers of the Arab world. The younger Haykal's book, *Nasser and the World*, published in 1971, has been serialized in more than twenty worldwide papers. His weekly column, *Frankly Speaking*, was considered to reflect the opinions of the Egyptian government, not only on foreign policy but also on domestic affairs. From his writings, Haykal may be judged to be first of all, an Egyptian nationalist, and secondly, a believer in positive neutralism as advocated by the late President Nasser. As such, he believes that diplomatic relations with the United States should be ongoing. With regard to Arab unity and Arab nationalism, he favors both, yet shows his Egyptian nationalist stance by emphasizing the difference between the Arabic terms *qawmiyah* (nationalism) and *wataniyah* (patriotism). He rationalized that one can be at the same time both an Arab nationalist and an Egyptian patriot. For him, patriotism is the love of the land in which one is reared and nationalism is the attachment and loyalty due to the whole Arab nation. In an interview published in the April 1972 edition of *Jeune Afrique*, Haykal was asked by Pierre Demeson where he stands vis-à-vis the West and the East. His reply was: "I am not for the West nor the East, I am for Egypt and the Arab nation; I am not a Communist, I am an Egyptian Arab nationalist."[5]

Haykal's career as a leading journalist, as well as his close association with President Nasser, placed him in a very influential position in Egypt. As such, he attempted to forward his ideas regarding Arab socialism (which he accepted as a viable system), Russia (with which an alliance must be maintained), and increased liberalism within the government. He recommended, upon the death of President Nasser, that Zakaria Muhiyyidin, a former pro-Western prime minister who had fallen from power because of his insistence on better relations with the United States, be returned to the premiership. Above all, he seemed to speak for the upper-middle class of which he is a part.

When speaking of religion, Haykal advocated partial separation of powers between church and state. Yet, because he is a practicing Muslim, he did not come out in favor of complete withdrawal of Islam from temporal matters. His position clearly indicated a middle-of-the-road stance where reform of Islam is necessary, yet it must be retained as the religion of the state.

There are other influential journalists in Egypt. Among this elite cadre is Lutfi al-Khuli. A lawyer by education, but a journalist by profession, he has not only contributed to the leading papers in Egypt but was also an editor of *Al-Tali'ah*, a monthly that speaks for the extreme left. He has been imprisoned several times for his affiliation with the Communist party. In January 1972, he was one of the principal speakers at the Lebanese Communist Party's Third Congress, held in Beirut. Al-Khuli has accommodated himself to Arab socialist ideology and in his articles, has defended Nasser's theories. This has caused many Egyptian Communists who are rigid in their beliefs and practices to part from him. Nevertheless, he continues to have some appeal to the students and the extreme leftists.

Ahmad Baha al-Din, editor since 1965 of *Al-Musawwar*, the oldest weekly in the Arab world, and board chairman of the Dar al-Hilal publishing house, has great ability for reportage and analysis of the news. He recently was elected president of the Arab Association of Journalists, whose members come from the entire Arab world. As an Arab socialist, he has devoted much time in his articles to explain to the public the general principles of Nasser's Arab socialism. He believes that the tenets of the Arab left are meaningless unless they are incorporated with Nasser's theories. The left was unable to accomplish anything alone, except to call attention to the threat of imperialism and will only succeed in achieving their goals by accepting Arab socialism and by being guided by the Arab socialists. However, he continues to revere Karl Marx as one of the great economists and sociologists in modern times.

In a recent discussion with President Qadhafi of Libya in which a number of leading Egyptian intellectuals participated, Baha al-Din stated that Islam is a religion that addresses itself to man's conscience, while its secular precepts are to be used only as guidelines. Communism as a religion has now become passé. From his statements, we can deduce that church and state should be separate. However, he has never directly come out and said this. He did attack the ideas of the Islamic League when it was first advocated by ex-King Faysal of Saudi Arabia, thereby strengthening the belief that religion should not be linked with politics.

Although jailed for his beliefs, he remains an ardent Egyptian nationalist and, on many subjects of domestic nature, a successful propagandist of the official line. His style is simplistic and is therefore more effective with the mass of readers than is Haykal, who writes in a more sophisticated and analytical way.

The Amin brothers have also reemerged into the journalistic limelight, one after having been jailed, the other after being exiled. Opposed to Nasser, they back the actions taken by Anwar al-Sadat. Since their return to the field of journalism is relatively new, their impact remains limited. Yet they, through their paper *Akhbar al-Yom*, have the potential to become great influencers in Egypt.

In Lebanon, the press has more freedom than anywhere else in the Arab world. Freedom of the press is guaranteed by law. However, certain restrictions are placed on it. For example, defamation of a foreign head of state or derogatory statements regarding official policy are banned. Licenses must be obtained before publication can begin; they can be withdrawn by the government if the publisher permits the above conditions to be printed, if publication is voluntarily suspended for six months, or if circulation falls below 1500 a month. The editor, too, must be a university graduate.

The Lebanese press displays a wide perspective of opinions ranging from the extreme right to the extreme left. Included in the ninety-six newspapers published in the country are those representing foreign interests. However, the large number reflects the denominational makeup of the state. Each religious community has at least one organ and one finds these papers published not only in Arabic but also in French, English, and Armenian.

There are numerous weeklies published in Lebanon that are widely distributed throughout the Middle East. *Al-Usbu'a al-'Arabi* sells more than 100,000 copies. Only *Al-Shabakah*, a weekly devoted to light and gossipy material, outsells *Al-Usbu'a al-'Arabi*. The latter is owned by George Abu'Adal, a wealthy businessman, with his editor-in-chief being Yasir Huwari. The editorials of *Al-Usbu'a al-'Arabi* are to be considered as moderate, reflecting the middle class business community. Emphasis of the weekly is on illustrated news reports, with behind-the-scenes coverage and analysis of important events taking precedence. Huwari is from a well-to-do Muslim family and is a graduate of the American University of Beirut and the University of London College of Journalism. Although moderate in his views, he does support Arab unity and decries communism. He does not believe in Arab socialism, though, as an economic or political system. His *bête noire* is Israel which he believes was established in the Middle East by the imperialist powers to be used as a base from which to strike against those who attempt to challenge their interest.

*Al-Hawadith*, a weekly publication having a format and approach similar to that of *Al-Usbu'a al-'Arabi*, enjoys a large audience located throughout the Middle East. Like *Al-Usbu'a al-'Arabi*, it caters to the middle class. Salim al-Lawzi, the editor, is vociferous on the Palestinian cause, which he supports. However, his championing of their movement has not prevented him from attacking the Palestinians, mainly for their activities in Lebanon.

Al-Lawzi advocates Arab unity yet does not adhere to Arab socialism as advanced by the Nasserites. To have viable socialism, democracy must be present. Furthermore, without democracy, the way is opened for the bureaucrats to infiltrate into the highest ranking government positions. Bureaucracy, to him, is as bad as security forces or power centers that cripple popular participation in the government.

Leftist attitudes are represented by several papers, among them the weeklies *Al-Akhbar* and *Al-Anba'*. The rightist papers are *Al-'Amal*, the organ of the Kata'ib party, and *Al-Hayat*, whose editor, Kamil Muruwah, was assassinated for his conservative points of view.

Perhaps the most forceful and influential communicator in Lebanon is Ghassan Tueni, at times referred to as the Lord Thompson of Lebanon because he owns two large newspapers, the Arabic daily *Al-Nahar* and the French daily *L'Orient*, and a number of other publications in Lebanon. Second only to *Al-Ahram*, *Al-Nahar* is the most widely read daily in the Arab world. Furthermore, *Al-Nahar* maintains its standards of excellence by employing some of the leading Lebanese columnists; for example, Michael Abu Jawdah, whose editorial columns on Arab international and internal affairs are widely read. Furthermore, *Al-Nahar* is the only Arabic newspaper whose editorial page usually includes three columns that express numerous, and at times contradictory, opinions.

Tueni, the son of a prominent journalist, was born into the upper middle class of Beirut society. Greek Orthodox in religion, and a graduate of the American University of Beirut and Harvard University, Tueni built the Dar al-Nahar publishing house into a huge financial concern. He was once elected to the Lebanese Parliament and became its youngest vice-president (1951-1953). He was also a member of the Lebanese delegation to the United Nations and the Minister of Education and Information in 1971. Although minister for only two months, he was influential in removing all censorship except on military news, a precautionary move originally taken by the government during the internal disorders in 1969.

Although a member of the Syrian Social Nationalist Party in his youth, Tueni is now skeptical of Arab unity. He firmly believes in the democratic process of government, with a separation of state and religion, and freedom of the press. Because of his strong Lebanese nationalism, his influence is greatest in his country, but less so in the more "progressive" countries whose leaders consider him to be too pro-Western.

Another influential Lebanese journalist is Sa'id Furayha. He, too, is the owner of a large publishing concern, which issues the daily *Al-Anwar*, the weekly *Al-Sayyad*, and the very popular *Al-Shabakah*. Although a Greek Orthodox, Furayha has defended Arab unity and Arab socialism.

Lebanon is host to numerous political refugees, connected with the press, from other Arab countries. For example, the former Ba'thist leader and prime minister of Syria, Salah al-Bitar, has often contributed written articles on the Arab world's political problems from his moderate Ba'thist viewpoint. Baland al-Haydari, an Iraqi Communist; the Sudanese poet Muhammad al-Fayturi; and the Palestinian journalist, Ghassan Kanafani, killed by Israeli agents, who was editor of *Al-Hadaf*, the organ of the Popular Front for the Liberation of Palestine all resided in Beirut and expressed their opinions freely.

One of the most influential publications found in the Middle East is *Al-'Arabi*, a monthly published in Kuwait by the Ministry of Information. Although a government magazine, it has great appeal for the Arab masses by combining the styles and format of the *Reader's Digest, National Geographic*, and the *Saturday Review*. Above all, it is filled with pictures and sold at a modest price enabling the poorer classes in the Arab world to purchase it. Its format seems to cover a multitude of subjects. A typical issue (March 1972) contains a long essay on the freedom of the press, a section on Islamic affairs concerning itself with personal opinion (*ijtihad*) in the *Shari'ah* or Sacred Law and Islam and social security; a section on language and literature that contains an article on the travels of the Arab-American writer Amin Rihani; a report on the Eighth Congress of Arab Writers; and a section of illustrations, including the Islamic holy places in Jerusalem under Israeli occupation, as well as the new Federation of Arab Amirates. In addition to the regular sections found in each issue, there are several special reports on medicine, education, economics, and poetry, as well as book reviews.

The editor of *Al-'Arabi* is Dr. Ahmad Zaki, an Egyptian scientist, who tries constantly to inculcate into the magazine's readers a scientific spirit. However, he also attempts, through his articles, to strengthen a liberal spirit throughout the Arab world based on the Islamic heritage. For this reason, one finds a permanent section in each issue on religion. There is no conflict between Islam and science, each one accommodating the other. Zaki is an advocate of Arab unity and through the illustrated travel section, he makes it possible for the masses to know and visualize distant parts of all the Arab lands. As a liberal, he is strongly against communism, but stresses moderate Arab socialism.

The press in the other Arab states does not play as important a role in the Arab world as does that of Lebanon, Egypt, and Kuwait. Circulation is smaller and, in several states, government control has turned the press into propagandist machinery for the central regime. Morocco's journalists have not been muted as much as those in the "progressive" states. The leading papers, however, are basically organs of the leading political parties and generally follow the function of advocate journalism commonly found in the Arab states. *L'Opinion*, the Moroccan paper having the largest circulation, is the Istiqlal Party's organ. As such, it strongly endorses the Palestinian guerrilla movement. It also gives full coverage of events taking place in the Maghrib, especially those dealing with matters relating to unity of the Maghrib states.

In summary, the Arab press in general acts, not as a collector and disseminator of information, but instead defends or advocates the points of view of its sponsors, be they the government, political parties, politicians, or founders. Criticism is permitted against policies taken by the governments. However, this is usually done within certain specified perimeters delineated by the government. Lebanon is the exception, where freedom of the press, except for military matters and criticism of foreign heads of state, is the general rule.

## The Writers

The writer, more than anyone else, should reflect a nation's heartbeat. He is the observer of life, the pulse taker so to speak of a nation, who expresses in words what is happening. If he is a dedicated person whose writings have impact, he can lead a people in their fight for decency and right. The adage, "The pen is mightier than the sword," would aptly apply to him. However, in the Arab world writers have, in general, little impact on the mainstream of life. They observe and they comment. It is probably because they themselves are in conflict with their own world and with themselves. Although emersing themselves in Western thought and techniques they have been unable to divorce themselves from their traditional upbringing. The results have been literary works instead of manuscripts to galvanize a society to action.

The modern Arab writer began to gain in prominence during the 1920s and 1930s with the publication of the works of Tawfiq al-Hakim, Muhammad Husayn Haykal, and Taha Husayn—all Egyptians. Although their writings are social in genre, they either conformed or were made to conform to the religious and social precepts in existence at that time. They wrote of the Egyptian countryside in which they grew up. They also wrote of themselves when experiencing the fruits of European culture. They did call attention to the plight of the *fellah* (peasant) but little was done to alleviate rural life's conditions until the military coup of 1952, which brought Nasser to power.

The 1952 Egyptian revolution, the defeats by Israel, and the Algerian revolution seem to have been the three catalysts that have encouraged Arab writers to speak out strongly against the ills of their own society, against imperialism, and for socialism and Palestinian rights. Censorship does tend to eliminate excesses of criticism. However, writers are beginning to realize that they have a duty—to change or revolutionalize Arab society, and to eliminate the traditional aspects of it by creating their own modern society. Egyptian writers such as Naguib Mahfuz and Ihsan 'Abd al-Qudus have criticized the regime and have analyzed the malaise existing in their country as stemming from the confusion by the government over what their national goals should be. In Lebanon, Halim Barakat and Leila Ba'albaki are writing on the social problems found in Lebanon, as well as on the Palestinian problem.

North African writers continue to face a perpetual dilemma. They feel betrayed by the West and therefore try to reject it. However, they are not accepted by their own countrymen because they are unable to identify with them and are unable to divest themselves of Western culture.[6] Elsewhere in the Arab world, however, some writers have successfully turned away from their Western tutors and have begun to express themselves in those ideals that are Arab. They are able to accommodate what is modern to Arab traditionalism. Others, too, have turned their backs completely on Western culture and ideas, rejecting the roots of modernity and taking up the traditional cause.

One precept that is very strong among most writers today is the belief in one strong Arab nation. This feeling for Pan-Arabism arose from the defeats inflicted by the Israelis on the Arabs, as well as the moral victory of the Arabs in 1973. Since any one Arab state is unable to eliminate the Israeli "imperialist" state, then it must be done through the concerted efforts of all Arab nations. However, since they are unable to cooperate sufficiently to defeat Israel, then it must be done by one nation, whose leaders control the destinies of all the Arabs.

Hand-in-glove with Pan-Arabism is the precept of Arab socialism. Only through a revolutionized society will the malaise existing in the Arab world be alleviated.

An editorial in the journal *Al-Udaba' al-Arab*, published by The General Union of Arab Writers, entitled "Hadhihi al-Majallah, li madha?" (*This Journal, Why?*), summarizes the position taken by the consensus of Arab writers today, whether they be novelists or journalists:

> The writers who constitute the educated and conscious vanguard of the Arab nation, have asserted their conviction that the Palestine Question is a reflection of the diabolical alliance against the Arab homeland and against the Palestinians' right to retrieve their land and their legitimate claims.
>
> The writers have also asserted that only substantial change in the Arab situation of division and backwardness is the only means to complete liberation and the elimination, from Arab lands, of all their enemies.[7]

Rightists, such as Muhammad al-Ka'ak, editor of *Al-Sha'ab wa al-Ard*, who is suspected of adhering to the cause of the MBA, as well as leftists, such as 'Ali Ahmad Sa'id, editor of the leftist journal *Mawaqif*, agree with the general consensus as stated in *Al-Udaba' al-Arab*. Incidentally, the new leftists are rejecting those ideals that are Western, as well as those that are Russian. They want only an Arab culture; an Arab society, based on the socialist precepts of Nasser and the Ba'thists, and one Arab nation. Nevertheless, even if Arab writers are unsuccessful in leading a crusade for social improvement or elimination of imperialism in their region, they at least are able to call attention to the shortcomings in their society and, thereby, create a greater degree of sympathy.

## Radio and Television

A huge communications network now covers the Arab Middle East. According to the *Americana Encyclopedia* 1972 *Yearbook*, a total of 11,832,000 radio receivers and 2,130,000 television sets are found in the region. When taking into account the fact that approximately 65 percent of the inhabitants in the Arab world are illiterate, radio and television media can be used to reach a vast audience which the press and the cinema cannot do. This fact has been recognized by the Arab governments and explains why all radio stations and television channels, except in Lebanon, are owned and run by those in power. Lebanon has three television channels that are privately owned. However, those rules that apply to press censorship are also in force for television.

Radio formats are varied, yet all contain similar programs. There are usually recitations from the Koran, news, music, poetry and play readings, and interviews. During times of crisis, martial music dominates the airs, punctuated by government communiques.

Some foreign language programs are broadcast at certain times, primarily for the enjoyment of the foreign communities in resident. These are limited, though, in time (usually a half hour), and in number (generally once or twice daily).

Because television is a recent acquisition of the Arab world, some experimentation is taking place. Locally produced shows are coming into prominence, yet the majority of the programs aired are from abroad. In Lebanon, most of the shows are either American, British, or French; and in Egypt, most come from the U.S.S.R. and other Eastern European countries. Those produced locally have included numerous panel discussions, some programs on the arts, and a few comedy situations. Egyptian cinema director Niazi Mustafa completed thirty-two half-hour programs on Islam—its inception, principal personalities, and historic events that led up to its ultimate triumph as the dominant religion from Afghanistan to Spain. It is interesting to note that the sound track of these segments was dubbed with English, Senegalese, and Urdu, and they were exported for world-wide consumption.[8]

The Egyptian government is capitalizing on Sawt al-Arab (Voice of the Arabs), the Middle East's largest and most influential radio station. It is being used by the government to disseminate information to all corners of the Arab world. It is also used extensively for propagandistic purposes. A typical daily program will include recitations from the Koran; a short religious sermon; music; summaries of major news items from the Cairo papers; two hours of "Radio Palestine"; and topical subjects such as "The Battle of Destiny," "The Arabs and the World," religion, Palestinian support, and the Israeli controversy—topics meant to weld the Arab nations together, with Egypt being in the pivotal role.

Music plays a tremendous role in the Arab world. Songs are used to emotionally affect the listening audience. Some carry political messages; others enumerate the glories of important personages such as the late President Nasser. Many of the most beautiful songs broadcast are related to the Palestine question. The best example is one recorded by Lebanon's leading singer, Fayruz, entitled *Sanarja'u* (We Shall Return), meaning the Palestinians will return to their land from which they were evicted by the Israelis.

Generally speaking, radio and television reflect a government's points of view and policies. For this reason and because more people are reached through radio and television, one of the first objectives of those staging a coup is to seize control of the stations and begin broadcasting their own policies to the public. Radio and television are, therefore, important enough to receive great attention, not only because they are instruments of communication used to reach the masses, but also because they reflect the power and prestige of the regime who controls them.

## The Cinema

The screen is a very popular and widespread communication medium in the urban centers of the Middle East. Except for Egypt, though, where the government has programmed movies to be shown in the rural areas, most of the hinterland in the Middle East remains devoid of movie houses or projectors. In Saudi Arabia and other parts of the Arabian peninsula, movies were forbidden to be shown to the public since it was considered a sin to portray man or even to see a picture of man who was made in God's image. Times are changing and the screen is now being introduced to the traditional areas of the Arab world and is, therefore, beginning to reach a large audience.

Many films shown in the urban centers are foreign in origin—French, American, British, Russian, Indian. Foreign movies are esteemed by the more sophisticated elites. However, locally produced films are preferred by the masses who are unable to understand a foreign language or even to read the Arabic subtitles.

Originally, movies made in the Arab world were produced with the purpose of entertaining their audiences. The basic themes were either melodramatic or comic. In the former, the most popular protagonist was the heroine, who, being a victim of circumstances, prostituted herself to save a distressed loved one. In comedies, the leading role was usually a man who continually found himself in trouble and who devised complicated yet comic means to extricate himself, in the mold of a Barber of Seville or a Charlie Chaplin.

Egypt has dominated the film industry in the Middle East since its introduction. Receptive to Western ideas and culture while containing the largest population and, therefore, the largest potential audience in the region, film-making rapidly expanded. Egyptian films, moreover, were and still are highly prized by Arab-speaking persons since Egyptian Arabic is the common language throughout the Arab world and is readily understood from Morocco to Iraq.

Most of the films produced in Egypt during the past two years have dealt with sociopolitical themes. They include both serious as well as comic plots, of which many are based on stories written by the principal Egyptian novelists—Najib Mahfuz, Yusuf Idris, Yusuf al-Siba'i, 'Abd al-Rahman al-Sharqawi, and Ihsan 'Abd al-Qudus. Most of these writers have followed the government's policy regarding Arab socialism, criticism of the monarchic regime, and defense of Egyptian and Arab causes. For the 1970 season, sociopolitical themes were predominant in the ten best pictures. In *Miramar*, considered to be the best film of the year, the author, Najib Mahfuz studied the effects, both social and psychological, which the Egyptian revolution has had on people who were prominent in the old regime. *Al-Ard* (The Earth) by al-Sharqawi, dealt with the tyranny of the feudalists over the peasants and the latter's love for the sustaining earth.

Religion was used only once as a theme for the 1970 season. However, the picture *Fajr al-Islam* (The Dawn of Islam) was produced on a large scale and in color. Nevertheless, religious attitudes and statements have appeared in numerous films, primarily as a sop to please the audience.

Documentary films are also made in Egypt. However, they reflect governmental themes emanating from the Ministry of Culture which produces them. Among such documentaries for the 1970 and 1971 seasons are found several on the war with Israel, including *Suez, My City*, which shows the destruction of Suez by Israeli bombardments; *Why?*, a documentary explaining why Palestinian commandos are fighting; and *The Mummies*, which deals with the looting of cultural finds from the archeological sites in Egypt. There were, of course, several shorts made on Nasser after his death.

The film industry elsewhere in the Middle East is still in its infancy. Lebanon has produced several films, as did Algeria. However, the Algerian cinema has been more interested in encouraging European producers to make movies in Algeria that deal purely with political problems than in producing their own. Two widely distributed movies of this type have been *The Algerian Revolution* and *Z.*

The Syrian cinema has begun to make a number of documentaries. Furthermore, it has hosted seminars on films and film-making, the most prominent being the International Congress for Young Movie Producers, held in Damascus in April 1972. During the sessions, several Syrian films were shown, among them being *A Song Along the Passage*, by 'Ali Salim, and a documentary entitled *We Are All Well*, which portrays the Arabs in Palestine who send to their relatives the message "We are all well," when in reality they are living in misery.

The congress, above all, revealed what Arab film producers thought should be the principal goals for their industry. The Lebanese producer and director George Shamshum, noted for his film *The Cats of al-Hamra Street*, continually insisted that movies are to be made for entertainment purposes. He was in the minority, however, since almost all the other participants agreed that they should commit themselves to produce works that carry political and social messages. Syria's leading producer, Karam Mutawi, summed up this attitude when he stressed that entertainment is ephemeral and provisional. A meaningful piece of art can be produced only when a man (in this case the producer or director) is aware of his surroundings and projects this awareness to his public. In other words, he should dedicate himself to a cause and tell his public about it.

It is from Egypt, though, that the producers and directors will most probably take their cues. Egyptian films are being sent abroad for viewing and some are receiving favorable receptions. Certainly one of the world's leading actors, Omar Sharif, who first gained prominence in the Egyptian film industry, is helping to publicize the Arab film industry, even if only by his acknowledgement of being a former Egyptian star. Propaganda will continue to play an important role in films. It is expected, therefore, that Egypt and other Arab countries will devote more attention to their film industries as a medium to reach their peoples.

## The Theater

The theater in the Arab world has only become a major category in communications within the past thirty years. The theatrical genre was not even considered to be part of the literary arts until it was given respectability by the Egyptian poet Ahmad Shawqi, and his fellow countryman, the author Tawfiq al-Hakim, in the 1920s and 1930s. Initially, the theater strove only to entertain its audiences. Messages were either absent from productions or played in a very low key so that they would not detract from a play's sole purpose—to entertain. Songs and dances were a mandatory part of each production.

Although the purpose of the theater today is still to entertain, many plays produced have important messages which the authors want to get across to the reviewers of their plays. An actor rarely cares for anything but his own success. He remains the medium through which the author and producer become communicators to the Arab public. As in the case of most communicators in the Middle East, the playwright's works are carefully scrutinized by the governments. Because of this, the majority of the theatrical writers has adopted the government line on whatever subject they want to relate.

The oldest theater in the Arab world is the Egyptian. However, it has only been in the last fifteen years that the theater has gained prominence. Among those contributing to the success of the theater have been the playwrights Nu'man 'Ashur, Lutfi al-Khuli, Yusuf Idris, 'Abd al-Rahman al-Sharqawi, Alfred Faraj, 'Ali Salim, and, of course, the father of Egypt's modern theater, Tawfiq al-Hakim. The latter continues to be a prolific writer, having produced in the past five years two plays: *Al-Sultan al-Ha'ir* (The Perplexed Ruler), and *Bank al-Qalaq* (The Worry Bank). The latter of the two plays is of great interest since the author approached his subject from a socialist point of view, thereby indicating an adherence to the government's Arab socialist policy.

Perhaps, the most significant development in the Egyptian theater has been the advent of the plays of 'Ali Salim. He began writing for the theater after the defeat of Egypt by Israel in 1967 and has aroused great interest in the country. Many plays following the June 1967 war dealt with the struggle against Israel and the subsequent defeat of their country. However, though the plays centered on the national struggle, struggle against tyranny, social injustice, and the question of Palestine, the authors were generally self-abusive in that they analyzed the causes for their loss, as well as the social injustices in their country, yet refrained from presenting positive action to overcome their country's faults. 'Ali Salim has gone much further than most in presenting a deeper insight into the ills of the Egyptian social and governmental systems. His first play of importance was the *Comedy of Oedipus* (subtitled *Ye Who Have Killed the Beast*) in which he strongly criticizes the entourage that surrounded President Nasser and created and augmented the myth of Nasser as a savior of his people. In this state of affairs, when the "beast" (Israel) attacked the city (Egypt) where Oedipus (Nasser) reigned, Oedipus was unable to kill the beast. The implication of course was that Nasser should purge himself of those surrounding him who led him to defeat and listen instead to the honest man of the street who will support him and give him victory. Salim's second play of importance is *A Song Along the Passage*, in which the author presents a realistic picture of the strengths and weaknesses of an Egyptian individual. The action of the play takes place during the June War when five Egyptian soldiers find themselves surrounded by the enemy. The reactions of the five to this situation make up the play's *raison d'être*. Each one is permitted to voice his attitudes toward nationalism and socialism, as well as courage and cowardice. The play symbolizes the plight in which the Egyptian people find themselves.

The play's success is derived from the fact that it is an honest presentation devoid of any idealization and misconceptions of the problems facing the people of the Arab world. Absent is the exhortative propaganda used to incite the public. As such, it could constitute a significant step toward a realistic approach to Egyptian existence and, therefore, could usher in a new dawn for the Egyptian theater.

The political theater in Lebanon is making great strides and, in many instances, has surpassed Egypt in this communication medium. Certainly, it is more daring and irreverent than Egypt's. The playwrights Isam Mahfuz and Jalal al-Khuri, among others, have fostered the Lebanese political theater, confronting directly and honestly the problems facing their country and the Arab world in general. Furthermore, the Lebanese theater has been experimenting with new forms and methods, thereby establishing its supremacy over all the Arab theaters.

The Lebanese theater has become known for its overt attacks on the government. One play to do this is *Carte Blanche*, produced in 1970. Overtly critical of American relations with the Lebanese government, it shows how satirical the Lebanese political theater has become. The symbolism in *Carte Blanche* is readily identifiable: the United States shares with the Lebanese government the responsibility of repainting an old house (Lebanon). While the old house is given a new facade, it is also converted into an elegant brothel. The price of the painting is the loss of spontaneity and the establishment of an unholy alliance between the Americans and the Lebanese government to exploit the old house.

Another play devotes itself to the Israeli question, *Jiha on the Front Line*, staged for the 1971 season. Jiha, the popular comic figure renowned throughout the Arab world, is this time placed on Lebanon's border with Israel. Throughout the play, the government is raked over the coals for its two-faced attitudes and activities with its enemy to the south, proclaiming deep-seated hatred but in reality carrying on clandestine relations.

Playwrights are beginning to gain some attention in four other Arab nations—Algeria, Syria, Iraq, and Tunisia. The Syrians have a national company, severely limited in their capabilities by government control. It usually presents versions of translated plays, for which it has come under heavy criticism for its uninspiring productions and lack of innovativeness. There have been a number of attempts to write political plays, the most renowned being Sa'dallah Wannus' *A Chat on the Night of June 6*. As the title suggests its setting is the 1967 June War, and its subject is the plight of the Palestinian refugee. The style of the play is similar to that of Bertolt Brecht and playwrights of the theater of the absurd. The outcome is forceful propaganda, meant to arouse patriotism.

The Tunisian theater could be described as artistic. Its leading personality, 'Ali Ben 'Ayad, who died in February 1972, set the tone for the entire industry. A leading actor and director of the National Theater, he exemplified the artist in the Arab world whose main interest is neither political nor educational, but art for art's sake. Ben 'Ayad's productions included such works as the Greek classic, *Oedipus Rex, Yerma* by Federico Garcia Lorca, and *Lost Love* by the Egyptian Taha Husayn.

The theater in Algeria is just now coming into its own. It is being used with some effect by the government for public relations purposes, by sending the national troup to other Arab countries to present plays written by Algerians and to exhibit Algerian cultural aspects, such as folklore and dancing. One Algerian playwright, Katib Yassin, one of his country's leading novelists, has taken the setting for his most recent play out of the Middle East and placed it in Vietnam. The tone of the play is anti-imperialist and therefore, propagandistic along government lines.

In general, the communicators of the theater seem to be going through a transitional period. Only in Lebanon and to some degree in Egypt has the breakthrough been made to present a message devoid of overt propaganda—one closer to realism. Playwrights are limited, however, by governmental control and by the fact that their audiences remain urban. Only in Egypt has there been an attempt to set up a touring company to reach the rural communities. The communication potential is present in each country, since a play can have great visual as well as auditory impact, combined with the emotional sense of being present at a live performance for the viewer. Even if used solely for propagandistic purposes, an actual performance should be able to influence an audience more than a radio or even a television program. This industry, nevertheless, must first improve and expand before it can be used successfully as a communication medium in the Arab world.

**Part III:
Conclusions**

# Conclusions

The conclusion reached after sifting through the existing data is that an informative approach toward a region may be undertaken by means of a systematic study of regional subcultures. Each region has definite and dynamic groups that affect individual countries as well as larger areas. However, whether or not each and every group in a single subculture acts in concert or independently of one another, yet reach identical conclusions, depends upon certain factors prevalent in the region. In the Middle East there are three factors which pervade all spectra of society—Islam, regionalism, and ideologies. Unless these are taken into consideration, any discussions on the Middle East become irrelevant.

Each one of the six regional subcultures discussed—the military, the Western-educated elites, the bureaucracy, the students, the professionals, and the communicators—has been examined with regard to regionalism, Islam, and ideologies; and certain themes have emerged. When speaking of regionalism, it was found that all subcultures supported the concept of one Arab nation encompassing all the Arab peoples. This concept of Arab unity, however, is basically an idealism. In reality, we find that the precept of state nationalism is just as strong as it was when the Arab nations gained their independence. Each regime jealously guards the sovereignty of the state, reluctant to surrender any right to another Arab state. The United Arab Republic was dissolved because Syrian nationalists refused to accept Egyptian domination of their homeland. The Federation of South Arabia never achieved sufficient organization because each amir and sultan would not relinquish sufficient sovereignty to a central government to make the federation workable. The present Federation of Arab Amirates of the Persian Gulf took three years to form and then only six of the former Trucial States agreed to participate. Threat of outside intervention forced the amirs to agree to federation. However, the continual internal bickering among the principal amirs makes one skeptical of the arrangement. Finally, the military regimes of Egypt, Syria, and Libya are attempting a federation of their own, too. Skeptics again believe that this federation will never "get off the ground."

We also see the cautious moves of the North African leaders who are exploring the possibility of a limited regional federation. However, talks have been going on for a single Maghrib state for many years. Certainly there are joint ventures undertaken by the three states. However, when one finds an autocratic monarch, a devout Muslim militant, and a civilian French-oriented socialist president thinking to unite their countries, doubts are immediately raised.

These have been comments on limited regional arrangements. On a wider sphere, one finds several organizations that have been formed to unite the eighteen independent states of the Arab region. Little, however, has been achieved from these various organizations. The Arab League is derided; the Arab common market is, for all intents and purposes, a paper organization. There are lesser bodies, such as those handling postal and telecommunications or customs regulations, which have worked fairly well. Perhaps the most effective area organization has been that of the Organization of Arab Petroleum Exporting Countries. Only oil producing states are members. However, they have acted in concert to stand fast against the Western oil companies and have come out the victors.

As was mentioned before, the various subcultures are working for Arab unity, some more than others. Students are the more idealistic and actively strive to achieve this goal. The other subcultures go along with the idea, primarily because their governments support it. Yet even the regimes favor lip service. It is a question of state sovereignty and who will be the leader.

Islam is, perhaps, the most difficult factor to discuss in relation to the various subcultural groups. Islam is, in reality, Arab culture. It is difficult for an Arab to deprive himself of his own culture. This is why one finds very few people willing to say that Islam must be divorced from politics. To do so would be heretical. Some communicators have dared, but they have been Christians. A few Muslims have come close to this but have always retreated from making the fateful pronouncement.

Islam is being used today to unify the Arab lands. It is also being used as a modernizing force in the region. By returning to the pure Islam, the Arab's past greatness will return. Some scholars have even concluded that many Western concepts, those that made the West the dominant force in the world, had their origins in Islam. These same concepts will raise the Arab states to their rightful place among the world powers.

Here again there is no uniformity in the degree of support for Islam. President Qadhafi of Libya is almost fanatic in his belief that Arabs must return to the true religion and that once purified, Islam will lead them all to victory over their enemies. President Sadat of Egypt attends the Friday prayers at the mosque yet continues to erode the powers of the religious institutions. President Bourguiba of Tunisia was forced to retreat when his people refused to go along with his more radical attempts to curtail some Islamic precepts. Even the Muslim Brotherhood proved to be ineffective.

Each subculture is affected by Islam, simply because Islam is their way of life. They cannot divorce Islam from their activities for to do so would anger the masses. Until the masses are made to realize that Islam should be separated from certain social and political activities, some subcultural groups will be hampered in their reformist campaign for a modern Arab world.

Ideology has played the most dynamic role in the Arab Middle East and has affected the subcultures to a great extent. It is Nasser's brand of Arab socialism that has created the most dissension within the ranks of the various subcultural groups. Those "progressive" states that advocate this ideology clash with those who advocate a more traditional and evolutionary form of development. Most inter-Arab subcultural group organizations have been captured by the "progressivists" and have forced their opponents to retire or to take a backseat in the activities of their organization.

Arab socialism has also played a prominent role in alienating both the Western-educated elite and the bureaucracy. Both of these groups were at one time supreme in the Middle East. Now they are constantly attacked and denigrated by the Arab socialists for holding onto Western ideas and techniques.

When researching the six subcultures, it was discovered that each had specific interests common to it alone, making it unique in the Middle Eastern region. At the same time, it was also found that each subculture had divisive forces at work. Although the six subcultures have been examined twice, from a theoretical and general approach, as well as a detailed survey, their most dynamic aspects will be briefly presented so that as the reader peruses the book, he will begin to fit into place the distinctive characteristics of each subculture with regards to the discussions on regionalism, Islam, and ideology.

Burdened by a conflict of values, the Western-educated elites find themselves alientated from their society. They neither belong to the West, from which they acquired their learning, nor are they accepted by the Arabs, who regard them with suspicion. They feel betrayed by the actions taken by the West in the Middle East. Because of this accusation hanging over their heads, those with a Western education, throughout the Arab world, have established a rapport among themselves. They recognize the failures in their countries and hope to create a consensus which would be used to tackle urgent problems in the region. Those who are now acquiring Western education do not have the same identity crisis as did their fathers. They are willing to accept the dynamics of Arab socialism and work as technocrats within the existing governmental structures of their countries. Moreover, they are more readily accepted by their own countrymen since they are a part of the new technocrat generation which is apolitical and dedicated to the advancement of Arab society.

It was found that the military were the most divisive of all the subcultures. As a group, they differed from country to country. They were also rent by internal factions. However, they hold in common numerous traits. Each military regime came to power ostensibly to create stability and social order. They derived their legitimacy from their predecessor's mistakes. However, once in power, except for the military regimes in Egypt and Algeria, the officers contributed little to education and technical training. They produced instability and economic stagnation. As a group they are the most nationalistic. It springs from their desire to retain power in their state instead of delegating authority to another Arab leader or to a multinational organization.

The subculture that is the most homogeneous of those researched is the bureaucracy. Each national subcultural group has traits in common with all the others throughout the Arab world. At the same time, as separate entities, they have the least contact with one another. Nevertheless, they can be described as *status quo*-oriented, Western-oriented, self-perpetuating, and self-aggrandizing. They have reluctantly accepted Arab socialism or other forces of change prevailing in the region and, whenever possible, have deliberately attempted to delay change that may affect their positions. The majority come from the middle class and had, during the colonial era, enjoyed prestige and favor. Now, however, they are being castigated and lowered in esteem.

The students are the most dynamic of all Middle Eastern subcultures. They are a highly politicized group and therefore politically motivated. They have a tendency to support both idealistic concepts as well as revolutionary causes. In the past, they formed the vanguard for change in the region. Presently, they are being subjected to suppressive measures and being used by the regimes in power. Because their numbers increase every year, jobs become harder to find. This adds to the restive spirit of the students. Some emigrate, while others try to "buck" the system and demand more opportunities for themselves.

Professionals as a subculture include many organized groups. However, for clarity, professionals are broken down into two categories: the laborers and the more educated classes. The latter groups are small in number and because of this, have, in general, proven to be ineffective. A few professional groups have attained importance, primarily the lawyers. Yet the regimes are suspicious of them and tend to keep close watch over their activities. By placing these groups under the one-party system, all initiative is lost. In contrast to the small elitist professional organizations, the trade unions are the best organized as well as the largest groups in the Middle East. However, the one-party system, once again, has debilitated the unions. Initiative is denied them, since they are not permitted bargaining powers, or in some cases, permission to strike. Where they were once the only means for political expression, now they are prevented from engaging in politics. Nevertheless, their size in number alone gives them an advantage over the other subcultural groups in attempting to achieve their goals.

As a subcultural group, the communicators have the most potential of any of the groups discussed to effect change in the Middle East. However, they have proven to be ineffective in reaching the public. This is partially explained by national laws that limit their powers. The regimes in power recognize their creative potential and therefore, stifle innovation. Instead, they force communicators to follow the government line. Egypt dominates the communications field. The largest transmitter in the Arab world is located in Cairo. Those papers having the largest circulation, at home and abroad, originated in Cairo. Egyptian playwrights are recognized as the most renowned. The Egyptian cinema is the most acceptable throughout the region. In spite of this domination of the communications media, Egyptian communicators find themselves just as handicapped as the other countries. Only in Lebanon is there freedom to create, to criticize fully, and to reach a public receptive to new ideas.

But what are the destinies of the subcultural groups discussed in this book?

Will the majority remain weak, dictated to by the military or autocratic regime, and forced to follow government policy? In the forseeable future, the rifts that exist in the various subcultures will remain unchanged, neither closing nor widening. This is due mainly to the divisive forces extant in the region as a whole—traditionalism vs. progressive socialism, modernization vs. Islam as it exists today, and Westernization vs. Eastern penetration.

A certain trend is noticeable and could considerably change the social and political context of the Arab world. One becomes aware of a turning inward among those elites discussed in this book. It is no longer a question of looking toward the West or the East for inspiration. Instead, the Arab leaders are looking inward at those things that are Arab. We find stressed the concepts of Arab socialism and Arab nationalism. We find being discussed rejuvenation of Islam.

Nevertheless, Arab society remains Western-oriented because of several factors. These are a legacy from the colonial era in which Western culture was anything and everything; Western-educated and bureaucratic subcultures who retain sufficient influence to project their cultural inheritance onto society in general; the vast admiration for Western technology and those technological inventions that the regimes in power feel must be acquired for the greatness of the Arab people; and a strong suspicion of communism and the Communist tactics that have begun to permeate the region. It should be mentioned that the positive outlook toward the West has been maintained in spite of Western economic "neocolonialism," Western "infamy" in establishing a Zionist state in the Arab homeland, and Western military penetration of the region.

It is expected that the military will continue in office, fostering their own power at the expense of other groups. However, it is discernible, too, that the military is being challenged. Labor has demanded better economic conditions. Communicators want more freedom to express themselves. It is the students, though, who have in the past been a revolutionary force and who may play a similar role in the future. Although used by political parties and the military for their own machinations, the students are beginning to rebel and to demand a say in their governments. However, they are still limited by the availability of jobs and must rely on government largesses for their education as well as for their future positions.

If students are instrumental in bringing down governments in some of the Arab countries and severely shake up the regimes in other countries, it is possible that they may force the military to return to their barracks and permit a civilian administration to preside over the affairs of Arab nations.

The revolutionary fervor of the students is abetted by the Arab-Israeli conflict and the Palestinian revolutionary movement. Both issues have exposed the impotency of the military regimes. And although the Palestinian cause is given a semblance of support by the majority of the military regimes, they realize that the movement is revolutionary in character and that it carries with it disruptive forces that could endanger their own regimes.

The study must not be considered to be definitive on subcultures in the Middle East since the region is undergoing dynamic and continuing changes. Furthermore, a dearth of material on the subcultures presented limits analysis as well as a full understanding of all the individual groups. The authors have come to the conclusion that extensive field work and data collection in the region could improve considerably a greater knowledge of the regional subcultural groups. Although the bibliography of this paper is extensive, and includes material in French and Arabic, as well as English, it is still insufficient in some cases for the purposes the authors wished to achieve.

As was stated before, the Middle East is constantly undergoing changes in its political, economic, and social forces. In some instances, material published as late as 1967 could easily be considered out of date, and therefore unusable except as historical reference. Changes in regimes—military coups and counter-coups—have certainly effected the publication of material on the region. The authoritative stand taken by some regimes, such as Syria and Iraq, have also had a limiting effect on the emanation of good analytical material from the two countries.

Then, too, it is only recently that the Arabian peninsula has begun to welcome the scholar. Besides travelogues and books on tribal structures, research reports are practically nonexistent. However, now that the peninsula is being opened to economic development, the researcher should be able to begin collecting data on subjects heretofore unpublished.

**Notes**

# Notes

**Chapter 1**
**The Dynamics of Arab Regionalism**

1. See Niyazi Berkes, *The Development of Secularism in Turkey* (Montreal: McGill University Press, 1964); and Sherif Mardin, *The Genesis of Young Ottoman Thought* (Princeton: Princeton University Press, 1962).

2. See Albert Hourani, *Arabic Thought in the Liberal Age, 1798-1939* (London: Oxford University Press, 1962); Sylvia Haim, *Arab Nationalism, an Anthology* (Berkeley and Los Angeles: University of California Press, 1962); and Hisham Sharabi, *The Arab Intellectuals and the West: The Formative Years, 1875-1914* (Baltimore: Johns Hopkins Press, 1970).

3. George Antonius, *The Arab Awakening, the Story of the Arab National Movement* (London: Hamish Hamilton, 1938), pp. 157-158.

4. Charles Gallagher, *The United States and North Africa* (Cambridge: Harvard University Press, 1963), pp. 84-115.

5. Ibid., p. 85.

6. Hourani, op. cit., pp. 37-38.

7. Mekki Shibeika, *The Independent Sudan* (New York: Robert Speller, 1959), p. 37.

8. George Lenczowski, *The Middle East in World Affairs* (Ithaca: Cornell University Press, 1962), pp. 476-484.

9. Antonius, op. cit., pp. 293-294.

10. Leonard Binder, *The Ideological Revolution in the Middle East* (New York: Wiley, 1964), p. 198.

11. Quoted in Haim, op. cit., p. 36.

12. Lenczowski, op. cit., pp. 633-652.

13. Kamel Abu Jaber, *The Arab Ba'th Socialist Party, History, Ideology, and Organization* (Syracuse: Syracuse University Press, 1966), pp. 23-32.

14. Anwar Chejne, "Egyptian Attitudes toward Pan-Arabism," *Middle East Journal* (Summer 1957), pp. 253-268.

15. George Lenczowski, "The Objects and Methods of Nasserism," *Modernization of the Arab World*, ed. by J.H. Thompson and R.D. Reischauer (Princeton: Van Nostrand, 1966), pp. 200-207.

16. Patrick Seale, *The Struggle for Syria, a Study of Post-War Arab Politics, 1945-1958* (London: Oxford University Press, 1965), pp. 37-131.

17. Lenczowski, *The Middle East in World Affairs*, p. 644.

18. Seale, op. cit., pp. 132-326.

19. Lenczowski, *The Middle East in World Affairs*, p. 369.

20. Malcolm Kerr, *The Arab Cold War, Gamal 'Abd al-Nasir and His Rivals, 1958-1970* (London: Oxford University Press, 1971), p. 11.

21. Ibid., pp. 12-13.

22. Ibid., pp. 44-76.

23. Ibid., pp. 96-105.

24. Robert Collins and Robert Tignor, *Egypt and the Sudan* (Englewood Cliffs, N.J.: Prentice-Hall, 1967), pp. 147-164.

25. Gallagher, op. cit., pp. 116-195.

26. Kerr, op. cit., pp. 137-140.

27. Ibid., pp. 145-146.

28. See text in *Middle East Journal* (Winter 1971), pp. 523-529.

29. Robert MacDonald, *The League of Arab States, a Study of the Dynamics of Regional Organization* (Princeton: Princeton University Press, 1965), pp. 202-220.

30. S.H. Schurr and P.T. Homan, et al., *Middle Eastern Oil and the Western World, Prospects and Problems* (New York: American Elsevier Publishing Co., 1971), pp. 123-127.

31. Ibid., pp. 139-140.

## Chapter 2
## Islam and Its Cultural Aspects

1. Jamal Hamdan, *al-'Alam al-Islami al-Mu'asir* (Contemporary Islamic World), Cairo: 'Alam al-Kutub, 1971, p. 26.

2. *Orient*, V (1958), p. 41.

3. Beirut: Dar al-Tali'ah, (1969).

4. M. Mahmud al-Sawwaf, *Ma'rakat al-Islam* (n.p., 1969), p. 177.

5. *al-Jihad fi`sabil Allah*, a pamphlet published by the International Islamic Federation of Student Organizations, (1970), pp. 5f.

## Chapter 3
## Middle East Ideologies

1. Ishaq, Musa al-Husayni, *Al-Ikhwan al-Muslimun* (Beirut, 1955), p. 33.

2. Ibid., pp. 113-114.

3. *Al-Mithaq* (The Charter) Chapter 5: "On Integral Democracy" (Cairo: Dar al-Ta'awun, 1962).

4. *Etudes Arabes*, 3rd-4th sem., no. 29 (Rome, 1971), p. 16.

5. As quoted in Michael Suleiman, *Political Parties in Lebanon* (Ithaca: Cornell University Press, 1967), p. 86.

6. *Al-Anwar* (Beirut), issues of January 7-10, 1972.

**Chapter 4**
**Subcultures in the Arab World**

1. Stephen Hallmark, "Subcultures as a Focus of Analysis," in Abdul A. Said (ed.), *Protagonists of Change* (Englewood Cliffs, N.J.: Prentice-Hall, 1971), pp. 10-20.
2. Daniel Lerner, *The Passing of Traditional Society* (London: Collier-Macmillan, 1964), pp. 251-258.


**Chapter 5**
**The Military**

1. Manfred Halpern, *The Politics of Social Change in the Middle East and North Africa* (Princeton, N.J.: Princeton University Press, 1963) John J. Johnson (ed.), *The Role of the Military in Underdeveloped Countries* (Princeton, N.J.: Princeton University Press, 1962).
2. Eliezer, Be'eri, *Army Officers in Arab Politics and Society* (New York: Praeger, 1970), pp. 326-332.
3. Charles Issawi, *Egypt in Revolution* (London: Oxford University Press, 1963), p. 309.
4. *New York Times, Magazine*, November 29, 1970, p. 30 and pp. 132-139.
5. *The Economist*, London, May 20, 1972, p. 52.
6. Guenter Lewy, *The Egyptian Revolution: Nasserism and Islam* (1968), passim.
7. *Al-Ahram* (Cairo, May 21, 1971), as quoted in Joseph P. O'Kane, "Islam in the New Egyptian Constitution: Some Discussions in *Al-Ahram*," *The Middle East Journal* (Spring 1972), p. 137.
8. Anouar Abdel-Malek, *Egypt: Military Society* "The Army Regime, the Left, and Social Change under Nasser. Translated from the French by Charles Lam Markmann" (New York: Vintage, 1968), pp. 246-287.
9. Abdel Rahman Azzam Pasha as quoted by Abdel Malek, op. cit., p. 251.
10. Be'eri, op. cit., pp. 326-332.
11. George M. Haddad, *Revolutions and Military Rule in the Middle East: The Arab States* (New York: Robert Speller and Sons, 1971), pp. 145-146.
12. Ibid., pp. 367-368.
13. Colonel Boumedienne's interview with *al-Ahram*, October 8-10, 1965, reprinted in *Revolution Africaine*, no. 143 (October 23, 1965, as reported in Ottoway), p. 178, f.t. #6.
14. J.C. Hurewitz, *Middle East Politics: The Military Dimension* (New York: Praeger, 1969), p. 341.

15. *Al-Fatih*, May 18, 20, 22, 25, and 27, 1974, as monitored by FBIS, May 21, 23, and 29, 1975.


# Chapter 6
## The Western-Educated Elites

1. Labib Zuwiyya Yamak, *The Syrian Social Nationalist Party: An Ideological Analysis*, Harvard Middle Eastern Monographs, XIV (Cambridge: Harvard University Press, 1966), p. 7.

2. John Badeau, "Islam and the Modern Middle East," *Foreign Affairs* 38, no. 1 (October 1959), pp. 64-70 passim.

3. C. Ernest Dawn, "Arab Islam in the Modern Age," *The Middle East Journal* 19, no. 4 (Autumn 1965), p. 443.

4. Anouar Abdel-Malek, "Introduction a la pensee Arabe contemporaine," *Civilisations* 15, no. 1 (1965), p. 71.

5. Ibid., p. 68.

6. C. Ernest Dawn, "Arab Islam," p. 442.

7. Cecil Hourani, "The Moment of Truth," *Encounter* 29, no. 5 (November 1967), p. 12.

8. Mark Tessler, "Cultural Modernity: Evidence from Tunisia," *Social Science Quarterly* 52, no. 2 (September 1971), p. 297.

9. A.B. Zahlan, "Wanted: A Great University," *MidEast* 9, no. 1 (January/February 1969), p. 12.

10. _____. "Arab Higher Education: the Next Decade," *MidEast* 8, no. 3 (May/June 1968), p. 7.

11. Louis Wiznitzer, "Algeria gives high priority to training of technicians," *Christian Science Monitor*, June 3, 1971, p. 5.

12. Saad Ibrahim, *Political Attitudes of an Emerging Elite: A Case Study of the Arab Students in the United States*, University of Washington, Ph.D. dissertation, 1968, p. 9.

13. Ibid., pp. 110 and 114.

14. "Al-Mu'tamar al-Sanawi li Munazamat al-talabah al-'Arab," *Shu'un Filastiniyah*, no. 6 (January 1972), p. 274.

15. Saad Ibrahim, op. cit., p. 11.


# Chapter 7
## The Bureaucracy

1. Samir Khalaf, "The Growing Pains of Arab Intellectuals," *Diogenes* 54 (Summer 1966), p. 67.

2. Stephen Longrigg, *The Middle East, A Social Geography*, 2nd ed. (Chicago: Aldine, 1970), p. 195.

3. John Badeau, "Islam and the Modern Middle East," *Foreign Affairs* 38, no. 1 (October 1959), p. 70.

4. C. Ernest Dawn, "Arab Islam in the Modern Age," *The Middle East Journal* 19, no. 4 (Autumn 1965), p. 445.

5. Amin Galal, "The Egyptian Economy and the Revolution," in P.J. Vatikiotis (ed.), *Egypt Since the Revolution* (London: George Allen and Unwin, 1968), p. 47.

6. *Al-Amal* (Cairo), September 1967, pp. 4-6.

7. Ibid.

8. Amos Perlmutter, "Egypt and the Myth of the New Middle Class: A Comparative Analysis," *Comparative Studies in Society and History* 10, no. 1 (October 1967), p. 64.

9. Ibid.

10. Ahmad Sadiq Sa'd, "Fi al-biruqratiyah wa al-Ishtirakiyah" (On Bureaucracy and Socialism), *al-Katib* (Cairo) 2, no. 124 (July 1971), p. 102.

11. Ibid., p. 100.

12. Clement Moore, *Politics in North Africa: Algeria, Morocco, and Tunisia* (Boston: Little, Brown and Co., 1970), p. 145.

13. John Waterbury, *The Commander of the Faithful; the Moroccan Political Elite—A Study of Segmented Politics* (London: Weedenfeld and Nicolson, 1970), p. 110.

14. Ibid., p. 6.

15. John Waterbury, "Marginal Politics and Elite Manipulation in Morocco," *Archives Europeennes de Sociologie* 8, no. 1 (1967), p. 110.

16. James Paul, "The Changing Basis of Moroccan Politics," *New Politics* 9, no. 2 (Summer 1970), p. 23.

17. Florence Carter, *Labor Law and Practice in Tunisia*, Department of Labor, Bureau of Labor Statistics, BLS Report #294 (June 1965), p. 25.

18. Farouk Luqman, *Yemen 1970*, (Aden: 1970), p. 27.

19. *L'Opinion* (Morocco), April 4, 1972, p. 1.

## Chapter 8
## The Students

1. Dr. Halim Barakat, "Al-Ightirab wa al-Thawrah fi al-'Arabiya," (Alienation and Revolution in Arab Life), (Beirut: Mawaqif, 1969), no. 9, pp. 18-44.

2. Elias Zain, "An Arab View," *Mid East* 9, no. 1 (January/February 1969), pp. 3-7.

3. "Emigration of Arab Technicians: Why and How?" in *al-Thawrah* (Dec. 8, 1970), p. 3; JPRS translation #52617 (March 15, 1971).

4. Barakat, Ibid.

5. Halim Barakat, "Social factors influencing attitudes of university students

in Lebanon towards the Palestinian resistance movement," *Journal of Palestine Studies* 1, no. 1 (Autumn 1971), pp. 87-112.

6. "Madha Yufakir Shabab al-Jami'ah" (What do university students think?), *Majallat al-tarbiyah al-hadithah–Journal of Modern Education* (Cairo) 44, no. 2 (December 1970), pp. 144-165.

7. P.J. Vatikiotis, *The Modern History of Egypt* (New York: Praeger, 1969), p. 420.

8. William H. Dorsey, "1968 Revisited: Student Power in Cairo," *New Middle East* (February 1972), p. 15.

9. Clement Henry Moore, *North Africa* (Boston: Little, Brown, 1970), p. 168.

10. John Norman, *Labor and Politics in Libya and Arab Africa* (New York: Bookman Associates, 1965), p. 178.

11. Clement Henry Moore and Arlie R. Hochschild, "Student Unions in North African Politics," *Daedalus* 97, no. 1 (Winter 1968), p. 26.

12. Moore and Hochschild, op. cit., p. 32.

13. Moore, *North Africa*, op. cit., p. 171.

14. *Africa Confidential*, June 28, 1968, pp. 5-7; and October 11, 1968, pp. 5-6.

15. "Taqrir min dakhil Tunis" (A report from inside Tunis) *al-Dastur* (Beirut) 2, no. 72 (February 28, 1972), p. 18; also *The New York Times*, February 10, 1972, p. 11.

16. Loc. cit.

## Chapter 9
## The Professionals

1. Samir Khalaf, "The Growing Pains of Arab Intellectuals," *Diogenes*, no. 54 (Summer 1966), p. 60.

2. Willard Beling, "Mobilization of Human Resources in Developing Nations: Algeria, Tunisia and Egypt," *Maghreb Digest* 5, no. 2 (April/June 1967), p. 19.

3. *Al-Ahram* (Cairo), March 16, 1972, p. 6.

4. "al-Muhamun al-'Arab wa al-Hurriyah" (Arab Lawyers and Freedom), *Mawaqif* 1, no. 1 (1968), pp. 200-207.

5. *Al-Haqq* (Cairo) 2, no. 3 (September 1971), pp. 241-253.

6. Ibid., pp. 174-190.

7. Ibid. (Translated by author)

8. J.A. Hallsworth, "Freedom of Association and Industrial Relations in the Countries of the Near and Middle East: Part I," *International Labour Review* 73, no. 5 (November 1954), p. 380.

9. Dankwart Rustow, *Middle Eastern Political Systems* (Englewood Cliffs, N.J.: Prentice-Hall, 1971), p. 85.

10. "Structure of Labor Unionism in Kuwait," *al-Tali'ah* (Kuwait) May 1, 1971, p. 10. (In Arabic.)

11. Harry Hopkins, *Egypt, the Crucible; the Unfinished Revolution in the Arab World* (Boston: Houghton Mifflin, 1969), p. 144.

12. Kamel Abu Jaber, "An Impetus to Egyptian Labor," *Mid East* 10, no. 6 (December 1970), p. 38.

13. Rustow, *Middle Eastern Political Systems*, p. 85.

14. John Cooley, "U.A.R. Labor Strikes at Iron, Steel Center," *The Christian Science Monitor*, August 31, 1971, p. 2.

15. Tareq Ismael, *Government and Politics of the Contemporary Middle East*, (Homewood, Ill.: Dorsey Press, 1970), p. 327.

16. Hopkins, *Egypt*, p. 145.

17. Cooley, "U.A.R. Labor," p. 2.

18. E.A. Alport, "Socialism in three countries; the record in the Maghrib," *International Affairs* (London) 43, no. 4 (October 1967), p. 683.

19. *L'Opinion* (Rabat), 22 March 1972, p. 1.

20. John Cooley, "Morocco takeover try showed shaky society," *The Christian Science Monitor*, July 31, 1971, p. 11.

21. Anisse Salah-Bey, "Trade Unions and Economic and Social Development in the Maghrib," *International Labour Review* 94, no. 4 (October 1966), pp. 375 and 396.

22. Florence Carter, *Labor Law and Practice in Tunisia*, Department of Labor, Bureau of Labor Statistics, BLS Report No. 294, June 1965, p. 33.

23. Charles Cecil, "The Determinants of Libyan Foreign Policy," *Middle East Journal* 19, no. 1 (Winter 1965), p. 31.

24. John Norman, *Labor and Politics in Libya and Arab Africa* (New York: Bookman Associates, 1965), p. 67.

25. Richard Ward, "The Long Run Employment Prospects for Middle East Labor," *The Middle East Journal* 24, no. 2 (Spring 1970), p. 147.

26. Baha Abu-Laban, "Social Change and Local Politics in Sidon, Lebanon," *The Journal of Developing Areas* 5, no. 1 (October 1970), p. 35.

**Chapter 10**
**The Communicators**

1. "The Arab Media, was it successful in awakening the masses' consciousness?" *Al-Arabi*, no. 158, January 1972, pp. 46-50.

2. Ibid.

3. Anouar Abdel-Malek, "Introduction á la penseé Arabe contemporaine," *Civilisation* 15, no. 1 (1965), p. 71.

4. *The Middle East and North Africa 1971-72*, 18th ed., (London: Europa Publications, 1971), p. 727.

5. *Jeune Afrique*, April 11, 1972, No. 587.

6. Yves Bourron, "Regards sur la littérature Maghrebine d'expression française," *Etudes* (Paris), May 1967, pp. 636-650.

7. *Al-Udaba'al-Arab*, April 1971, Editorial, 2nd issue.

8. "Azamat al-Islam" (The Greatness of Islam), *Al-Nahda* (Kuwait), April 29, 1972, p. 65.

# Selected Bibliography

# Selected Bibliography

**A Regional Assessment**

*The Dynamics of Arab Regionalism*

Abu Jaber, Kamel. *The Arab Ba'th Socialist Party, History, Ideology, and Organization.* Syracuse: Syracuse University Press, 1966.

Adams, Charles. *Islam and Modernism in Egypt.* New York: Russell and Russell, 1968.

Ahmed, Jamal. *The Intellectual Origins of Egyptian Nationalism.* London: Oxford University Press, 1960.

Amin, Samir. *The Maghreb in the Modern World.* Baltimore: Penguin, 1970.

Antonius, George. *The Arab Awakening, the Story of the Arab National Movement.* London: Hamish Hamilton, 1938.

Badeau, John. *The American Approach to the Arab World.* New York: Harper & Row, 1968.

Berkes, Niyazi. *The Development of Secularism in Turkey.* Montreal: McGill University Press, 1964.

Binder, Leonard. *The Ideological Revolution in the Middle East.* New York: Wiley, 1964.

Brown, Leon. *State and Society in Independent North Africa.* Washington, D.C.: Middle East Institute, 1966.

Collins, Robert, and Tignor, Robert. *Egypt and The Sudan.* Englewood Cliffs, N.J.: Prentice-Hall, 1967.

Gallagher, Charles. *The United States and North Africa.* Cambridge: Harvard University Press, 1963.

Haim, Sylvia. *Arab Nationalism, an Anthology.* Berkeley and Los Angeles, University of California Press, 1962.

Hourani, Albert. *Arabic Thought in the Liberal Age, 1798-1939.* London: Oxford University Press, 1962.

Hurewitz, J.C., ed. *Soviet-American Rivalry in the Middle East.* New York: Praeger, 1969.

Husry, Khaldun. *Three Reformers, a Study in Modern Arab Political Thought.* Beirut: Khayats, 1966.

Karpat, Kemal. *Political and Social Thought in the Contemporary Middle East.* New York: Praeger, 1968.

Kerr, Malcolm. *The Arab Cold War, Gamal Abd al-Nasir and His Rivals, 1958-1970.* London: Oxford University Press, 1971.

_____. *Islamic Reform, the Political and Legal Theories of Muhammad Abduh and Rashid Rida.* Berkeley and Los Angeles: University of California Press, 1966.

Khalil, Muhammad. *The Arab States and the Arab League, a Documentary Record.* 2 vols. Beirut: Khayats, 1962.

Lenczowski, George. *The Middle East in World Affairs.* Ithaca: Cornell University Press, 1962.

_____ , ed. *The Political Awakening in the Middle East.* Englewood Cliffs, N.J.: Prentice-Hall, 1970.

Lewis, Bernard. *The Middle East and the West.* Bloomington: Indiana University Press, 1964.

MacDonald, Robert. *The League of Arab States, a Study in the Dynamics of Regional Organization.* Princeton: Princeton University Press, 1965.

Mansfield, Peter. *Nasser's Egypt.* Baltimore: Penguin, 1969.

Mardin, Sherif. *The Genesis of Young Ottoman Thought.* Princeton: Princeton University Press, 1962.

Nuseibeh, Hazem. *The Ideas of Arab Nationalism.* Ithaca: Cornell University Press, 1956.

Rustow, Dankwart. *Middle Eastern Political Systems.* Englewood Cliffs, N.J.: Prentice-Hall, 1971.

Saab, Hassan. *The Arab Federalists of the Ottoman Empire.* Amsterdam: Djambatan, 1958.

Safran, Nadav. *Egypt in Search of a Political Community, an Analysis of the Intellectual and Political Evolution of Egypt, 1804-1952.* Cambridge: Harvard University Press, 1961.

Sayegh, Fayez, ed. *The Dynamics of Neutralism in the Arab World.* San Francisco: Chandler, 1964.

Schmidt, Dana Adams. *Yemen, the Unknown War.* New York: Holt, Rinehart and Winston, 1968.

Seale, Patrick. *The Struggle for Syria, a study of Post-War Arab Politics, 1945-1958.* London: Oxford University Press, 1965.

Sharabi, Hisham. *The Arab Intellectuals and the West: The Formative Years, 1875-1914.* Baltimore: Johns Hopkins Press, 1970.

Shibeika, Mekki. *The Independent Sudan.* New York: Robert Speller, 1959.

Smith, Wilfred Cantwell. *Islam in Modern History.* Princeton: Princeton University Press, 1957.

Stevens, Georgiana. *The United States and the Middle East.* Englewood Cliffs, N.J.: Prentice-Hall, 1965.

Thompson, J.H., and R.D. Reischauer, eds. *Modernization of the Arab World.* Princeton: Van Nostrand, 1966.

Zuwiyya-Yamak, Labib. *The Syrian Social Nationalist Party: An Ideological Analysis.* Cambridge: Harvard University Press, 1966.

Zeine, Zeine. *Arab-Turkish Relations and the Emergence of Arab Nationalism.* Beirut: Khayats, 1958.

*Islam and its Cultural Aspects*

## Books

Al Yasin, M. Hasan. *Hawamish 'ala Kitab Naqd al-Fikr al-Dini* (Marginal Notes on the Critique of Religious Thinking). Beirut: Maktabi Lubnan, 1971.

Anderson, J.N.D. *Islamic Law in the Modern World.* New York: New York University Press, 1959.

Arberry, A.J., ed. *Religion in the Middle East.* Cambridge: Cambridge University Press, 1969.

al-'Azm, Sadiq Jalal. *Naqd al-Fikr al-Dini* [Critique of Religious Thinking]. Beirut: Dar al-Tali'ah, 1969.

'Azzam, Abd-ar-Rahman. *The Eternal Message of Muhammad.* Translated by Ceasar E. Farah. New York: Devin-Adair, 1964.

Charnay, Jean Paul, ed. *Normes et valeurs dans l'Islam contemporain.* Paris: Payot, 1966.

Coulson, Noel J. *Conflicts and Tensions in Islamic Jurisprudence.* Chicago: University of Chicago Press, 1969.

Faruqi, Isma'il. *On Arabism, 'Urubah and Religion.* Amsterdam: Djambatan, 1962.

Fattal, A. *Le statut legal des non-Musulmans en pays d'Islam.* Beirut: Catholic Press, 1958.

Gardet, Louis. *L'Islam, Religion et Communaute.* Paris: Desclee de Brouwer, 1967.

Gibb, Sir Hamilton. *Modern Trends in Islam.* Chicago: The University of Chicago Press, 1945.

International Islamic Federation of Student Organizations. *al-Jihad fi Sabil Allah* [Struggle for the Cause of God]. N.P. 1970.

Khan, Sir Muhammad Zafrullah. *Islam, Its Meaning for Modern Man.* New York: Harper & Row, 1962.

Morgan, Kenneth, ed. *Islam, the Straight Pass: Islam Interpreted by Muslims.* New York: Roland Press, 1958.

Nasrallah, M. 'Izzat. *al-Radd 'ala Sadiq al-'Azm* [A Reply to Sadiq al-'Azm]. Beirut: Dar Filastin, 1970.

Qutb, Sayyid. *Ma'rakat al-Islam wa al-Ra'smaliyah* [The Battle of Islam and Capitalism]. 4th ed. Jeddah, Saudi Arabia: al-Dar al-Sa'udiyah, 1969.

Rosenthal, E.I.J. *Islam in the Modern National State.* Cambridge: Cambridge University Press, 1965.

Sa'b, Hasan. *Al-Islam tijah tahaddiyat al-Hayat al-'Asriyah* [Islam in Front of the Challenges of Modern Life]. Beirut: Dar al-Adab, 1965.

al-Sawwaf, M. Mahmud. *Ma'rakat al-Islam* [The Battle of Islam]. Jeddah, Saudi Arabia: Published by the author, 1969.

Smith, Wilfred Cantwell. *Islam in Modern History*. Princeton, N.J.: Princeton University Press, 1957.

Von Grunebaum, Gustave E. *Modern Islam: The Search for Cultural Identity*. Berkeley: University of California Press, 1962.

Yamani, Ahmad Zaki. *Islamic Law and Contemporary Issues*. Jeddah, Saudi Arabia: Saudi Publishing House, 1958.

## Articles

Badeau, John. "Islam and the Modern Middle East." *Foreign Affairs* 38, no. 1 (October 1959), pp. 61-75.

Bonderman, D. "Modernization and Changing Perceptions of Islamic Law." *Harvard Law Review* 81, no. 6 (April 1968), pp. 1169-1193.

Borthwick, Bruce M. "The Islamic Sermon as a Channel of Political Communication." *The Middle East Journal* 21, no. 3 (Summer 1967), pp. 299-313.

Cahen, C. "L'Islam et les minorite confessionelles au cours de l'histoire." *Table Ronde*, no. 126 (June 1958), pp. 61-72.

Dawn, C. Ernest. "Arab Islam in the Modern Age." *Middle East Journal*, 19, no. 4 (August 1965), pp. 435-446.

Najjar, Fauzi. "Islam and Modern Democracy." *Review of Politics*, Vol. 20 (April 1958), pp. 164-180.

Nasr, Sayyed H. "The Immutable Principles of Islam and Western Education." *Muslim World* 56, no. 1 (January 1966), pp. 4-9.

Rahman, Fazlur. "The Impact of Modernity on Islam." *Islamic Studies* (Karachi) 5, no. 2 (1966), pp. 113-128.

*Middle East Ideologies*

## Books

Abu Jaber, Kamel S. *The Arab Ba'th Socialist Party: History, Ideology and Organization*. New York: Syracuse University Press, 1966.

Agwani, M.S. *Communism in the Arab East*. New York: Asia Publishing House, 1970.

Ahmed, Jamal Mohammed. *The Intellectual Origins of Egyptian Nationalism*. London: Oxford University Press, 1960.

Antonius, George. *The Arab Awakening*. New York: Capricorn Books, 1965.

al-Bazzaz, 'Abd al-Rahman. *On Arab Nationalism*. London: S. Austin, 1965.

Berkes, Niyazi. *The Development of Secularism in Turkey*. Montreal: McGill University Press, 1964.

Binder, Leonard. *Iran, Political Development in a Changing Society*. Berkeley and Los Angeles: University of California Press, 1962.

_____. *The Ideological Revolution in the Middle East*. New York: Wiley, 1964.

Cottam, Richard W. *Nationalism in Iran*. Pittsburgh: University of Pittsburgh Press, 1964.

Dabbas, Hashim Ahmed. *Arab Unity: Prospects and Problems*. Ph.D. dissertation, Missouri, 1964.

Dekmejian, R. Hrair. *Egypt under Nasir*. Albany: State University of New York Press, 1971.

Duclos, Louis Jean, et al. *Les Nationalismes Maghrebins*. Paris: Fondation Nationale des sciences politiques, 1966.

al-Faruqi, Ismail R. *On Arabism*. Vol. 1 *'Urubah and Religion*. Amsterdam: Djambatan, 1962.

Gokalp, Ziya. *The Principles of Turkism*. Translated and annotated by Robert Devereux. Leiden: E.J. Brill, 1968.

Haim, Sylvia G., ed. *Arab Nationalism, an anthology*. Berkeley: University of California Press, 1962.

Halpern, Manfred. *The Politics of Social Change in the Middle East and North Africa*. Princeton: Princeton University Press, 1963.

Harris, Christina (Phelps). *Nationalism and Revolution in Egypt: The Role of the Muslim Brotherhood*. The Hague: published for the Hoover Institution by Mouton, 1964.

Heyd, Uriel. *Foundations of Turkish Nationalism: The Life and Teachings of Ziya Gokalp*. London: Luzac and Co., 1950.

Hourani, Albert H. *Arabic Thought in the Liberal Age, 1798-1939*. London: Oxford University Press, 1962.

Karpat, Kemal H., ed. *Political and Social Thought in the Contemporary Middle East*. New York: Praeger, 1968.

Kerr, Malcolm. *The Arab Cold War 1958-1967: A Study of Ideology in Politics*. 2nd ed. London: Oxford University Press, ca. 1967.

Khadduri, Majid. *Political Trends in the Arab World: The Role of Ideas and Ideals in Politics*. Baltimore: Johns Hopkins Press, 1970.

Laqueur, Walter Z. *Communism and Nationalism in the Middle East*. 2nd ed. London: Routledge and K. Paul, 1957.

Lewis, Bernard. *The Emergence of Modern Turkey*. London: Oxford University Press, 1962.

Mahr, Horst. *Die Baath-Partei, Portrait einer panarabischen Bewegung*. Munchen: Gunterolzog Verlag, 1972.

Mardin, Sherif. *The Genesis of Young Ottoman Thought: A Study in the Modernization of Turkish Political Ideas*. Princeton: Princeton University Press, 1962.

Mitchell, Richard P. *The Society of the Muslim Brothers*. London: Oxford University Press, 1969.

Murqus, Ilyas. *Naqd al-fikr al-qawmi: Sati' al-Husri* [Criticism of the Idea of Nationalism, Sati' al-Husri]. Beirut: Dar al-Tali'ah, 1966.

Naji, Amin. *Falsafat al-'aqidah al-kata'ibiyah* [The Philosophy of the Phalangist Ideology]. Beirut: Phalangist Publications, 1966.

Nouschi, Andre. *La Naissance du nationalisme algerien.* Paris: Editions de Minuit, 1962.

Nuseibeh, Hazem Zaki. *The Ideas of Arab Nationalism.* Ithaca: Cornell University Press, 1956.

Palmer, Monte. *Arab Unity: Problems and Prospects* [Ph.D. dissertation]. Wisconsin, 1964.

Qubain, Fahim. *Inside the Arab Mind; a Bibliographic Survey of Literature in Arabic on Arab Nationalism and Unity. With an Annotated List of English-Language Books and Articles.* Arlington, Virginia: Middle East Research Associates, 1960.

al-Razzaz, Munif. *The Evolution of the Meaning of Nationalism.* Translated by Ib. Abu Lughad. Garden City, N.Y.: Doubleday, 1963.

Sayegh, Fayiz. *Arab Unity, Hope, and Fulfillment.* New York: Devin-Adair, 1958.

Seale, Patrick A. *The Struggle for Syria: A Study of Post-War Arab Politics, 1945-1958.* London: Oxford University Press, 1965.

Sharabi, Hisham. *Nationalism and Revolution in the Arab World.* Princeton, N.J.: Van Nostrand, 1966.

Torrey, Gordon. *Syrian Politics and the Military 1945-1958.* Columbus: University of Ohio Press, 1964.

Ule, Wolfgang. *Bibliographie zu Fragen des Arabischen Sozialismus, des Nationalismus und des Kommunismus unter dem Gesichtspunkt des Islams.* Hamburg: Deutschen Orient-Institut, 1967.

Zuwiyya-Yamak, Labib. *The Syrian Social Nationalist Party: An Ideological Analysis.* Cambridge, Mass.: Harvard University Press, 1966.

## Articles

Abu Jaber, Kamel. "Salamah Musa: Precursor of Arab Socialism." *The Middle East Journal* 20, no. 2 (September 1966), pp. 196-206.

'Allush, Naji. "Yasar la ya'rif al-yamin min al-yasar" [The Left That Does Not Know Right from Left]. *Al-Adab* 15, no. 10 (October 1967), pp. 5-9.

Chejne, Anwar. "Egyptian Attitudes Toward Pan-Arabism." *The Middle East Journal* 11, no. 3 (1957), pp. 253-268.

Dawn, C. Ernest. "From Ottomanism to Arabism: The origin of an ideology." *The Review of Politics* 23, no. 3 (1961), pp. 378-400.

_____. "The Rise and Progress of Middle Eastern Nationalism." *Social Education* 25, no. 1 (1961), pp. 20-25.

_____. "The Rise of Arabism in Syria." *The Middle East Journal* 16, no. 2 (1962), pp. 145-168.

Gallagher, Charles F. "Language, Culture, and Ideology: The Arab World." *Expectant Peoples: Nationalism and Development.* Edited by K.H. Silvert. New York: Vintage Books, 1967.

Gardner, G.H., and S.A. Hanna. "Islamic Socialism." *The Muslim World* 56, no. 2 (August 1966), pp. 71-86.

Golino, Frank R. "Patterns of Libyan National Identity." *The Middle East Journal* 24, no. 4 (Summer 1970), pp. 338-352.

Haim, Sylvia. "Islam and the Theory of Arab Nationalism." *The Middle East in Transition.* Edited by Walter Z. Laqueur. New York: Praeger, 1958.

Hanna, Sami. "al-Takaful al-Ijtima't and Islamic Socialism." *The Muslim World* 59, nos. 3-4 (July-October 1969), pp. 275-286.

Hanna, Sami, and George H. Gardner. "Al-Shu'ubiyyah Updated." *The Middle East Journal* 20, no. 3 (Summer 1966), pp. 335-351.

Hourani, Albert. "Near Eastern Nationalism, Yesterday and Today." *Foreign Affairs* 42, no. 1 (October 1963), p. 123ff.

Karpat, Kemal H. "Socialism and the Labor Party of Turkey." *The Middle East Journal* 21, no. 2 (September 1967), pp. 157-172.

Kenny, L.M. "Sati' al-Husri's Views on Arab Nationalism." *The Middle East Journal* 17, no. 3 (1963), pp. 231-256.

al-Khuli, Lutfi. "Hawl bina' wihdat al-qiwah al-taqaddumiyah fi al-watan al-'Arabi" [On Building the Unity of the Progressive Forces in the Arab Fatherland]" *Al-Tali'ah* 3, no. 6 (June 1967), pp. 17-42.

Major, John. "The Search for Arab Unity." *International Affairs* (London) 39, no. 4 (October 1963), p. 551ff.

Pennar, Jaan. "The Arabs, Marxism, and Moscow." *The Middle East Journal* 22, no. 4 (August 1968), pp. 433-447.

Rustow, Dankwart. "The Development of Parties in Turkey." *Political Parties and Political Development.* Edited by J. LaPalombara and M. Weiner. Princeton: Princeton University Press, 1966.

Sayfal-Dawlah, 'Ismat. "Al-Wihdah wa al-ishtirakiyah fi al-watan al-'Arabi" [Unity and Socialism in the Arab Fatherland] *Al-Tali'ah* 2, no. 2 (February 1966), pp. 61-67.

Shamir, Shimon. "The Question of a 'National Philosophy' in Contemporary Arab Thought." *Asian and African Studies.* Vol. 1. Jerusalem; Israel Oriental Society, 1965.

Sharabi, Hisham. "The Transformation of Ideology in the Arab World." *The Middle East Journal* 19, no. 4 (August 1965), pp. 471-486.

Torrey, Gordon. "The Ba'th—Ideology and Practice." *The Middle East Journal* 23, no. 4 (August 1969), pp. 445-470.

Viennot, Jean Pierre. "Le Ba'th entre la theorie et la pratique." *L'Orient*, (Paris) no. 30 (1964), pp. 13ff.

## Subcultures

### Books

Abboushi, W.F. *Political Systems of the Middle East in the 20th Century*. New York: Dodd, Mead, 1970.

Abdel-Malek, Anouar. *Egypt: Military Society, the Army Regime, the Left and Social Change under Nasser*. New York: Random House, 1968.

Abu Jaber, Kamel S. *The Arab Ba'th Socialist Party: History, Ideology, and Organization*. Syracuse: Syracuse University Press, 1966.

Adams, Michael, ed. *The Middle East: A Handbook*. New York: Praeger, 1971.

Agwani, M.S. *Communism in the Arab East*. Bombay: Asia Publishing House, 1969.

Al-Akhrass, Mouhamad Safouh. *Revolutionary Change and Modernization in the Arab World: A Case from Syria*. Ph.D. dissertation. Berkeley: University of California Press, 1969.

Amin, Samir. *L'Economie du Maghreb*. Paris: Les Editions de Minuit, 1966.

Arab Information Center. *Education in the Arab States*. New York: Arab Information Center, January 1966. (Information Paper #25).

Ashford, Douglas. *National Development and Local Reform in Morocco, Tunisia, and Pakistan*. Princeton: Princeton University Press, 1967.

Baer, Gabriel. *Studies in the Social History of Modern Egypt*. Chicago: University of Chicago Press, 1969.

Be'eri, Eliezer. *Army Officers in Arab Politics and Society*. New York: Praeger, 1970.

Berger, Morroe. *Bureaucracy and Society in Modern Egypt: A Study of the Higher Civil Service*. New York: Russell & Russell, 1969.

_____. *Islam in Egypt Today: Social and Political Aspects of Popular Religion*. Cambridge: Cambridge University Press, 1970.

_____. *Military Elite and Social Change: Egypt since Napoleon*. Princeton: Center for International Studies, Princeton University Press, 1960.

Binder, Leonard, ed. *Politics in Lebanon*. New York: Wiley, 1966.

Bourges, Herve. *L'Algerie: A l'Epreuve du Pouvoir (1962-1967)*. Paris: Editions Bernard Grasset, 1967.

Brown, Leon Carl, ed. *State and Society in Independent North Africa*. Washington, D.C.: Middle East Institute, 1966.

Carter, Florence. *Labor Law and Practice in Tunisia*. Department of Labor, Bureau of Labor Statistics, BLS Report #294 (June 1965).

Clarke, Joan. *Labor Law and Practice in the United Arab Republic (Egypt)*. Department of Labor, Bureau of Labor Statistics, BLS Report #275 (March 1965).

Debbasch, Charles. *Mutations Culturelles et Cooperation au Maghreb*. Paris: Centre National de la Recherche Scientifique, 1969.

Dekmejian, R. *Egypt under Nasir: a Study in Political Dynamics.* Binghamton, N.Y.: State University of New York Press, 1972.

Fisher, Sydney, ed. *The Military in the Middle East.* Revised ed. Columbus: Mershon Center for Education in National Security, 1967.

Haddad, George H. *Revolutions and Military Rule in the Middle East: The Arab States.* Vol. 2. New York: Robert Speller & Sons, 1971.

Haim, Sylvia. *Arab Nationalism: an Anthology.* Berkeley: University of California Press, 1962.

Halpern, Manfred. *The Politics of Social Change in the Middle East and North Africa.* Princeton: Princeton University Press, 1963.

Hanna, Sami. *Arab Socialism: a Documentary Survey.* Leiden, Holland: Brill, 1968.

Hawley, Donald. *The Trucial States.* London: Allen & Unwin, 1970.

Hayes, R.C. *Labor Law and Practice in the Hashimite Kingdom of Jordan.* Department of Labor, Bureau of Labor Statistics, BLS Report #322 (1967).

Hoffman, Bernard. *The Structure of Traditional Moroccan Rural Society.* The Hague: Mouton, 1967.

Hopkins, Harry. *Egypt, the Crucible; the Unfinished Revolution in the Arab World.* Boston: Houghton Mifflin, 1969.

Hudson, Michael. *The Precarious Republic: Political Modernization in Lebanon.* New York: Random House, 1968.

Humbaraci, Arslan. *Algeria: A Revolution that Failed.* New York: Praeger, 1966.

Huntington, Samuel, ed. *Changing Patterns of Military Politics.* New York: Free Press, 1962.

_____. *Political Order in Changing Societies.* New Haven: Yale University Press, 1968.

Hurewitz, J.C. *Middle East Politics: the Military Dimensions.* New York: Praeger, 1969.

Hussein, Mahmoud. *La Lutte de Classes en Egypte de 1945 a 1968.* Paris: Francois Maspero, 1969.

Ibrahim, Saad E.M. *Political Attitudes of an Emerging Elite: A Case Study of the Arab Students in the United States.* Ph.D. dissertation. University of Washington, 1968.

Ismael, Tareq. *Governments and Politics of the Contemporary Middle East.* Homewood, Ill.: Dorsey Press, 1970.

Isnard, Hildebert. *Le Maghreb.* Paris: Presses Universitaires de France, 1966.

Issawi, Charles P. *Egypt in Revolution: an Economic Survey.* London: Oxford University Press, 1963.

Khadduri, Majid. *Political Trends in the Arab World; the Role of Ideas and Ideals in Politics.* Baltimore: Johns Hopkins Press, 1970.

_____. *Republican Iraq, a Study in Iraqi Politics since the Revolution of 1958.* New York: Oxford University Press, 1969.

Kimche, Jon. *The Second Arab Awakening.* New York: Holt, Rinehart and Winston, 1970.

Koury, Enver M. *The Patterns of Mass Movements in Arab Revolutionary Progressive States.* The Hague: Mouton, 1970.

Lacheraf, Mostefa. *L'Algerie: Nation et Societe.* Paris: Maspero, 1965.

Laroui, Abdallah. *L'Histoire du Maghreb, un essai de synthese.* Paris: Francois Maspero, 1970.

_____. *L'Ideologie Arabe Contemporaine.* Paris: Francois Maspero, 1967.

Lasswell, Harold, and Daniel Lerner, eds. *World Revolutionary Elites: Studies in Coercive Ideological Movements.* Cambridge: M.I.T. Press, 1966.

Leiden, Carl. *The Conflict of Traditionalism and Modernism in the Muslim Middle East.* Austin: University of Texas Press, 1968.

Lenczowski, George. *The Political Awakening in the Middle East.* Englewood Cliffs, N.J.: Prentice-Hall, 1970.

Lewy, Guenter. *The Egyptian Revolution: Nasserism and Islam* (Religion and Revolution—A Study in Comparative Politics and Religion. Technical Report #5). Amherst: Department of Government, University of Massachusetts, 1968.

Little, Tom. *South Arabia: Arena of Conflict.* New York: Praeger, 1968.

Longrigg, Stephen. *The Middle East: A Social Geography.* 2nd ed. London: Duckworth, 1970.

Luqman, Farouk M. *Yemen 1970.* Aden, 1970.

Lutfiyya, Abdulla, and Charles Churchill. *Readings in Arab Middle Eastern Societies and Culture.* The Hague: Mouton, 1970.

Meynaud, Jean, and Anisse Salah-Bey. *Le Syndicalisme Africain.* Paris: Payot, 1963.

*Middle East and North Africa 1971-72, The.* 18th ed. London: Europa Publications, Ltd. 1971.

*Military Balance 1971-1972, The.* London: The International Institute for Strategic Studies, 1971.

Moore, Clement Henry. *Politics in North Africa: Algeria, Morocco, and Tunisia.* Boston: Little, Brown, 1970.

Nasser, Gamal Abdel. *The Philosophy of the Revolution.* Washington, D.C.: Public Affairs Press, 1955.

Neguib, Mohammed. *Egypt's Destiny.* London: Victor Gollancz; New York: Doubleday, 1955.

Norman, John. *Labor and Politics in Libya and Arab Africa.* New York: Bookman Associates, 1965.

O'Brien, Patrick. *A Revolution in Egypt's Economic System.* London: Oxford University Press, 1966.

Ottaway, David and Marina. *Algeria: the Politics of a Socialist Revolution.* Berkeley: University of California Press, 1970.

Quandt, William. *Revolution and Political Leadership, Algeria 1954-1968.* Cambridge, Mass.: M.I.T. Press, 1969.

Qubain, Fahim. *Education and Science in the Arab World.* Baltimore: Johns Hopkins Press, 1966.

Rosenthal, E.I.J. *Islam in the Modern National State.* Cambridge: Cambridge University Press, 1965.

Rustow, Dankwart A. *Middle Eastern Political Systems.* Englewood Cliffs, N.J.: Prentice-Hall, 1971.

_____. *The Military in Middle Eastern Society and Politics.* Washington, D.C.: Brookings Institute, 1967 (reprint).

Sadat, Col. Anwar El. *Revolt on the Nile.* London: Wingate, 1957.

Sayegh, Kamal. *Oil and Arab Regional Development.* New York: Praeger, 1968.

Seale, Patrick. *The Struggle for Syria: A Study of Post War Arab Politics.* London: Oxford University Press, 1965.

Stephens, Robert. *Nasser: A Political Biography.* New York: Simon and Schuster, 1972.

*Strategic Survey 1970.* London: The Institute for Strategic Studies, 1971.

Suleiman, Michael. *Political Parties in Lebanon; the Challenge of a Fragmented Political Culture.* Ithaca: Cornell University Press, 1967.

Thompson, Jack, and Robert C. Reischauer, eds. *Modernization of the Arab World.* Princeton: Van Nostrand, 1966.

Torrey, Gordon H. *Syrian Politics and the Military 1945-1958.* Columbus: Ohio State University Press, 1964.

United Nations Educational, Scientific, and Cultural Organization. *Statistical Yearbook, 1968.* Paris: 1969.

United Nations. *Statistical Yearbook, 1970.* New York: 1971.

Van Nieuwehnuije, C.A.O. *Social Stratification and the Middle East.* Leiden, Holland: E.J. Brill, 1965.

Vatikiotis, P.J., ed. *Egypt Since the Revolution.* New York: Praeger, 1968.

_____. *Politics and the Military In Jordan: A Study of the Arab Legion 1921-1957.* New York: Praeger, 1967.

_____. *The Egyptian Army in Politics: Pattern for New Nations.* Bloomington: Indiana University Press, 1961.

_____. *The Modern History of Egypt.* New York: Praeger, 1969.

Vernier, Bernard. *Armee et Politique au Moyen-Orient.* Paris: Payot, 1966.

Von Grunebaum, Gustave. *Modern Islam: The Search for Cultural Identity.* Berkeley: University of California Press, 1962.

Waterbury, John. *The Commander of the Faithful: the Moroccan Political Elite—A Study in Segmented Politics.* New York: Columbia University Press, 1970.

Ziadeh, Farhat. *Lawyers, the Rule of Law and Liberalism in Modern Egypt.* Stanford: Hoover Institution Publication 75, 1968.

Zuwiyya-Yamak, Labib. *The Syrian Social Nationalist Party: An Ideological Analysis* (Harvard Middle Eastern Monographs XIV). Cambridge: Harvard University Press, 1966.

Zuzik, Michael B. *Labor Law and Practice in the Kingdom of Libya.* Department of Labor, Bureau of Labor Statistics, BLS Report #297 (June 1966).

## Articles

Abadir, Akef, and Roger Allen. "Nagib Mahfuz, His World of Literature." *The Arab World* 17, nos. 1-9 (August-September 1971), pp. 81-89.

Abdel-Malek, Anouar. "Introduction a la pensee arabe contemporaine." *Civilisations* (Paris) 15, no. 1 (1965), pp. 45-72.

Abu Jaber, Kamel. "An Impetus to Egyptian Labor." *Mid East* 10, no. 6 (December 1970), pp. 37-41.

Abu-Laban, Baha. "Factors in Social Control of the Press in Lebanon." *Journalism Quarterly* 43, no. 3 (Autumn 1966), pp. 510-518.

_____ . "Sources of College Aspirations of Lebanese Youth." *The Journal of Developing Areas* 2, no. 2 (January 1968), pp. 225-240.

Abu-Lughod, Ibrahim. "Retreat from the Secular Path? Islamic Dilemmas of Arab Politics." *The Review of Politics* 28, no. 4 (October 1966), pp. 447-476.

"Al-Kitabah al-Ibda'iyah wa al-Kitabah al-Wazifiyah" [Creative Writing and Official Writing]. *Al-Usbu' al-'Arabi* (Beirut), no. 625, May 31, 1971, pp. 52-56.

Alexander, Mark. "Left and Right in Egypt." *Twentieth Century*, February 1952, pp. 119-128.

"Algeria: Another Turbulent Summer?" *Africa Confidential*, no. 14 (July 12, 1968), pp. 5-6.

"Al-Muhamun al-'Arab wa al-hurriyah" [Arab Lawyers and Freedom]. *Mawaqif*, 1, no. 1 (1968), pp. 200-207.

"Al-Mu'tamar al-Sanawi li munazamat al-Talabah al-'Arab." *Shu'un Filastiniyah*, no. 6 (January 1972), pp. 273-274.

Alport, E.A. "Socialism in Three Countries; the Record in the Maghrib." *International Affairs* (London) 43, no. 4 (October 1967), pp. 678-692.

Al-Qazzaz, A. "Military Regimes and Political Stability in Egypt, Iraq, and Syria." *Berkeley Journal of Sociology* 12 (1967), pp. 44-54.

"Al-Tabaqah al-Wusta wa dawriha fi al-Mujtama' al-Misri" [The Middle Class and Its Role in Egyptian Society]. *Al-Tali'ah* (Cairo) 8, no. 3 (March 1972), pp. 61-72.

"Al-Wihdah al-Arabiyah fi Majal al-Fikr Wa al-thaqafah" [Arab Unity in the Realm of Thought and Culture]. *Al-Hilal* (Cairo), February 1972, pp. 2-15.

Ashford, Douglas. "Organizations of Cooperatives and the Structure of Power in Tunisia." *Journal of Developing Areas* 1 (April 1967), pp. 317-332.

" 'Azamat al-Islam" [The Greatness of Islam]. *Al-Nahda* (Kuwait), April 29, 1972, p. 65.

Aziz, Qutubuddin. "Islam shows growing unity commitment." *The Christian Science Monitor*, January 5, 1971, p. 14.

Badeau, John. "Islam and the Modern Middle East." *Foreign Affairs* 38, no. 1 (October 1959), pp. 61-74.

_____ . "The Revolt Against Democracy." *International Affairs* (London) 13, no. 2 (1959), pp. 149-156.

Barakat, Halim. "Al-ightirab Wa al-Thawrah fi al-hayat al-Arabiyeh" [Alienation and Revolution in Arab Life]. *Mawaqif* (Beirut), no. 5 (1969), pp. 18-44.

_____. "Social Factors Influencing Attitudes of University Students in Lebanon towards the Palestinian Resistance Movements." *Journal of Palestine Studies* 1, no. 1 (Autumn 1971), pp. 87-112.

Barbot, M., ed. "Literature Syrienne d'aujourd'hui." *L'Orient* (Paris) 40 (1966), pp. 51-128.

"Bayanat al-Ittihad" [Statements by the Arab Lawyers Union]. *Al-Haqq* (Cairo) 2, no. 3 (September 1971), pp. 241-253.

Beling, Willard. "Modernization of Human Resources in Developing Nations: Algeria, Tunisia and Egypt." *Maghreb Digest* 5, no. 2 (April-June 1967), pp. 5-26.

_____. "Political Trends in Arab Labor." *The Middle East Journal* 15, no. 1 (Winter 1961), pp. 29-39.

Ben-Tzar, Abrahan. "The Neo-Ba'th Party of Syria." *New Outlook* 12, no. 1(103) (January 1969), pp. 21-37.

Berger, Morroe. "Social and Political Change in the Moslem Arab World." *World Politics*, July 10, 1958, pp. 629-638.

Bill, James A. "The Military and Modernization in the Middle East." *Comparative Politics* 2, no. 1 (October 1969), pp. 41-63.

Bourron, Yves. "Regards sur la litterature Maghrebine d'expression francaise." *Etudes* (Paris), May 1967, pp. 636-650.

Breyer, Karl. "Morocco Awaits." *To The Point* (Johannesburg) 1, no. 11 (June 3, 1972), pp. 41-42.

Britt, George. "Lebanon's Popular Revolution." *The Middle East Journal* 7, no. 1 (Winter 1953), pp. 1-17.

Bujra, A.S. "Political Conflict and Stratification in the Hadramawt." *Middle East Studies* 3, no. 4 (1967), pp. 355-375; 4, no. 1 (October 1967), pp. 2-28.

Cecil, Charles. "The Determinants of Libyan Foreign Policy." *Middle East Journal* 19, no. 1 (Winter 1965), pp. 20-34.

Childs, Marquis. "Boumedienne's Goals." *The Washington Post.* December 16, 1970, p. A-15.

Cooley, John K. "Major Questions about Moroccan Revolt still Unanswered." *The Christian Science Monitor*, July 14, 1971, p. 3.

_____. "Morocco Take-Over Try Showed Shaky Society." *The Christian Science Monitor*, July 31, 1971, p. 11.

_____. "Student Activists prod Sadat to retake Sinai Peninsula." *The Christian Science Monitor*, January 22, 1972, p. 4.

_____. "U.A.R. Labor Strikes at Iron, Steel Center." *The Christian Science Monitor*, August 31, 1971, p. 2.

Craig, A.J.M. "Egyptian Students." *The Middle East Journal* 7, no. 3 (Summer 1953), pp. 293-299.

Crecilius, Daniel. "Al-Azhar in the Revolution." *The Middle East Journal* 20, no. 1 (Winter 1966), pp. 31-49.

Damis, John. "The Moroccan Political Scene." *The Middle East Journal* 26, no. 1 (Winter 1972), pp. 25-36.

Dawn, C. Ernest. "Arab Islam in the Modern Age." *The Middle East Journal* 19, no. 4 (Autumn 1965), pp. 435-446.

"Decision has many Meanings." *The Economist* (London), January 29, 1972, p. 40.

Dorsey, William H. "1968 Revisited: Student power in Cairo." *New Middle East* (February 1972), pp. 13-15.

Dullforce, William. "Cairo Policies Challenged by Student Protest." *The Washington Post*, January 21, 1972, p. A-16.

_____. "Sadat Appoints New Cabinet." *The Washington Post*, January 18, 1972, p. A-10.

_____. "Sadat sees top Ministers to consult on Student Protests in favor of War." *The Washington Post*, January 20, 1972, p. A-27.

_____. "Students May Affect Suez Peace." *The Washington Post*, January 22, 1972, p. A-11.

"Egypt: More than Student Unrest." *Africa Confidential*, no. 24 (December 6, 1968), pp. 3-5.

"Egypt: Nasser's Dilemma." *Africa Confidential*, no. 25 (December 19, 1969), pp. 1-3.

El Kodsy, Ahmad. "Nationalism and Class Struggles in the Arab World." *Monthly Review* 22, no. 3 (July-August 1970), pp. 1-61.

Flinn, Peter. "The Impact of the Technological Era." *Journal of Contemporary History* 3, no. 3 (July 1968), pp. 53-68.

Gabrieli, F. "Contemporary Arabic Fiction." *Middle East Studies* 2, no. 1 (1965), pp. 79-84.

Gallagher, C.F. *The Maghrib and the Middle East*. Santa Monica: The Rand Corporation, October 1969 (Monograph).

Gendzier, Irene L. "Socialism graced by Tradition's Veil." *The Christian Science Monitor*, September 19, 1970, p. 9.

Glubb, John B. "The Conflict between Tradition and Modernism in the Role of Muslim Armies." In *Conflict of Traditionalism and Modernism in the Middle East*. Edited by Carl Leiden from papers delivered March 29-31, 1965. Austin: University of Texas, 1966, pp. 9-21.

Goleno, Frank. "Patterns of Libyan National Identity." *The Middle East Journal* 24, no. 3 (Summer 1970), pp. 338-352.

Hagopian, Elaine. "Conceptual Stability, the Monarchy, and Modernization in Morocco." *Journal of Developing Areas* 1, no. 2 (January 1967), pp. 199-214.

Hallsworth, J.A. "Freedom of Association and Industrial Relations in the Countries of the Near and Middle East: I." *International Labour Review* 70, no. 5 (November 1954), pp. 363-384.

Halpern, Manfred. "Middle Eastern Armies and the New Middle Class." In *Role of the Military in Underdeveloped Countries.* Edited by John J. Johnson. Princeton: Princeton University Press, 1962, pp. 277-317.

_____. "Egypt and the New Middle Class: Reaffirmation and New Explorations." *Comparative Studies in Society and History* 11, no. 1 (January 1969), pp. 97-108.

Harbison, Frederick. "Two Centers of Arab Power." *Foreign Affairs* 37 (July 1959).

Hasanayn, Jamal Majdi. "Al-fiat al-Wustah fi al-duwal al-Namiyah" [The Middle Classes in the Developing Countries]. *Al-Katib* (Cairo) 12, no. 131 (February 1972).

Hess, Clyde G., Jr., and Herbert L. Bodman, Jr. "Confessionalism and Feudality in Lebanese Politics." *The Middle East Journal* 8, no. 1 (Winter 1954), pp. 10-26.

"Hiwar al-tahaddi hayn mithahyat al-tullab wa waqi 'iyat al-dawlah" [The Dialogue of Challenge between the Idealism of Students and Realism of the State]. *Al-Jumhar al-Jadid* 36, no. 919 (January 26, 1972), pp. 10-11.

Hourani, Cecil. "The Moment of Truth." *Encounter* 29, no. 5 (November 1967), pp. 3-14.

Hudson, M. "Democracy and Social Mobilization in Lebanese Politics." *Comparative Politics* 1, no. 2 (January 1969), pp. 245-263.

Iskandar, Amir. "Al-Masrah wa Ma'rakat al-Masir" [The Theater and the Battle of Destiny]. *Al-Ishtiraki* [The Socialist] (Cairo), no. 164 (April 7, 1971), pp. 18-21, 23.

Kelider, A. "Shifts and Changes in the Arab World." *World Today* 24 (December 1968), pp. 503-511.

Khadduri, Majid. "The Role of the Military in the Middle East." *American Political Science Review* 27 (June 1953), pp. 511-524.

Khalaf, Samir. "The Growing Pains of Arab Intellectuals." *Diogenes*, no. 54 (Summer 1966), pp. 59-80.

Khalidi, Tarif. "A Critical Study of the Political Ideas of Michel Aflak." *Middle East Forum* 42, no. 2 (1966), pp. 55-68.

Khetab, Mahmud. "Fawa'id al-sawm al'askariyah" [The Military Benefits of Fasting]. *Al-Wa'i al-Islam* (Kuwait), October 20, 1971, pp. 32-37.

Khuri, Fuad I. "Changing Class Structure in Lebanon." *The Middle East Journal* 23, no. 1 (Winter 1969), pp. 29-44.

Kinsman, James. "Strange Bed-Fellows and New Alignments in the Maghreb." *New Middle East* (Great Britain), February 1971, pp. 23-26.

Le Gassick, Trevor. "A Malaise in Cairo: Three Contemporary Authors." *The Middle East Journal* 21, no. 2 (April 1967), pp. 145-156.

_____. "Arab Prose and Poetry." *Mid East* 9, no. 5 (October 1969), pp. 6-13.

Lenczowski, George. "Arab Radicalism: Problems and Prospects." *Current History* 60 (January 1971), pp. 32-37.

_____. "Radical Regimes in Egypt, Syria and Iraq: Some Comparative

Observations on Ideologies and Practices." *Journal of Politics* 28, no. 1 (February 1966), pp. 29-56.

Lewis, Jesse W., Jr. "Corruption May Be Key to Morocco Coup Bid." *The Washington Post*, July 18, 1971, p. A-19.

_____ . "Moroccan King Faces Urgent Tasks." *The Washington Post*, July 15, 1971, pp. A-19 and A-22.

Lewis, William. "Algeria Against Itself." *Africa Report* 12, no. 9 (December 1967), pp. 9-15.

"Libya: After the Coup." *Africa Confidential*, no. 18 (September 5, 1969), pp. 7-8.

"Libya: Arms and the Men." *Africa Confidential* no. 3 (January 30, 1970), pp. 6-8.

"Libya: Egypt and the Economy." *Africa Confidential*, no. 8 (April 17, 1970), pp. 1-3.

"Libya: Question Marks Remain." *Africa Confidential*, no. 19 (September 19, 1969), pp. 1-2.

"Libya: Softly, Softly." *Africa Confidential*, no. 20 (October 10, 1969), pp. 1-3.

"Libya: Trials and Plan." *Africa Confidential*, no. 24 (December 5, 1969), pp. 5-7.

Long, C.W.R. "Taufiq al-Hakim and the Arabic Theater." *Middle Eastern Studies* 5, no. 1 (January 1969), pp. 69-74.

"Madha Yufakkir Shabab al-Jamiah" [What do University Students Think?]. *Majallat al-tarbiyah al-hadithah* [Journal of Modern Education, Cairo] 44, no. 2 (December 1970), pp. 144-165.

Mahmud, Dr. Zaki Najib. "Mawqaf al-thaqafah al-'Arabiyah al-hadithah fi muwajahat al-'Asr" [The Attitudes of Modern Arabic Culture Towards Modernization]. *Al-Adab* 19, no. 11 (November 1971), pp. 6-12.

Maksoud, Clovis. "The Arab Revolution in Quest of a Direction." *Review of International Affairs* 3 (November 15, 1954), pp. 15-16.

Marais, Octave. "Les Relations entre la monarchie et la classe dirigeante au Maroc." *Revue Francaise de Science Politique* 19, no. 6 (December 1969), pp. 1172-1186.

Masannat, George S. "Modernization in the Arab Middle East." *Social Studies* vol. 60 (January 1969), pp. 12-20.

Micaud, Charles. "Leadership and Development; the Case of Tunisia." *Comparative Politics* 1, no. 4 (July 1969), pp. 468-484.

Miller, N.B. (pseud.). "Social Revolution in the Arab World." In *Monthly Review* 19 (February 1968), pp. 20-32.

Moore, Clement H., and Arlie R. Hochschild. "Student Unions in North African Politics." *Daedalus* 97, no. 1 (Winter 1968), pp. 21-50.

Murad, Dr. Muhammad Helmi. "Ma Yajib Taghyiruhi fi al-bi'ah wa dawr Jama'at al-Khirriyin wa al-naqabat" [What Needs Change in the Environment and the Role of the Graduates and Unions]. *Al-Mudir al-'Arabi* (Cairo), no. 36 (November 1971), pp. 13-20.

Musrey, Alfred. "First Steps toward Arab economic Integration." *International Development Review* 13, no. 1 (1971), pp. 13-18.

Najjar, F. "Islam and Socialism in the United Arab Republic." *Journal of Contemporary History* 3, no. 3 (July 1968), pp. 183-199.

"Nasser fights back." *Africa Confidential*, no. 11 (May 31, 1968), pp. 1-3.

Newman, K.J. "The New Monarchies of the Middle East." *Journal of International Affairs* 13, (1959), pp. 157-168.

Nordell, Roderick. "Cairo's Thriving Theater World." *The Christian Science Monitor*, May 27, 1972, p. 9.

Ottaway, David B. "Algeria: Back to Islam." *The Washington Post*, March 21, 1971, p. B-1.

Paul, James A. "The Changing Basis of Moroccan Politics." *New Politics* 9, no. 2 (Summer 1970), pp. 11-26.

Perlmutter, Amos. "Egypt and the Myth of the new Middle Class: A Comparative Analysis." *Comparative Studies in Society and History* 10, no. 1 (October 1967), pp. 46-65.

_____. "From Disunity to Rule: the Syrian Army and the Ba'th Party." *Western Political Quarterly* 22, no. 4 (December 1969), pp. 827-845.

_____. "Sources of Instability in the Middle East: Two Decades of Nationalism and Revolution." *Orbis* 12, no. 3 (Fall 1968), pp. 718-753.

Petrov, R. "Arab Unity: Lessons and Prospects." *New Times* (Moscow), May 1, 1971, pp. 22-23.

Pfaff, R.H. "The Functions of Arab Nationalism." *Comparative Politics* 2, no. 2 (January 1970), pp. 147-168.

Polk, William R. "The Middle East: Analyzing Social Change." *Bulletin of the Atomic Scientists* 23, no. 1 (January 1967), pp. 12-19.

_____. "The Nature of Modernization: the Middle East and North Africa." *Foreign Affairs* 44, no. 1 (October 1965), pp. 100-110.

Quandt, William. "Algeria: the Revolution Turns Inward," *Mid East* 10, no. 4 (August 1970), pp. 9-12.

Ramazani, R.K. "Cultural Change and Intellectual Response in Algeria, Tunisia and Iran." *Comparative Studies in Society and History: an International Quarterly* 6, no. 2 (January 1964), pp. 219-229.

Randal, Jonathan C. "Morocco since the Near-Coup: Reform is Slow Motion." *The Washington Post*, December 12, 1971, p. C-2.

Rif'at, Kamal ad-Din. "Bureaucracy is a Disease which threatens the whole political System." *Al-Amal* (Cairo), September 1967, pp. 4-6.

"Rijal al-Amal wa naql al-sultah ila Jamahir al-'Amilin" [The High Administration and the Transfer of Power to the Labor Masses]. *Al-Mudir al-'Arabi* (Cairo), no. 36 (November 1971), pp. 55-58.

Robert, J. "Opposition in the Maghreb." *Government and Opposition* 1, no. 3 (May 1966), pp. 389-404.

"Sadat is not the Man." *The Economist* 242, no. 6703 (February 12, 1972), pp. 17-19.

Schaar, Stuart H. "A New Look at Tunisia." *Mid East* 10, no. 1 (February 1970), pp. 43-46 and 48.

Saint John, P. "Independent Algeria from Ben Bella to Boumedienne." *World Today* 24, no. 7 (July 1968), pp. 290-296; 24, no. 8 (August 1968), pp. 339-345.

Salah-Bey, Anisse. "Trade Unions and Economic and Social Development in the Maghreb." *International Labour Review* 94, no. 4 (October 1966), pp. 375-397.

"Saudi Arabia." *Emergent Nations* 2, no. 2 (1966), pp. 1-65.

Serag el Din, I. "The Search for Identity among Muslim Youth: the case of the UAR." *Nonaligned Third World Annual* (1970), pp. 245-251.

Sfeir, George. "The Contemporary Arabic Novel." *Daedalus* 95, no. 4 (Fall 1966), pp. 941-960.

Sharabi, H.B. "Parliamentary Government and Military Autocracy in the Middle East." *Orbis* 4 (Fall 1960), pp. 338-355.

Sheehan, Edward R.F. "Colonel Qadhafi—Libya's Mystical Revolutionary." *The New York Times Magazine*, February 6, 1972, pp. 10-11, 56-59, and 68.

_____ . "The Second Most Important Man in Egypt—and possibly the World's most powerful Journalist." *The New York Times Magazine*, August 22, 1971, pp. 12, 53-54, 58-62.

_____ . "Who Runs Egypt?" *The New York Times Magazine*, November 29, 1970, pp. 30 and 132-139.

Shils, Edward. "Intellectuals in the Political Development of the New States," *World Politics* 12, no. 3 (April 1960), pp. 329-368.

"Student despair follows Moroccan Walkout end." *The Christian Science Monitor*, April 1, 1971, p. 8.

Suleiman, Michael W. "The Role of Political Parties in a Confessional Democracy: the Lebanese Case." *Western Political Quarterly* 20, no. 3 (September 1967), pp. 682-693.

"Swirling Signposts." *The Economist* (London), May 20, 1972, p. 52.

Szyliowicz, Joseph. "Education and Political Development in Turkey." *Comparative Education Review* 13 (June 1969), pp. 150-166.

"Taqrir min dakhil Tunis" [A Report from Inside Tunis]. *Al-Dustur* (Beirut) 2, no. 72 (February 28, 1972), p. 18.

Tessler, Mark. "Cultured Modernity: Evidence from Tunisia." *Social Science Quarterly* 52, no. 2 (September 1971), pp. 292-308.

"The Arab Media, Was It Successful in Awakening the Masses Consciousness?" *Al-Arabi*, no. 158 (January 1972), pp. 46-50.

"Tullab al-Jil al-da'i' yathurun 'ala' Burguiba wa al-Mistiri" [The Students of the Lost Age Revolt against Bourguiba and al-Mistiri]. *Al-Sayyad* (Beirut), no. 1432 (February 24, 1972), pp. 36-37.

"Tunisia: after the Deluge, Bourguiba." *Africa Confidential*, no. 23 (November 21, 1969), pp. 1-3.

"Tunisia: l'Affaire ben Salah." *Africa Confidential*, no. 8 (April 17, 1970), pp. 5-6.

Vatikiotis, P.J. "Dilemmas of Political Leadership in the Arab Middle East." *International Affairs* 37, no. 2 (April 1961), pp. 189-202.

"Ventriloquism." *The Economist* 243, no. 6719 (June 3, 1972), p. 45.

Wadi, Dr. Taha'Umran. "Azmat al-Burjwaziyah al-Misriyah" [The Crisis of the Egyptian Bourgeoisie]. *Al-Katib* (Cairo) 12, no. 133 (April 1972), pp. 122-128.

Ward, Richard. "The Long Run Employment Prospects for Middle East Labor." *The Middle East Journal* 24, no. 2 (Spring 1970), pp. 147-162.

Waterbury, John. "Marginal Politics and Elite Manipulation in Morocco." *Archives Europeennes de Sociolgie* 8, no. 1 (1967), pp. 94-111.

_____ . "The Coup Manque: American Universities Field Staff Reports." *North Africa Series* (Morocco) 15, no. 1 (July 1971).

Wiznitzer, Louis. "Algeria: from Words, Slogans to Efficiency Experts." *The Christian Science Monitor*, May 20, 1971, pp. 1-2.

_____ . "Algeria Gives High Priority to Training of Technicians." *The Christian Science Monitor*, June 3, 1971, p. 5.

_____ . "Algeria's President Speaks Out . . ." *The Christian Science Monitor*, May 8, 1971, p. 9.

_____ . "Boumedienne Steers Algeria away From Flamboyant Policy." *The Christian Science Monitor*, June 17, 1971, p. 12.

Yodfat, Aryeh. "The End of Syria's Isolation." *The World Today*, August 1971, pp. 329-339.

Zahlan, A.B. "Wanted: a Great University." *Mid East* 9, no. 1 (January/February 1969), pp. 10-14.

_____ . "Arab Higher Education: the Next Decade." *Mid East* 8, no. 3 (May/June 1968), pp. 3-9.

Zartman, William. "Political Pluralism in Morocco." *Government and Opposition* 2, no. 4 (July-October 1967), pp. 568-583.

Zein, Elias. "An Arab View." *Mid East* 9, no. 1 (January/February 1969), pp. 3-7.

## Extensively Used Newspapers

*Al-Ahram* (Cairo), January 1971 to May 1972.
*Al-Nahar* (Beirut), January 1971 to May 1972.
*L'Opinion* (Rabat, Morocco), October 1971 to May 1972.
*The Daily Star, Sunday Supplement* (Beirut), June 6, 1971.
*The Christian Science Monitor*, January 1971 to June 1972.
*The New York Times*, January 1965 to June 1972.
*The London Times*, January 1965 to March 1972.

# Index

# Index

Abd al-Nasser, Gamal, 16, 17, 18, 19,
35, 51, 52, 54, 60, 61, 62, 75, 76,
97, 98, 99, 102, 113, 117, 131, 132,
133, 155, 156, 160, 162, 165, 166
'Abd al-Qudus, Ihsan, 163
'Abdun, Muhammad, 8, 10, 41, 98
Abdullah ibn Hussayn, 13, 15, 16
Abu 'Adal, George, 157
Abu Jawdah, Michael, 158
Afghani, Jamal al-Din al-, 8, 41
Aflaq, Michel, 56, 59, 102
Ahl al-Shura (people of counseling),
53
Ait Ahmad, Hocine, 108, 136
'Alawites, 59, 104, 106
Algeria, 62, 76, 78, 79, 86, 90, 94,
106, 107-110, 118, 123, 134, 135,
136, 137, 144, 147, 148, 160, 164,
166, 167, 173
Ali, 30
Ali, Mohammed, 131
American University of Beirut, 84,
115, 140, 157, 158
Amin, Mustafa, 89, 156
Arab Association of Journalists, 156
Arab Cold War, 18
Arab Common Market, 23
Arab Engineer Congress, 142
Arab federalism, 13-21, 103
Arab Peninsula, 62, 163, 176
Arabic, 116
Arab ideologies, general
characteristics, 48-51
Arabism, 31-32, 55, 85, 100, 113,
128, 145
Arab-Israeli conflict, 76, 93, 113, 115,
128, 137, 140, 160, 162, 164, 165,
175
Arab Lawyers Union, 143
Arab League, 13, 14, 15, 16, 23, 172
Arab nationalism, 56-57, 59, 62, 63,
65, 80, 100, 130, 155, 175
Arab Nationalist Movement (Harakat
al-Qawmiyun al-'Arab), 58-66
Arab Nationalists (al-Qawmiyun
al-'Arab), 59
Arab socialism, 18, 61, 86, 87, 98,
117, 143, 145, 155, 156, 157, 159,
161, 163, 165, 173, 174, 175
Arab Socialist Union (ASU), 58, 60,
78, 86, 87, 88, 96, 122, 132, 133,
145, 146, 154
Arab society, 33-34
Arab Student Organization, 118-119
'Arif, 'Abd al-Rahman, 102
'Arif, 'Abd al-Salaam, 101, 102
'asabiyya (social solidarity), 7
As'ad, Hafiz al-, 59, 104, 105
'Ashur, Nu'man, 165
Association of Social Reform, 54
Azhar, al-, 37, 38
'Azm, Sadiq Jalal al-, 39

Ba'albaki, Leila, 160
Baghdad Pact, 16, 17
Baghdady, Abdel Latif el-, 97
Bahrain, 58, 148
Bakr, Ahmad Hasan, 102
Banna, Hassan al-, 52, 53
Barakat, Halim, 130, 160
Ba'thism. *See* Ba'th Party
Ba'th (Ba'ath) Party, 14, 16, 17, 18,
59-60, 66, 67, 68, 78, 81, 86, 87,
101, 103, 105, 106, 127, 130
Bazzaz, Abd al-Rahman al-, 56
Ben 'Ayad, 'Ali, 167
Ben Barka, Mehdi, 134, 135, 137
Ben Bella, Ahmad, 108, 109, 137
Berbers, 107, 111, 112
bid'a (innovation), 8
Bitar, Salah al-, 158
Bizri, Afif al-, 105
Boumedienne, Houari, 107, 108, 109,
137
Bourguiba, Habib, 107, 116, 139, 172
bureaucracy, 85-87, 121-125, 157, 173
Bustani, Butrus al-, 9, 115

Charter of National Action
(al-Mithaq), 58, 88; precepts, 61-62
China, 85, 106
cinema, 161, 163-164
colonialism. *See* Western impact
communicators, 87-89, 153-167, 174,
175
communism in the Arab world, 39, 40,

211

# About the Contributors

**Alan R. Taylor** is currently Professor of International Relations at the School of International Service of The American University in Washington, D.C. He received his undergraduate degree from Columbia University and took his master's and doctorate degrees from Georgetown University. Prior to his coming to The American University, he taught several years at the American University in Beirut, Lebanon, and at Howard University. Dr. Taylor's publications include his authorship of *Prelude to Israel* and coeditorship of *Palestine: A Search for Truth*. Furthermore, he has contributed articles to such scholarly journals as the *Middle East Journal, Commonweal,* and *Journal of Palestine Studies.*

**George N. Atiyeh** is Head of the Near East Section of the Library of Congress. He matriculated for his B.A. and M.A. at the American University in Beirut, Lebanon. He received his doctorate from the University of Chicago. Dr. Atiyeh has published in several languages: *Three Historical Essays* (Arabic), *Contemporary Philosophy* (Spanish), and two books in English, *Al-Kindi, Philosopher of the Arabs* and *Medieval Political Philosophy*, in which he was a co-author. He has also contributed several articles to such journals as the *Middle East Forum*, the *Middle East Journal*, and the *Journal of the American Oriental Society.*

**Abdul A. Said** is currently Professor of International Relations at the School of International Service of The American University in Washington, D.C. Having first being educated in Syria and France, Dr. Said came to The American University in Washington, D.C. for his doctorate. He is often called upon by the government to give lectures on the Middle East and on theories of international relations. His publications include: *Concepts of International Politics* (coauthor), *African Phenomenon, America's Role in the 1970's* (editor), *Revolutionism* (coauthor), *Protagonists of Change* (editor), *The New Sovereigns: Multinational Corporations As World Powers* (coauthor), and *Drugs, Politics, and Diplomacy* (coauthor). In addition to his numerous books and articles, he is associate editor of *Society* magazine.

# About the Authors

**Mr. William Hazen** has been employed with the American Institutes for Research since 1967. He took his B.A. degree from the University of Virginia and his M.A. from the American University in Beirut, Lebanon. At the present time, he is a Ph.D. candidate at Johns Hopkins School of Advanced International Studies. While with the American Institutes for Research, Mr. Hazen has coauthored several works on the Middle East, including *Six Clashes: An Analysis of the Relationships between the Palestinian Guerrilla Movement and the Governments of Jordan and Lebanon* and *Selected Minority Groups of the Middle East.* Furthermore, he has worked on projects involving prisoners of war and AIR's Social Science Review.

**Mohammed Mughisuddin** is currently employed by the American Institutes for Research (AIR), and was a lecturer of Middle East Studies at the School of International Service of The American University in Washington, D.C. In addition to teaching at The American University, he has also taught Middle East and South Asian courses at the University of Virginia (1970), and at the St. Albans International Seminars (1968-1970). Mohammed Mughisuddin's publications include the foreign relations chapters for the Foreign Area Studies Area Handbooks on Morocco, India, and Jordan. He is coauthor of *The Soviet Union and the Middle East* (AIR, 1974) and *Cooperation and Conflict: Egyptian, Iraqi and Syrian Objectives and U.S. Policy* (AIR, 1975). He received his Ph.D. from the School of International Studies at The American University.

# Related Lexington Books

Sadik, Muhammed and Snavely, William P., *Bahrain, Qatar and the United Arab Emirates*, 208 pp., 1972

Micaud, Charles, and Gellner, Ernest, *Arabs and Berbers*, 448 pp., 1973

Bull, Vivian A., *The West Bank—Is It Viable?*, 192 pp., 1975